DATE DUE

ILL 4-16-90	

JC
319   Taylor, Peter J.
T34   (Peter James)
19
                              phy

$2

D1064322

POLITICAL GEOGRAPHY

World-economy, nation-state and locality

POLITICAL GEOGRAPHY

WORLD-ECONOMY, NATION-STATE AND LOCALITY

PETER J. TAYLOR

Department of Geography
University of Newcastle upon Tyne

Longman
London and New York

Longman Group Limited
Longman House, Burnt Mill, Harlow
Essex CM20 2JE, England
Associated companies throughout the world

*Published in the United States of America
by Longman Inc., New York*

© **Longman Group Limited 1985**

First published 1985
Reprinted 1986

British Library Cataloguing in Publication Data
Taylor, Peter J. (Peter James)
    Political geography.
    1. Geography, Political
    I. Title
    320.1′2   JC319
ISBN 0-582-30088-6

Library of Congress Cataloging in Publication Data
Taylor, Peter J. (Peter James), 1944–
    Political geography.

    Bibliography: p.
    Includes index.
    1. Geography, Political.   2. Geopolitics.
    I. Title.
    JC319.T34   1985   320.1′2   84-5790

ISBN 0-582-30088-6

Set in Linotron 202 Baskerville Roman
Produced by Longman Singapore Publishers (Pte) Ltd.
Printed in Singapore

This book is dedicated to

KARL LIEBNECHT

1871–1919

CONTENTS

PREFACE

As an undergraduate geography student at Liverpool University from 1963 to 1966 I was not able to attend any lectures on political geography for the simple reason that they did not exist. The Liverpool geography department was by no means exceptional – the 1960s represent the nadir of political geography. This subject was more likely to be kept off honours geography syllabuses than to be put on them. Nevertheless on train journeys back to digs I always made a point of reading those articles in journals to which we had *not* been referred to in lectures. Hence I 'found' political geography. I soon discovered the latest text book, Norman Pound's *Political Geography*, and was fascinated by what were, to me, new topics. I remember enjoying especially the debates concerning the Heartland Theory. But it was soon back to work to earn my degree.

As a post-graduate I carried out a typical piece of quantitative geography research which was fashionably apolitical. One of my research themes, however, led me back to political geography. Regionalization or region-building had as one of its practical examples electoral districting. And so I became hooked on gerrymandering, a concept which neatly linked my spatial analysis interest with political geography. While at Iowa in 1970–71 I was able to follow the redistricting process daily as the Iowa legislature reduced its congressional districts from seven to six. I finished up producing a bibliography on districting as an appendix to a report to the Iowa legislature. Back in England I teamed up with Graham Gudgin with the avowed intention of technically solving the mysteries of the spatial organization of elections. This was further developed in collaboration with Ron Johnston as a more general interest in electoral geography. At the same time I was asked to write annual progress reports on political geography for *Progress in Human Geography* from which I learnt two things: that I had developed a dissatisfaction with current political geography (the reports were more negative than positive) but this was based in large part on my ignorance of the subject-matter. It's a long way from the narrow perspective of electoral geography to the broad vistas of political geography.

These broad vistas were forced upon me when I visited Clark University in 1978–79 as I was assigned to take over Saul Cohen's introductory political geography course. I soon decided that there was no text book suitable for my needs (negative again) but I had no general framework of my own to supersede what I found to be inadequate. The political geography graduates at Clark exposed me on this count and I am continually grateful to them for that. But it was at this time that I was slowly finding a way forward. It seemed to me that Immanuel Wallerstein's world-systems approach provided an answer to many of the questions I had been asking. The last few years have been spent trying to restructure political geography as part of the holistic framework that Wallerstein and his associates have proposed. This book is the result of these endeavours.

In the meantime political geography has shown all the signs of, in Rostow's terms, 'taking off'. International conferences at Lancaster, Haifa and Oxford have allowed me to try out my ideas on my peers drawn from all five continents. As part of this growth I have been involved in launching *Political Geography Quarterly*. As the editor many papers have now passed through my hands and my original fascination with all aspects of political geography has been rekindled. This has had an important effect on this book. Several recent statements on political geography have attempted to distance 'modern' political geography from 'traditional' political geography. Hence capital cities and boundaries are out, social choice theory and location conflicts are in. I feel strongly that we cannot just dismiss our past as if it did not exist. Most of the chapters below start with a 'heritage section' – for geopolitics I discuss an ideological heritage, for imperialism a revolutionary heritage, for electoral geography a liberal heritage and for urban political geography an ecological heritage. These are not meant to be of mere antiquarian interest. Quite simply if you do not know your past you do not understand your present. And of course many themes of the past are of direct relevance today. The neglect of the Heartland Theory in modern political geography in the light of current international tensions is nothing short of criminal. It is not a matter of whether the theory is right or wrong, it is a major component of the world-views of international decision-makers and that makes it real enough for me. I want to survive.

The book is written from a particular viewpoint. I have avoided an approach that reviews and discusses ideas and finishes up sitting on fences after praising the 'best bits' of what are often incompatible theories. My political geography is a world-systems political geography with all that that entails. Ideas are developed in a radical, holistic political-economy framework. Both old and new political geography is reinterpreted in world-systems terms. For instance, capital cities are discussed as core, periphery and semi-periphery political strategies in state management and modern concern for state theory is extended to a theory of *states* since the world-economy by definition has multiple states not one. I present a definite viewpoint but I hope not an unfair one. I do not use the straw-man technique of debate by setting up a false and simplified view of the ideas of others and then knocking them down. Where I use ideas from other than world-systems work, Stein Rokkan's models for instance, they are only included because I consider them worthy of discussion and criticism. This is how I hope those readers who do not accept my premises will treat this work. It can be used directly as a set of ideas that comprise a political geography to aid teaching or research or it can be used indirectly as a set of ideas against which other ideas can be compared, contrasted and, hopefully, refined or even improved. I have attempted to produce a theoretically respectable political geography which maintains the broad vista and general interest of the best political geographies of the past. I have really enjoyed writing this book. I hope reading it is as enjoyable an experience.

Peter Taylor

November 1983

Chapter 1

A WORLD-SYSTEMS APPROACH TO POLITICAL GEOGRAPHY

THE WORLD-SYSTEMS APPROACH

The challenge: bringing history back in

1. The myth of universal laws
2. The poverty of disciplines
3. The error of developmentalism

Systems of change

1. Mini-systems and the reciprocal-lineage mode of production
2. World-empires and the redistributive-tributary mode of production
3. World-economy and the capitalist mode of production

Types of change

1. Transformation
2. Discontinuities
3. Continuities

The basic elements of the world-economy

1. A single world market
2. A multiple state system
3. A three-tier structure

A SPACE-TIME MATRIX OF THE WORLD-ECONOMY

The dynamics of the world-economy

1. Kondratieff cycles
2. 'Logistic' waves

The spatial structure of the world-economy

1. The geographical extent of the system
2. The concepts of core and periphery
3. The semi-periphery category

A space-time information matrix for political geography

POWER AND POLITICS IN THE WORLD-ECONOMY

What is a strong state? – overt and covert power relations

1. Actual and latent force
2. Non-decision making
3. Structural position
4. Power and appearance

A political geography perspective on the world-economy

1. Ideology separating experience from reality
2. World-economy, nation-state and locality

Chapter 1

A WORLD-SYSTEMS APPROACH TO POLITICAL GEOGRAPHY

Cancun is a fashionable holiday resort on Mexico's Yucatan coast. In October 1981 it became the centre of world attention as the venue of a meeting between 'first world' and 'third world' governments. President Reagan led the 'first world' group which included the presidents and prime ministers of all the major 'western' countries. Third-world countries were represented by government leaders of seventeen countries from all three 'southern' continents. What transpired at this meeting was referred to as nothing less than 'global negotiations'. Even allowing for journalistic exaggeration, the Cancun meeting is symptomatic of current concern for world-wide perspectives and global thinking. Inkeles (1975: 467) has captured this concern very succinctly:

> The widespread diffusion of this sense of a new, emergent global interrelatedness is expressed in numerous ideas, slogans and catchphrases which have wide currency, such as 'world government', 'the global village', 'spaceship earth', 'the biosphere', and the ubiquitous cartoon of a crowded globe with a lighted fuse protruding from one end, the whole labelled 'the world population bomb'.

Inkeles sees the 'new sense' as indicating the development of an emerging social structure of the world. His particular approach to studying the global scale is just one of many to emerge in recent years. The Cancun conference itself grew out of pressure resulting from the very influential Brandt Report on North–South differences in material well-being. Other, more radical, researchers have emphasized the existence of a new international division of labour with the industrialization of certain third-world countries. And of course there are the large number of studies of multi-national corporations which emphasize the international powers of large private companies. One such study even begins with the assertion that 'The men who run the global corporations are the first in history with the organization, technology, money and ideology to make a credible try at managing the world as an integrated unit' (Barnett and Muller 1974: 13).

World-wide problems and global issues are therefore on the agenda of modern social science. The approach I have chosen to adopt in this study, however, does not emphasize the global uniqueness of the current situation. Presentday global problems and issues are only considered in the light of past processes. For political geographers global concerns are by no means a new theme. The heritage of the various geopolitics and the continuing study of the world political map will make any political geographer wary of the recent 'discovery' of the global scale in both the popular perception and modern social science. Eighty years ago one of the founding fathers of political geography was expressing similar global concerns:

> From the present time forth, in the post-Columbian age, we shall again have to deal with a closed political system, and none the less that it will be one of world-wide scope. Every explosion of social forces, instead of being dissipated in a surrounding circuit of unknown space will be sharply re-echoed from the far side of the globe. (Mackinder 1904: 422)

In fact Mackinder was expressing a very common global concern at the turn of the century. Multi-national corporation managers may be devising global strategies today but so too were the men who were 'painting the world map pink' in the late nineteenth century to ensure that the sun would never set on the British Empire. In fact there were three rival political ideologies of this period each of which had its own world model. The imperialists adhered to a competitive inter-state viewpoint in which the strong would prosper at the expense of the weak. Such thinking ultimately produced two world wars and 24 million battle deaths. Liberals opposed such militarism and suggested an alternative world model of free-trading countries each prospering under its own 'comparative advantage' to produce the goods it exported. They devised international clubs for countries to join and help keep the peace, first the League of Nations and then the United Nations. The socialists were even more explicitly international with their initial emphasis on class rather than country. Their 'Internationals' live on although divided since 1914. Global problems were paramount in many people's minds around the turn of the century at about the time of the emergence of political geography. It is therefore not surprising that political geography has a global heritage. We attempt to maintain this tradition in this study.

We could of course go back further to illustrate earlier 'global concerns'. European colonialism and settlement and the many extra-European wars between European powers before the twentieth century bear witness to the existence of such global conflicts and strategies. In the nineteenth century several European powers were involved in the famous 'Scramble for Africa'. In the eighteenth century Britain and France were fighting on battlefields as far apart as Canada and India. In the seventeenth century the Netherlands were challenging Spain on both sides of the globe in the West and East Indies. And during the sixteenth century Portugal and Spain operated in a global system arranged by Pope Alexander VI and largely confirmed at the Treaty of Tordesillas (1494) in which the non-European world was divided between them along the 47th parallel. Clearly global concerns have a long history.

The question of how far back we trace global concerns is not a trivial one. Any decision on where to start looking for the emergence of the modern world will be based upon a theory, implicit or explicit, about the nature of our modern world. Many studies, such as those briefly referred to at the very beginning of the chapter, involve theoretical frameworks which justify treating the current world situation as distinct from previous situations. In this study we employ Wallerstein's (1979) world-systems approach which provides a much longer temporal perspective. This involves a framework centred upon the capitalist world-economy which emerged in Europe in the period after 1450 and expanded to encompass the whole world by 1900. Both Pope Alexander VI in 1492 and President Reagan at Cancun in 1981 are part of this single story.

Wallerstein's world-systems approach has stimulated a massive literature in recent years. This involves both substantive and theoretical additions to the original ideas and criticisms from a range of alternative perspectives. I do not intend to enter this debate here. In simplest terms my choice of Wallerstein's framework is based on the fact that I have found it to be most useful for ordering and understanding the subject-matter of political geography (Taylor 1981a, 1982b). The remaining chapters of this book are an attempt to illustrate this point. The remainder of this chapter describes the world-systems approach and my particular adaption of it to political geography.

THE WORLD-SYSTEMS APPROACH

The second half of the twentieth century has seen a massive growth in the social sciences. Although firmly based upon European roots this growth has been largely American-led. The world-systems approach is first and foremost a challenge to this modern social science and this is the way we introduce it below. This challenge is a fundamental one because it questions the whole system of concepts and categories employed by modern social science. This is most clearly seen in their alternative treatments of social change and these are highlighted in the following discussion.

THE CHALLENGE: BRINGING HISTORY BACK IN

Of course the world-systems approach is not the first venture to challenge orthodox thinking in the social sciences. In fact Wallerstein is consciously attempting to bring together two previous challenges. First he borrows ideas and concepts from the French *Annales* school of history. These historians deplored the excessive detail of early twentieth century history with its emphasis upon political events and especially diplomatic manoeuvres. They argued for a more holistic approach in which the actions of politicians were just one small part in the unfolding history of ordinary people. Different politicians and their diplomacies would come and go but the everyday pattern of life with its economic and environmental material basis continued. The emphasis was therefore on the economic and social roots of history rather than the political facade emphasized in orthodox writings. This approach is perhaps best summarized by Fernand Braudel's phrase *longue durée* which represents the materialist stability underlying political volatility (Wallerstein 1977: 5).

The second challenge which Wallerstein draws upon is the neo-Marxist critique of the development theories of modern social science. The growth of social science after the Second World War coincided with a growth of new states out of the former European colonies. It was the application of modern social science to the problems of these new states which more than anything else exposed its severe limitations. In 1967 Gunder Frank published a cataclysmic critique of social scientific notions of 'modernization' in these new states which showed that ideas developed in the more prosperous parts of the world could not be transferred to poorer areas without wholly distorting the analysis. Frank's main point was that different economic processes operate in different parts of the world. Whereas western Europe and America may have experienced *development* most of the remainder of the world had experienced *the development of underdevelopment*. This latter phrase encapsulates the main point of this school, namely that for the new states it is not a matter of 'catching up' but rather one of changing the whole process of their development.

The world-systems approach attempts to combine selectively critical elements of Brandel's materialist history with Frank's neo-Marxist development studies as well as adding several new features to develop a comprehensive *historical social science*. As Goldfrank (1979) has put it, Wallerstein is explicitly 'bringing history back in' to social science. And, we might add, with the development of Frank's ideas he is also 'bringing geography back in' to social science. Quite simply there is more to understanding the world we live in than can be derived from study of the 'advanced' countries of the world in the late twentieth century, however rigorous or scholarly the conduct of such study is.

Drawing on this previous work Wallerstein challenges modern social science on three basic grounds.

1. The myth of universal laws

Modern social science is the culmination of a tradition that attempts to develop general laws for all times and places. A well-known example of this is the attempt to equate the decline of the British Empire with the decline of the Roman Empire nearly two millenia earlier. Similarly assumptions are often made that 'human nature' is universal so that motives identified today in 'advanced' countries can be transferred to other periods and cultures. An important example of this is the profit motive in price-fixing markets which is historically limited to modern society. To transfer this motive to past societies is to commit an error which Polanyi

(1977) terms the 'economistic fallacy'. Nevertheless Wallerstein does not retreat into an idiographic position emphasizing the uniqueness of events. Wallerstein does identify order which is not universal. The important point is to specify the scope of generalizations which we do below.

2. The poverty of disciplines

Modern social science is divided into different sectors of knowledge which are relatively self-contained and normally referred to as 'disciplines'. This division of knowledge is a very recent phenomenon and was only fully institutionalized in the twentieth century. The major 'disciplines' are economics, sociology and political science, each of which specialize in economic, social and political explanations respectively. The problem is that in the increasing complexity of the modern world, with massive growth of state activity, it is becoming increasingly difficult to identify problems as distinctively economic, social or political. By studying events separately in disciplines the type of solutions to problems that can be found is severely curtailed. There is, therefore, increasing awareness that the disciplines are more a hindrance than a help to understanding our world. One reflection of this feeling is the return of the pre-social science concept of 'political-economy' with its more holistic tradition. Wallerstein's approach is part of this new synthesis with perhaps more emphasis on overcoming the most basic division in the study of human society, that between all the social sciences and history.

3. The error of developmentalism

Modern social science has very many 'stage models' of development. The most famous is Rostow's *stages of economic growth*. This generalizes British economic history into a ladder of five stages from 'traditional society' at the bottom to 'the age of high mass consumption' at the top. Rostow uses this model to locate different countries on different rungs of his ladder. 'Advanced' countries are at the top whereas most of the new states are on the lower rungs. This way of conceptualizing the world has been very popular in geography where stage models are applied to a wide range of phenomena such as demographic change and transport networks. All assume that the new states can follow a path of development essentially the same as that pursued by the current 'advanced' states. This completely misses out the overall context in which development occurs. When Britain was at the bottom of Rostow's ladder there was no 'high mass consumption' going on at the top. Wallerstein's basic point is that states or countries are inappropriate units for studying change. They are not self-contained systems developing separately from one another but are all part of a larger whole. To treat them separately and to model change accordingly is to make the fundamental *error of developmentalism*. More than anything else the world-systems approach is a challenge to developmentalism.

SYSTEMS OF CHANGE

If modern social science is studying the wrong unit of change by concentrating on states or countries, what is the correct unit? Wallerstein argues that change can only be adequately understood if the object of analysis is a self-contained system which he terms an *entity*. Such entities are defined by their mode of production. For Wallerstein mode of production is broadly conceived as the organization of the material basis of a society. This is a much broader concept than the orthodox Marxist definition in that it includes not only the way in which productive tasks are divided up but also decisions concerning the quantities of goods to be produced, their consumption and/or accumulation along with the resulting distribution of goods. Using this broad definition Wallerstein identifies just three basic ways in which the material base of societies have been organized. These three modes of production are each associated with a type of entity or system of change.

1. Mini-systems and the reciprocal-lineage mode of production

This is the original mode of production based upon very limited specialization of tasks. Production is by hunting, gathering or rudimentary agriculture, exchange is reciprical between producers and the main organizational principle is age and gender. These are small extended families or kin-groups which are essentially local in geographical range and exist for just a few generations before destruction or fissure. There have been countless such mini-systems but none have survived to the present having been taken over and incorporated into larger world-systems. By 'world' Wallerstein does not mean 'global' but merely systems larger than the local day-to-day activities of particular members. Two such world-systems are identified by mode of production.

2. World-empires and the redistributive-tributary mode of production

World-empires have appeared in many political forms but they all share the same mode of production. This consists of a large group of agricultural producers whose technology is advanced enough to generate a surplus of production beyond their immediate needs. This surplus is sufficient to allow the development of specialized non-agricultural producers as artisans and administrators. Whereas exchange between agricultural producers and artisans is reciprocal the distinguishing feature of these systems is the appropriation of part of the surplus to the 'administrators' who form a military-bureaucratic ruling class. Such tribute is channelled upwards to produce large scale material inequality not found in mini-systems. This redistribution may be maintained in either a unitary political structure such as the Roman Empire or a fragmented structure such as feudal Europe. Despite such political contrasts Wallerstein argues that all such 'civilizations' from the Bronze Age to the recent past have the same material basis to their societies: they are all world-empires. These are less numerous than mini-systems but nevertheless there have been dozens of such entities since the Neolithic Revolution.

3. The world-economy and the capitalist mode of production.

The capitalist mode of production is based upon production for exchange so that the final distribution of production is determined by the market. The criterion for production is profitability and the basic drive of the system is accumulation of the surplus as capital. There is no overarching political structure so that the basic rule is accumulate or perish. Competition between different units of production is ultimately controlled by the cold hand of the market. In this system the efficient prosper and destroy the less-efficient by under-cutting their prices in the market. This mode of production defines a world-economy.

Historically such entities have been extremely fragile and have been incorporated and subjugated to world-empires before they could develop into capital-expanding systems. The great exception is the European world-economy that emerged after 1450 and survived to take over the whole world. A key date in its survival is 1557 when both the Spanish–Austrian Habsburgs and their great rivals the French Valois dynasty went bankrupt in their attempts to dominate the nascent world-economy (Wallerstein 1974a: 124). It is entirely appropriate that the demise of these final attempts to produce a unified European world-empire should fail not because of military defeat but at the hands of 'international' bankers. Clearly by 1557 the world-economy had truly arrived and survived its most vulnerable period to become the only historical example of a fully developing world-economy. As it expanded it eliminated all remaining mini-systems and world-empires to become truly global about 1900.

TYPES OF CHANGE

The error of developmentalism can be avoided by choosing the correct object of analysis. For the study of contemporary social change there is only one such entity, the world-economy. The current world-wide recession is evidence of this reality. But the world-systems approach allows us to specify much more than the study of contemporary social change. Three types of change can be identified.

1. Transformation

This occurs between different modes of production. There have been numerous transformations from mini-systems to world-empires as the latter have waxed and waned. There has been just one major transformation to the capitalist mode of production which started in Europe and spread to the rest of the world with the expansion of the world-economy.

2. Discontinuities

This occurs between different entities at approximately the same location where both entities share the same mode of production. The system breaks down and a new one is constituted in its place. For world-empires the sequence of Chinese states is the classic example. The periods between these separate world-empires are anarchic with some reversal to mini-systems and are commonly referred to as 'Dark Ages'. The most famous is that which occurred in western Europe between the collapse of the Roman Empire and the rise of feudal Europe.

3. Continuities

These occur within systems. Despite the popular image of 'time-less' traditional cultures all entities are dynamic and continually changing. Such changes are of two basic types – linear and cyclic. All world-empires have displayed a large cyclical pattern of 'rise and fall' as they expanded into mini-systems until bureaucratic-military costs lead to diminishing returns resulting in contraction. In the world-economy linear trends and cycles of growth and stagnation form an integral part of our analysis and they are described in some detail below.

From this point onwards we will concentrate on the world-economy entity as the basis of our political geography. It should be emphasized, therefore, that the remainder of the book is about the political geography of this one entity; the generalizations and analyses will not be relevant to other entities such as the Roman Empire. That would be to fall prey to the myth of universal laws – a political geography of the Roman Empire requires a different analysis and another book.

THE BASIC ELEMENTS OF THE WORLD-ECONOMY

Now that we have set the study of our world into the overall world-systems framework we can summarize the basic elements of our system which will underlie all our subsequent analyses. Wallerstein identifies three such basic elements.

1. A single world market

The world-economy consists of a single world market which is capitalist. This means that production is for exchange rather than use: producers do not consume what they produce but exchange it on the market for the best price they can get. These products are known as commodities whose value is determined by the market. It is for this reason that the capitalist market is a price-setting institution unlike pre-capitalist markets which are based upon traditional fixed-prices (Polanyi 1977). Since the price of any commodity is not fixed there is economic competition between producers. In this competition the more efficient producers can undercut the prices of other producers to increase their share of the market and to eliminate rivals. In this way the world market determines in the long run the quantity, type and location of production. The concrete result of this process has been uneven economic development across the world. Since the Second World War the world market has been dominated by multi-national corporations.

2. A multiple state system

In contrast to one economic market there has always been a number of political states in the world-economy. This is part of the definition of the system since if one state came to control the whole system the world market would become politically controlled, competition eliminated and the system would transform into a world-empire. Hence the international state system is a necessary element of the world-economy. Nevertheless single states are able to distort the market in the interests of their national capitalist group within their own boundaries and powerful states can distort the market well beyond their boundaries for a short time. This is the very stuff of 'international politics'. The concrete result of this process is a competitive state system in which a variety of 'balance of power' situations may prevail. Since the Second World War the balance of power has been bi-polar organized around the USA and USSR.

3. The three-tier structure

This third essential element is also 'political' in nature but is more subtle than the previous one. Wallerstein argues that the exploitative processes that operate through the world-economy always operate in a three-tiered format. This is because in any situation of inequality three tiers are more stable than two tiers of confrontation. Those at the top will always manoeuvre for the 'creation' of a three-tier structure whereas those at the bottom will emphasize the two tiers of 'them and us'. The continuing existence of the world-economy is due in part therefore to the success of the ruling groups to sustain three-tiered patterns throughout various fields of conflict. An obvious example is the existence of 'centre' parties between right and left in many political systems. The most general case is the promotion of the notion of a 'middle class' between capital and labour. In other contexts the acceptance of 'middle' ethnic groups such as 'poor whites' helps ruling groups to maintain stability and control.

Geographically the most interesting example is Wallerstein's concept of the 'semi-periphery' which separates the extremes of material well-being in the modern world-economy which Wallerstein terms the core and the periphery. We define these terms in the next section.

A SPACE–TIME MATRIX OF THE WORLD-ECONOMY

If we are bringing history back into political geography the question obviously arises as to 'what history?'. Several recent studies have shared our concern for the neglect of history in geography and have attempted to rectify the situation by presenting brief résumés of world history over the last few hundred years in the opening chapter of their work. The dangers and pitfalls of such writing are obvious: how can such a task be adequately achieved in just a few pages of text? The answer is that we must be highly selective. The selection of episodes to be covered will be directly determined by the purpose of the 'history'. This is nothing new of course; it is true of all history. It is just that the exigencies are so severe for our purpose here.

We are fortunate that our problem has been made manageable by the publication of *The Times Atlas of World History* (Barraclough 1979). Applying Wallerstein's world-systems approach to any subject assumes a level of general historical knowledge which is probably an unreasonable expectation of most students. It is well worth a trip to the library to browse through *The Times Atlas* and obtain a sense of the movement of world history. This is recommended to all readers of this book.

Of course this atlas does not itself employ a world-systems approach. It is divided into seven sections in the following chronological order:

1. The world of early man
2. The first civilizations
3. The classical civilizations of Eurasia
4. The world of divided regions (approximately 600–1500)
5. The world of the emerging west (1500–1800)
6. The age of European dominance (nineteenth century)
7. The age of global civilization (twentieth century)

The product is explicitly global in intent and it avoids the Eurocentric basis of many earlier attempts at world history. Nevertheless it does bear the mark of traditional historiography with its impress of progress from stone age to global civilization. Hence Wallerstein's (1980b) conclusion that the *The Times Atlas of World History* represents the culmination of a tradition rather than being a pathbreaker. The seven sectors could be termed, stone age, bronze age, classical iron age, dark ages, age of exploration, nineteenth-century age of trade and imperialism and twentieth-century age of global society and world wars, with not too much distortion of the flow of ideas. Wallerstein (1980b) looks forward to a new product in which the waxing and waning of world-empires into and out of zones of mini-systems is gradually replaced after 1450 by the geographical expansion of the capitalist world-economy. That product is not yet available. In the meantime *The Times Atlas* provides an indispensable set of facts catalogued on maps using a traditional model which can be used to bounce world-systems ideas off.

One of the advantages of adopting the world-systems approach is that it enables us to be much more explicit in the theory behind our history. The purpose of this section is to construct just such a historical framework for our political geography which does not simply reflect the weak sense of progress to be found in the other texts referred to at the beginning of this discussion. In place of a linear reconstruction of history we will emphasize the ups and downs of the world-economy. Furthermore the different parts of the world-economy will be affected differentially by these movements. The way we will present these ideas is as a space–time matrix of the world-economy. This is an extremely poor relation to *The Times Atlas* but it does provide a succinct description of the major events relevant to our political geography.

The matrix we generate is not an arbitrary, artificial creation. We are trying to describe the concrete historical entity of the world-economy. Both dimensions of the matrix are calibrated in terms of the system properties of the world-economy. Neither space nor time are treated as in any sense separate from the world-economy. They are *not* space–time containers through which the world-economy 'travels'. Rather they are both interpreted as the product of social relations. The time dimension is described as a social product of the *dynamics* of the world-economy. The space dimension is described as a social product of the *structure* of the world-economy. Our space–time matrix is a simple model which combines the dynamics and structure to provide a framework for political geography.

THE DYNAMICS OF THE WORLD-ECONOMY

One reason for current interest in the global scale of analysis is the fact that the whole world seems to be suffering from an economic recession. It is clear that it is not an American problem or British problem or the problem of any single state; rather is is a world problem. Furthermore it seems that this is not the first time the 'world' has experienced such a general recession. About fifty years ago similar problems occurred in the 'Great Depression'. As we go back in time such events are less clear but economic historians also identify economic recessions in the late Victorian era and before 1850 – the famous 'hungry forties'. Between each recession there was recovery and growth, the most recent example being the world-wide post-Second World War boom. It is but a short step from these simple observations to the idea that the world-economy has developed in a cyclical manner. The first person to propose such a scheme was a Russian economist, Kondratieff, and today such fifty-year cycles are named after him.

1. Kondratieff cycles

Kondratieff cycles consist of two phases, one of growth (A) and one of stagnation (B). It is generally agreed that the following four cycles have occurred (exact dates will vary):

I	1780/90	_____	A	_____	1810/17	_____	B	_____	1844/51
II	1844/51	_____	A	_____	1870/75	_____	B	_____	1890/96
III	1890/96	_____	A	_____	1914/20	_____	B	_____	1940/45
IV	1940/45	_____	A	_____	1967/73	_____	B	_____	?

These have been identified in time-series data for a wide range of economic phenomena including industrial and agricultural production and trade statistics for many countries. On this interpretation we are currently experiencing the B-phase of the fourth Kondratieff cycle.

Whereas identification of these cycles is widely agreed the actual causes of their existence is more problematic. They are certainly associated with technological change and the A-phases can be easily related to major periods of the adaption of technological innovations. The first A-phase coincides with the original 'industrial revolution' with its steam engines, cotton industry and wrought iron. Subsequent 'new industrial revolutions' also fit the pattern well, consisting of railways and steel (IIA), chemicals (oil) and electricity (IIIA) and aerospace and electronics (IVA). Of course technology itself cannot explain anything. Why did these technical adoptions occur as 'bundles' of innovations and not on a more regular, linear basis? Wallerstein's answer is that cyclical behaviour is inherent in the capitalist mode of production. Contradictions in the organization of the material base means that linear growth is impossible and intermittent phases of stagnation are necessary. Let us briefly consider this argument.

A basic feature of the capitalist mode of production is the lack of any central control, political or otherwise. The market relies on competition to order the system and competition implies multiple decentralized decision-making. Such entrepreneurs make decisions for their own short-term advantage. In good times, A-phases, it is in the interests of all entrepreneurs to invest in production (new technology) since profits are good. With no central planning of investment, however, such short-term decision-making will inevitably lead to over-production and the cessation of the A-phase. Conversely in B-phases profits are poor and there will be under-investment in production. This is rational for each individual entrepreneur but it is irrational for the system as a whole. This contradiction is usually referred to as the *anarchy of production* and will produce cycles of investment. After extracting all the surplus value out of a particular set of production processes based on one bundle of technology in an A-phase, the B-phase becomes necessary to reorganize production to generate new conditions for expansion based on a new bundle of technological innovations. Hence the ups and downs of the world-economy as described by the Kondratieff waves.

There is a lot more that could be said about the generation of these cycles, not least the political inputs into the process. These will be the subject-matter of the next chapter and for the time being it is sufficient for us to accept that the nature of the world-economy produces cyclical growth which has been adequately described by Kondratieff waves. This will provide the main part of the metric for the time dimension for our matrix.

2. 'Logistic' waves

What about before 1780? We have indicated that the world-economy emerged after 1450 but we have as yet no metric for this early period. Of course as we go back in time data sources become less plentiful and less reliable, leading to much less consensus on the dynamics of the early world-economy. Some researchers, including Braudel, claim to have found Kondratieff waves before 1780 but such hypotheses for this earlier period do not command the same general support as the sequence reported above. There is, however, more support for longer waves of up to three hundred years which have been referred to as 'logistics'. Just like Kondratieff waves these longer cycles have A- and B-phases. Two logistics of particular interest to world-systems analysis are as follows:

c1050 _____ A _____ c1250 _____ B _____ c1450
c1450 _____ A _____ c1600 _____ B _____ c1750

The dates are much less certain than for the Kondratieff waves but there does seem to be enough evidence in terms of land-use and demographic data to support the idea of two very long waves over this general time span.

It will have been noticed that these logistics take us back beyond the beginning of the world-economy. The first logistic is of interest, however, because it encompasses the material rise and decline of feudal Europe, the immediate predecessor of the world-economy. There is a massive literature on the transformation from this feudalism to the capitalist mode of production which is beyond the scope of this text. Wallerstein's (1974a) explanation, however, is relevant since it relates to this first logistic wave and the emergence of the world-economy. The B-phase of the first logistic reflects a real decline in production as indexed by the contraction of agriculture throughout Europe. This is the so-called crisis of feudalism. B-phases terminate when a solution to a crisis is generated. In this case the solution was nothing less than the development of a new mode of production. This emerged gradually out of European exploration and plunder in the Americas, the development of new trade patterns, particularly the Baltic trade, and technological advances in agricultural production. The result was, according to Wallerstein, a new entity or system – the European world-economy based upon agricultural capitalism. This system itself generates a logistic wave of expansion in its emergence in the 'long sixteenth century' followed by stagnation in the 'crisis' of the seventeenth century. However Wallerstein emphasizes the fact that this second B-phase in agricultural capitalism is different in kind from the

B-phase of late feudalism. Unlike the real decline that occurred in feudal Europe, the world-economy B-phase is more one of stagnation. This involved the reordering of the materialist base so that some groups and areas gained while others lost. There was no general decline like the crisis of feudalism but rather a consolidation of the system into a new pattern. In this sense the second logistic B-phase is more like the B-phase of the later Kondratieff waves.

Just as there is a dispute over whether Kondratieff waves extend back before 1780 there is a similar disagreement about whether logistic waves can be extended forward to the present. If either set of cycles is extended then we come across the thorny problem of how they relate to one another. For the purposes of our matrix we will avoid this problem by just using the waves generally accepted in the literature and described above. Our time metric for the world-economy therefore consists of ten units, A- and B-phase for the logistic wave after c1450 and four A- and B-phases in the Kondratieff waves. These two different treatments of time may be thought of as relating to agricultural capitalism and industrial capitalism as consecutive production forms of the world-economy.

THE SPATIAL STRUCTURE OF THE WORLD-ECONOMY

I have dealt with the dynamic property of the world-economy first because the term 'spatial structure' usually conjures up a static picture of an unchanging pattern. The spatial structure we are dealing with here is part and parcel of the same processes that generate the cycles described above. Spatial structure and temporal cycle are two sides of the same mechanisms which produce a single space–time framework. Space and time are separated here for pedagogic reasons so that in what follows it must always be remembered that the spatial structures we describe are essentially dynamic.

1. The geographical extent of the system

Our first task is to consider the geographical expansion of the world-economy. We have mentioned that it emerged as a European world-economy after 1450 and covered the globe by about 1900 but have not indicated how this varying size is defined. Basically all entities are defined in concrete terms by the geographical extent of their division of labour. This is the division of the productive and other tasks which are necessary for the operation of the system. Hence some distribution and trade is a necessary element of the system whereas other trade is merely ephemeral and has little relevance beyond those directly participating in it. For instance luxury trade between the Roman and Chinese Empires was ephemeral and we would not suggest they be combined to form a single 'Eurasian' system because of this trade. In Wallerstein's terminology China is part of Rome's external arena and vice versa.

Using this criteria Wallerstein delimits the initial European world-system as consisting of western Europe, eastern Europe and those parts of south and middle America under Iberian control. The rest of the world was an external arena. This included the ring of Portuguese ports around and Indian and Pacific Oceans which were concerned with trade in luxury goods. The development of this Portuguese trade had minimal effects in Asia (they merely replaced Arab and other traders) and Europe. In contrast Spanish activity in America – especially bullion exports – was fundamentally important in forming the world-economy. For Wallerstein therefore Spain was much more important than Portugal in the origins of the world-economy despite the latter's more global pattern of possessions.

From this period the European world-economy has expanded by incorporating the remainder of the world roughly in the order Caribbean, North America, India, East Asia, Australia, Africa and finally the Pacific Islands. These incorporations take several forms. The simplest was plunder. This could only be a short-term process to be supplemented by more productive activities involving new settlement. This sequence occurred in Latin America. Elsewhere aboriginal systems were also destroyed and completely new economies built as in North America and Australia. Alternatively existing societies remained intact but they were *peripheralized* in the sense that their economies were reorientated to serve wider needs within the world-economy. This could be achieved through political control as in India or directly through 'opening up' an area to market forces as in China. The end result of these various incorporation procedures was the eventual elimination of the external arena.

2. The concepts of core and periphery

The concept of peripheralization implies that these new areas did not join the world-economy as 'equal partners' with existing members but that they were joining on unfavourable terms. They were, in fact, joining a particular part of the world-economy which we will term the periphery. It is now common-place to define the modern world in terms of core (meaning the rich countries of North America, Western Europe and Japan) and periphery (meaning the poor countries of the 'third world'). Although the 'rise' of Japan to such status has been quite dramatic in this century, this core–periphery pattern is often treated as a static, almost natural, phenomenon. The world-economy use of the terms core and periphery is entirely different. Both refer to complex processes and *not* directly to areas, regions or states. The latter only become core-like because of a predominance of core *processes* operating in that particular area, region or state. Similarly peripheral areas, regions or states are defined as those where peripheral *processes* dominate. This is not a trivial semantic point but directly relates to the way in which the spatial structure is modelled (Agnew 1981). Space itself can be neither core nor periphery in nature. Rather there are core and periphery processes which structure space so that at any point in time one or other of the two processes predominate. Since these processes do not act randomly but generate uneven economic development, broad zones of 'core' and 'periphery' are found. Such zones exhibit some stability – parts of Europe have always been in the core – but also show dramatic changes over the lifetime of the world-economy notably in the rise of non-European areas – first the USA and then Japan.

How does Wallerstein define these two basic processes? Like all core–periphery models there is an implication that 'the core exploits and the periphery is exploited'. But this cannot occur as zones exploiting one another, it occurs through the different processes operating in different zones. Core and periphery processes are opposite types of complex production relations. In simplest terms core processes consist of relations that incorporate *relatively* high wages, advanced technology and a diversified production mix whereas periphery processes involve low wages, more rudimentary technology and a simple production mix. These are general characteristics, the exact nature of which changes constantly with the evolution of the world-economy. It is important to understand that these processes are not determined by the particular product being produced. Frank (1978) provides two good examples to illustrate this. In the late nineteenth century India was organized to provide Lancashire with cotton and Australia to provide Yorkshire with wool. Both were producing raw materials for Britain's textile industry so that their economic function within the world-economy was broadly similar. Nevertheless the social relations embodied in these two productions were very different with one being an imposed peripheral process and the other a transplanted core process. The outcomes for these two countries have clearly depended on these social relations and not the particular type of product. Frank's other example of similar products leading to contrasting outcomes due to production relations is the contrast between the tropical hardwood production of central Africa and the softwood production of North America and Scandinavia. The former combines expensive wood and cheap labour, the latter cheap wood and expensive labour.

3. The semi-periphery category

Core and periphery do not exhaust Wallerstein's concepts for structuring space. Although these processes occur in distinctive zones to produce relatively clear-cut contrasts across the world-economy not all zones are easily designated as primarily core or periphery in nature. One of the most original elements of Wallerstein's approach is his concept of the semi-periphery. This is neither core nor periphery but combines particular mixtures of both processes. Notice there are *no* semi-peripheral processes. Rather the term semi-periphery can be directly applied to zones, areas or states when they exhibit neither a predominance of core nor peripheral processes. This means that the overall social relations operating in such zones involves exploiting peripheral areas while the semi-periphery itself suffers exploitation by the core.

The semi-periphery is interesting because it is the dynamic category within the world-economy. The restructuring of space during recessions involves zones rising and sinking through the semi-periphery. Opportunities for change occur during recessions but these are only limited opportunities – not all the semi-periphery can evolve to become core. Political processes are very important here in the selection of success and failure in the world-economy. Wallerstein actually considers the semi-periphery's role to be more political than economic. It is the crucial middle zone in the spatial manifestation of his three-tiered characterization of the world-economy. For this reason it will figure prominently in much of our subsequent discussions.

A SPACE–TIME MATRIX FOR POLITICAL GEOGRAPHY

The above discussion produces a 10×3 matrix involving ten phases of growth and stagnation and three types of spatial zone. In Table 1 this framework is used to portray those features of the evolving world-economy that are necessary for understanding our political geography. This table should be read and referred to as necessary for subsequent chapters. It is largely self-explanatory but a brief commentary will illustrate the ways in which this information will be related to our discussion.

The establishment of the world-economy as a system operating from eastern Europe to the 'New World' involved the development of both Atlantic trade and the Baltic trade. The former initiated from Iberia but gradually came to be financially controlled from the incipient core of north-west Europe on which the Baltic trade was based. Once this core becomes established Iberia is relegated to a 'conveyor belt' for the transfer of surplus from its colonies to the core. It is during the logistic B-phase that the basic elements of the world-economy identified above become consolidated. First, there is a single world-market organized and controlled from north-west Europe. Second, a multiple state system emerges epitomized by the initiation of 'international law' to regulate relations between states. Third, a three-tiered spatial structure clearly emerges and can be identified in the new division of labour for agricultural production: 'free' wage labour developing in the north-west European core; partially free 'sharecropping' arrangements in the Mediterranean semi-periphery and, in the periphery, two different forms of coerced labour – slavery in the New World and the so-called 'second feudalism' in eastern Europe. Despite massive changes in the world-economy since this time these three essential features have remained and are just as important today as they were in the seventeenth century.

Following the consolidation of the world-economy it has grown economically and geographically in fits and starts as described by the four

Kondratieff waves. Some degree of symmetry in these changes can be identified from Table 1 by designating British and American 'centuries'. These relate to the rise of these two states, defeat of their rivals (France and Germany respectively), their dominance of the world-economy (including their promotion of free-trade) and finally their decline with new rivalries emerging (including the rise of protectionism and/or imperialism). We consider such patterns in some detail in the next chapter.

In order to illustrate the rest of the matrix let us highlight the route of today's major states through this matrix. Britain became part of the core by the time of the logistic B-phase when it restructured its state in the civil war. It has maintained that position despite relative decline since the second Kondratieff B-phase. France's early position is similar to Britain's but defeat in the periphery and relative decline in the logistic B-phase led to a restructuring of the French state in the revolution. However, subsequent defeat in the core of the first Kondratieff wave led to a second relative decline but within the core. The USA and Germany (Prussia) have had much more volatile histories. Both carved out semi-peripheral positions in the logistic B-phase but their positions were unstable. In the USA peripheralization was prevented by the War of Independence. This victory was consolidated by the civil war in the second Kondratieff A-phase when southern cotton became part of an American periphery (rather than part of a British periphery) in a restructured American state. From this point onwards the USA prospered to become the major power of the twentieth century. Initially its major rival was Germany which also restructured its state in the second Kondratieff A-phase under Prussian leadership but subsequent economic prowess was set back in the third Kondratieff wave by military defeat. Today Germany is again a major economic challenger of the USA in the core. But the major economic challenger is Japan which only entered the world-economy in the second Kondratieff wave. It also restructured its state, suffered military setbacks but has now finally come through towards economic leadership. Russia, on the other hand, entered the world-economy earlier but declined in the second Kondratieff wave. This was halted by a reorganization of the Russian state as the USSR which has emerged as a major military power but remains economically semi-peripheral. Finally China entered the world-economy in the periphery at the end of the first Kondratieff wave and has attempted to rise to semi-peripheral status with reorganizations of the state in the third and fourth Kondratieff A-phases. This has been successful as the People's Republic of China.

This description emphasizes the role of state reorganization in the rise of these states. But we should not imply that a state merely needs to reorder its political apparatus to enjoy world-economy success. By only describing the success stories – today's major states – we omit the far greater number of failures: while Germany and the USA were reorganizing in the second

Table 1 A space–time information matrix

		Core
Logistic Curve	A	Initial geographical expansion based on Iberia but economic advances based on north-west Europe.
	B	Consolidation of north-west European dominance, first Dutch and then French–English rivalry
Kondratieff Wave I	A	Industrial revolution in Britain, 'national' revolution in France. Defeat of France
	B	Consolidation of British economic leadership. Origins of socialism in Britain and France
Kondratieff Wave II	A	Britain as the 'workshop of the world' in an era of free trade
	B	Decline of Britain relative to USA and Germany. Emergence of the Socialist Second International
Kondratieff Wave III	A	Consolidation of German and USA economic leadership. Arms race
	B	Defeat of Germany, British Empire saved. USA economic leadership confirmed
Kondratieff Wave IV	A	USA as the greatest power in the world both military and economically. New era of free trade
	B	Decline of USA relative to Europe and Japan. Nuclear arms race

Kondratieff A-phase so too was the Ottoman Empire to much less effect.
In fact political reorganization has become a way of life in many semi-
peripheral states as lack of success in the world-economy brings forth
pressure for change again and again. We are now ready to consider this
power and politics in the world-economy.

POWER AND POLITICS IN THE WORLD-ECONOMY

One common criticism of Wallerstein's approach is that it neglects the

Semi-periphery	Periphery
Relative decline of cities of central and Mediterranean Europe	Iberian empires in 'New World', second 'feudalism' in eastern Europe
Declining areas now include Iberia and joined by rising groups in Sweden, Prussia and north-east USA	Retrenchment in Latin America and East Europe. Rise of Caribbean sugar. French defeat in India and Canada
Relative decline of whole semi-periphery. Establishment of USA	Decolonization and expansion – formal control in India but informal controls in Latin America
Beginning of selective rise in North America and central Europe	Expansion of British influence in Latin America. Initial opening up of East Asia
Reorganization of semi-periphery: civil war in USA, unification of Germany and Italy, entry of Russia	The classic era of 'informal imperialism' with growth of Latin America
Decline of Russia and Mediterranean Europe	Expansion – scramble for Africa. The classical age of imperialism
Entry of Japan and Dominion states	Consolidation of new colonies (Africa) plus growth in trade elsewhere (especially China)
Socialist victory in Russia – establishment of USSR. Entry of Argentina	Neglect of periphery. Beginning of peripheral revolts. Import-substitution in Latin America
Rise of eastern Europe and 'cold war'. Entry of OPEC	Socialist victory in China. Decolonization leading this time to 'neo-colonialism'
Entry of 'Little Japans' in East Asia and new regional powers – China, Brazil, Mexico, India. Rise of debts to core	Severe economic crisis and conflict. Expansion of poverty

political dimension. Zolberg (1981), for instance, claims that politics is the 'missing link' in the world-systems approach. By now the reader should be aware that such criticisms represent a misunderstanding of the framework we have adopted. Quite simply an emphasis upon the materialist base of society as defined by a mode of production does not necessarily mean that politics is ignored or devalued. In the section on basic elements of the world-economy above, two of the three characteristics described were pre-eminently political in nature – the multi-state system and the three-tier structure. It is the purpose of this final section of our introductory chapter to develop the argument concerning politics in the world-economy in order to derive our political geography perspective on the world-economy.

The position we take in interpreting political events in the world-economy is based upon Chase-Dunn (1981, 1982). As we have seen the capitalist mode of production involves the extraction of economic surplus for accumulation within the world-economy. This surplus is expropriated in two related ways. The distinguishing feature of our system is the expropriation via the market. But the traditional expropriation method of world-empires is not entirely eliminated. The use of political and military power to obtain surplus is the second method of expropriation. Of course this second method cannot dominate the system or else the system would be transformed into a new mode of production. But neither should it be under-valued as a process in the world-economy from the initial Spanish plunder of the New World to today's support of multi-national corporation interests by their 'home' country, usually the USA. The important point is that these two methods of expropriation should not be interpreted as two separate processes – or 'two logics' as Chase-Dunn (1981) terms them – one 'political' and the other 'economic'. In our framework they are but two aspects of the same overall political-economy logic. Chase-Dunn (1982: 25) puts the argument as follows:

> The interdependence of political military power and competitive advantage in production in the capitalist world-economy reveals that the logic of the accumulation process *includes* the logic of state building and geopolitics.

Political processes lie at the heart of world-systems analysis but they are not located there separately in isolation.

WHAT IS A STRONG STATE? OVERT AND COVERT POWER

The measurement of the relative power of states has been a perennial problem in political geography. It is a problem because 'power' is one of those concepts which cannot be directly measured. The usual solution has been to identify some salient characteristics of states which are then combined to produce an index of power for each state. A simple example is Fuck's index where power is computed by cubing a country's gross national product and then multiplying the cube by the square root of its population (Muir 1981: 149). The result provides an intuitively reasonable measure of power but it is hardly satisfactory. Why use just production and population variables? Why combine them in this specific manner? Such questions cannot be answered without explicit recourse to the theory behind the measurement. We have to go back to the question – what makes a particular characteristic salient to this measurement problem?

Most studies of state power have been inductive in nature to the severe neglect of theory. The theory implicit in this work is usually some notion of war potential. But the defeat of the 'super power' USA by the 'medium power' of Vietnam has required a complete rethink. Even more intriguing has been the recent experience of Britain – defeated in a North Atlantic

War by a 'small power' Iceland in the 1970s (the so-called Cod War) but victorious in a South Atlantic War over a 'medium power', Argentina, in the 1980s. What do we make of these recent exercises of state power on the international scene? One solution is to lower our sights and admit that 'it seems unlikely that a complete measure will ever be obtained' (Muir 1981: 149). We then retreat into 'rough estimates' which are dependent upon the 'situation' in which the power is employed. Muir (1981: 150) uses five variables – area, population, steel production, size of army and number of nuclear submarines – to provide his rough estimates of power. Again the results are intuitively correct but what use are they if they imply a US victory in Vietnam or a British triumph over Iceland? It is not enough to say that state power depends on the situation in which it is employed.

We need a completely fresh approach to studying state power. This can be achieved through the world-economy approach by employing the concepts of overt and covert power relations. Whereas the former is what we normally understand by power as reflected in conflict we will argue that covert power, the ability to forward particular interests without resort to coercion or threat, is much more pervasive and important. We identify four types of power relations, two overt and two covert.

1. Actual and latent force

Overt power is the political relation observed in conflict. If two actors A and B have opposing interests in a situation then whichever interest prevails indicates which of the two actors is most powerful. In the American civil war we would say that the north was basically more powerful than the south or that in the Second World War the allies were ultimately more powerful than the axis powers. This is a very important demonstration of power as witnessed by the 224 wars each causing more than one thousand battle deaths between 1816 and 1980 listed by Small and Singer (1982).

Overt power need not consist of an actual use of force. Violent coercion can be seen as a last resort after persuasion has been attempted. Such diplomacy does not normally rely on the logic of argument, however, but is backed up by the threat of force. This latent force is especially well illustrated in the Cuban missile crisis of 1962 when Soviet vessels were turned back without any actual use of force. Such brinkmanship is rare but more modest 'gunboat diplomacy' has been a hallmark of both British and American foreign policy at different times in the last two centuries. Between 1945 and 1976, for instance, Blechman and Kaplan (1978) record 215 incidents when American armed forces were used politically to further American interests but without appreciable violence – what they call 'force without war'. A typical example would be the visit of the most powerful warship in the US Navy, uss *Missouri*, to Turkey in 1945 at a time of USSR claims on Turkish territory. As Blechman and Kaplan (1978: 2) put it:

The meaning of this event was missed by no one; Washington had not so subtly reminded the Soviet Union and others that the United States was a great military power and that it could project this power abroad, even to shores far distant.

Blechman and Kaplan identify four periods of American use of latent force which are shown in Table 2 along with a geographical allocation of the incidents to eight political arenas. It can be seen that early American concern for Europe in the first period gives way to involvement in East Asia in the second period. In the third period Middle America/Caribbean and South-east Asia dominate the picture whereas the Middle East/North Africa and South-east Asia are the important arenas in the final period. Obviously these peaks of incidents revolve around important crises of the post-Second World War era, notably Berlin in the first period, Korea in the second period, Cuba in the third period, Vietnam in the third and fourth periods and Israel in the third and fourth periods. The interesting point is the quantity of such incidents in comparison to just the two major examples of actual force employed by the USA in Korea and Vietnam.

Of course, the USA is not alone in 'flexing its muscles' in this way. The foreign policy of the other 'super power', USSR, has been studied in a

Table 2   366 examples of latent force: USA and USSR armed forces used as political instruments 1946–75 (Derived from data presented in Blechman and Kaplan (1978) and Kaplan (1981))

Arenas	Time Periods							
	1946–8		1949–55		1956–65		1966–75	
	USA	USSR	USA	USSR	USA	USSR	USA	USSR
Europe/Mediterranean	15	10	6	24	13	24	5	23
Middle East/North Africa	3	2	2	2	18	5	15	23
South Asia	0	0	0	0	2	0	1	3
South-east Asia	0	0	4	0	26	5	12	1
East Asia	1	6	8	5	7	3	5	6
Africa south of the Sahara	0	0	1	0	8	3	1	6
Middle America/Caribbean	2	0	3	0	35	2	6	2
South America	3	0	0	0	9	0	0	0
Total	24	18	24	31	118	42	45	64

similar manner by Kaplan (1981) who identifies 190 'incidents' when Soviet armed forces were used as political instruments between 1944 and 1979. 155 of these incidents which occurred between 1946 and 1975 have been added to Table 2 for comparative purposes. In this case the data show the emergence of the USSR as a global power. In the first two periods all incidents occurred in arenas adjacent to the USSR but in the final two periods the political influence of USSR armed forces spreads to all arenas except South America. But we are jumping ahead in our argument – we deal with geopolitics in the next chapter. The point of Table 2 is to illustrate the existence of latent force and to show its quantitative importance.

2. Non-decision making

The most well-known form of covert power is described by the strange term 'non-decision making'. This derives from Schattschneider's (1960) study of American democracy in which he argued that 'all organization is bias'. By this he means that in any politics only some conflicts of interest will be represented on the political agenda. All other conflicts will be 'organized out of politics' so that they do not become the subject of any overt power relations. Schattschneider's examples relate to political parties and in particular the rather limited range of options offered to the American electorate. We will consider his ideas in Chapter 5 below. His work is now most well known as the source for Bachrach and Baratz's (1962) concept of non-decision-making in urban studies. They argue that just to study overt decision-making in urban government misses out the agenda-setting process when what will be and what will not be considered occurs. This is essentially a form of manipulation which allows decisions to be steered along certain directions normally favourable to maintaining the status quo. The power is covert in that 'decisions' on non-agenda matters do not have to be made (hence non-decision making). This view takes us a long way along the road to understanding the strength of the status quo in the world-economy.

A most sustained attempt to change the agenda of world politics occurred at the United Nations after the achievement of a third world majority in the General Assembly in the wake of the decolonization of the post-Second World War period. The United Nations Conference on Trade and Development has spawned two 'development decades' and we have had the Brandt commission culminating with the Cancun conference in which 'global negotiations' took place. But despite the lip-service paid to development of the poorer countries at Cancun the agenda of world politics has not changed. It is not North–South issues that dominate current inter-state relations, instead the East–West conflict continues at the top of the agenda. UN pressure seems merely to have weakened the position of that body in the eyes of the dominant states, notably the USA. The lesson is simple – once established, agendas are very difficult to shift since they represent the very assumptions upon which politics is based. Both 'old cold war', 'detente' and 'new cold war' share the same assumptions which omit the massive material inequalities of our world from the main agenda. This is non-decision making because it leaves the status quo untouched by the mainstream of world politics.

3. Structural position

Non-decision making is not the only form of covert power relations. It is important for understanding that power games are not played out in some neutral arena but it is only one relatively minor aspect of covert power-relations. If indeed the UN was successful in defusing the East–West conflict and focusing all attention on third world poverty, there is no guarantee that material inequalities will be successfully tackled. Getting an issue on the agenda is a start but it is only a beginning. The vested interests of the status quo will have to combat the periphery directly but they need not have to use overt force to maintain their position.

The most important form of power relation is structural. It derives directly from the operation of the world-economy as a system. Consider the two states of Brazil and Switzerland. On almost every power index Brazil will appear more powerful than Switzerland – on Muir's criteria it has more area, population, steel production and soldiers, for instance. But this is only a war potential measure and Brazil and Switzerland have not gone to war with one another and are unlikely to do so in the future: the Swiss government are not that silly. In fact Switzerland has not gone to war with anybody since the Napoleonic era. But in the hierarchical spatial structure of the world-economy Switzerland is core and Brazil is only semi-periphery. By definition, therefore Switzerland can be said to 'exploit' Brazil because the world-economy is structured in such a way as to favour Switzerland at Brazil's expense. Switzerland does not have to engage in any overt actions to impose its domination beyond 'normal' trading relations: Swiss bankers are part of an international banking community imposing conditions on Brazil to reschedule its debts. And Swiss multinationals such as Nestlé are involved in profitable enterprises for the ultimate benefit of Swiss shareholders. Quite simply the operation of the world market and Swiss and Brazilian relations to that market ensure Swiss predominance and a resulting flow of surplus to Switzerland. This is a far cry from the original Spanish plunder of the Americas based on a very overt use of power but it is none the less real for all that. In fact it is much cheaper and efficient exploitation. It is also very different from the covert use of power in agenda-setting. The Swiss are involved in no manipulation of the system; quite the opposite. They are playing the rules of the game as they are meant to be played. It is just those rules, the operation of the world-economy, are in their favour as a state whose economy is based upon core production relations. With more efficient production they can call the tune in countries that cannot directly compete economically with them such as Brazil.

4. Power and appearance

We can now return to our original question concerning the power of states. In the world-economy approach power is a direct reflection of the ability of a state to operate within the system to its own material advantage. This depends on the efficiency of its production processes which is measured by our categories of core, semi-periphery and periphery. If power is overtly expressed then we can expect a core–semi-periphery– periphery sequence of success chances in a given conflict. But most expressions of this power will be covert and structural. Although this is essentially an 'economic' definition of power it can be directly related to the notion of the 'strong state' as a complementary expression of power.

Generally speaking there is a tendency for core states to be relatively liberal in their characteristics since their power is based primarily on their economic prowess. The seventeenth-century Dutch state was the first state to reach such a fortunate position. As a politically weak federation of counties it never *appeared* to be the most powerful state in the world – but for a short period that is exactly what it was. Britain and America have subsequently become leading 'liberal' states. In the next chapter we shall refer to such states as hegemonic. In contrast the semi-periphery tends to be occupied by authoritarian states which *appear* to be politically powerful. The absolute monarchies of the early world-economy right through to the authoritarian regimes of today's semi-periphery (for example, Brazil and Russia) illustrate this characteristic. Their political postures can be interpreted in part as attempts to compensate for their relative economic weakness. Remember the semi-periphery is the most dynamic category in world-economy and these states have to employ political processes to restructure the system in their favour. Usually, of course, they are unsuccessful. Finally there are the weakest element in the system, the peripheral states. For much of the history of the world-economy this zone has not been in political control of its own territory but has had colonial status. This is obviously the weakest possible position to hold in the world-economy. Even with political independence, however, economic dependence will remain, leading to concepts such as 'informal imperialism' and 'neo-colonialism' whereby the destiny of the country remains almost wholly outside its own control. The main problem of the state is internal security leading to repression and often ephemeral regimes. Informal imperialism and peripheral states are both dealt with in later chapters. The point to make here is that despite the tanks and guns they are essentially weak states. Overt political power is attempting to compensate for the lack of 'real' power in the world-economy.

A POLITICAL GEOGRAPHY PERSPECTIVE ON THE WORLD-ECONOMY

We have described the way in which we will interpret politics in the world-economy but have not dealt with political *geography*. Given our holistic stance we will not be attempting to devise a sub-discipline of political geography with its own subject matter. We recognise only historical social science in the political economy tradition in which there are no disciplines or sub-disciplines. What we offer is a political geography perspective on the world-economy. The only justification for devising this perspective in preference to other viewpoints is that it seems to provide an interesting arrangement of ideas and suggests insights into the operation of the world-economy which have not been so clearly shown elsewhere.

What is this political geography perspective? At its simplest it just involves viewing the world-economy through different geographical scales of analysis. In nearly all of our previous discussion we have treated topics at the international scale. This should not be taken to mean that the world-economy approach deals *only* with global-level activities, however. For the purposes of our exposition it has been convenient to stay largely at this one geography scale. Since the world-economy is a holistic concept, however, it follows that one scale of analysis cannot be hived off and studied separately any more than economic or political processes can be treated in isolation. The world-economy approach must treat activities at all geographical scales.

If we briefly return to our problem examples in the measurement of power we will soon see the need for an integrated approach to geographical scales. American defeat in Vietnam or the contrasting fortunes of Britain in the North and South Atlantic conflicts cannot be properly considered at the level of state power comparisons. These inter-state conflicts must be seen in relation to the overall international context in which they occurred and in their interactions with intra-state processes. Obviously American policy in Vietnam in the early 1970s – so-called Vietnamization of the war – was a response to internal pressures on the US government. In order to avoid the separation of foreign and domestic policy which occurs in much political analysis the political geography perspective uses geographical scale as its principle of organization. In this way continuities across scales can be identified and assessed.

Political geographers of the current generation have come to accept geographical scale as the main way of ordering their studies. Numerous books since 1975 have employed a framework that employs three scales of analysis – international or global, national or state level and an intra-national usually urban metropolitan scale. Although this framework represents a consensus of opinion it is particularly disappointing that this

position has been reached with no articulation of theory to justify a trilogy
of geographical scales (Taylor 1982a). Two questions immediately arise –
'Why just three scales?' and 'why these particular three scales?' These
questions have not been answered because they have not been asked.
Instead the three scales are accepted merely as 'given': as one author puts
it these 'three broad areas of interest seem to present themselves' (Short,
1982: 1). Well, of course, they do no such thing. These three scales do not
just happen to appear so that political geographers have some convenient
hooks upon which to hang their information. In fact recognition of three
scales is implicit in many social science studies beyond political geography
(Taylor 1981b). It represents a particular way of viewing the world which
is a subtle form of developmentalism. The scales pivot around the basic
unit of the state – hence the inter*national*, *national* and intra-*national*
terminology. The problem is that if it is taken at face value it destroys the
holism of the world-economy. Hence Short (1982: 1) is able to write about
'distinct spatial scales of analysis' and Johnston (1973: 14) even refers to
'relatively closed or self-sufficient systems' at these different scales. If
political geography is to use geographical scale it cannot just accept this
organization as given: the framework must explain why these scales exist
and how they relate one to another.

1. Ideology separating experience from reality

Why three scales? This immediately brings to mind Wallerstein's three-tier
structure of conflict control. We have already come across his geographical
example of core–semi-periphery–periphery. We can term this a horizontal
three-tier geographical structure. Our scales form a vertical three-tier
geographical structure pivoting about the nation-state. The role of all
three-tier structures is the promotion of a middle category to separate
conflicting interests. In our model, therefore, the nation-state becomes the
mediator between global and local scales. We will treat this arrangement
as a classic example of ideology separating experience from reality. The
three scales therefore represent a national scale of ideology, a local scale of
experience and a global scale of reality. This is illustrated schematically in
Figure 1 where it is compared to Wallerstein's original horizontal
geographical structure.

Let us consider this interpretation in more detail. The scale of
experience is the scale at which we live our daily lives. It encompasses all
our basic needs including employment, shelter and consumption of basic
commodities. For most people living in the core countries this consists of a
daily urban 'system'; for most people elsewhere it consists of a local rural
community. But the day-to-day activities we all engage in are not
sustained locally. By the fact that we live in a *world*-system the arena that
affects our lives is much larger than our local community whether urban
or rural. In the current world-economy the crucial events that structure
our lives occur at a global scale. This is the ultimate scale of accumulation

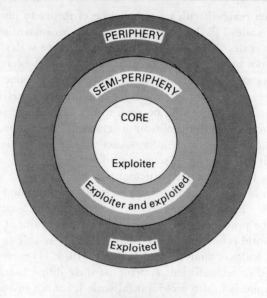

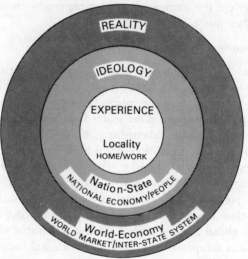

1. Alternative three-tiered structures of separation and control (a) Horizontal division by area (b) Vertical division by scale.

where the world market defines values which ultimately impinge on our local communities. But this is not a direct effect, the world market is filtered through particular aggregations of local communities which are nation-states. For every community the precise effects of these global processes can be reduced or enhanced by the politics of the nation-state in which it is located. Such manipulation can be at the expense of other communities with the state or else at the expense of communities in other states. But the very stuff of politics in this framework is in this filter between world market and local community.

But why talk of 'ideology' and 'reality' in this context? The notion of scale of experience seems unexceptional enough but in what sense are the other scales related to ideology and reality? In this model we have very specific meanings for these terms. By 'reality' we are referring to the holistic reality that is the concrete world-economy which incorporates the other scales. It is in this sense the totality of the system. Hence ultimate explanations within the system must be traced back to this 'whole'. It is the scale that 'really matters'. In our materialist argument the accumulation that is the motor of the whole system operates through the world market at this global scale. In contrast ideology is a partial view of the system which distorts reality into a false and limited picture. In our model the reality of the world-system is filtered through nation-centred ideologies to provide a set of contrasting and often conflicting 'world views'. We will argue below that such nation-centred thinking has become pervasive in modern politics. This has the effect of diverting political protest away from the key processes at the scale of reality by ensuring that they stop short at the scale of ideology – the nation-state. It is in this sense that we have a geographical model of ideology separating experience from reality.

A simple example may clarify the argument at this point. I have drawn from my own political experience of the late 1970s. Wallsend is a shipbuilding town in north-east England. With the onset of the current recession there was much local concern for the future of the shipyards. As the major employer in the town any closure of the industry would have major repercussions throughout the local community. This is the scale of experience. It is at the scale of ideology that policy emerges, however. Following pressure from, among others, the local Labour Party, the British (Labour) government nationalized shipbuilding including the Wallsend yards. But this is ideological because it reflects only a partial view of the problem. It may protect jobs in the short term but it does not tackle the problem of Wallsend's shipyards over the long term. These derive from the scale of reality – both supply and demand for ships is global in scope. The current problem in the industry stems from the fall in demand for world shipping in the wake of the 1973/74 oil price rise and the increase in supply with the emergence of new shipyards in other countries such as South Korea. Clearly a policy of nationalization within Britain is a long way from solving the problems of Wallsend's shipping industry. Rather it represents a political solution which stops at the state scale so that there is no challenge to the processes of accumulation at the global scale.

Nelund (1978) provides another more general example of this distortion of politics. In a study of a broad range of thirteen countries, survey respondents were asked about political issues at various scales. The issue of war and peace was, not surprisingly, viewed predominantly as one

concerning the world as a whole. But as Nelund points out, this means it
is despatched to a level 'where nobody can reach it'. Hence even if it is of
greatest concern to an individual he or she can do very little about it. War
and peace have been, and remain, largely the concern of politicians and
diplomats. Hence the difficulty of the anti-nuclear peace movement in
breaking into the world of global politics. Nelund (1978: 278) concludes
that

> the national world picture does not provide us with a language which we can
> use in our daily life to deal with our concerns. It is a mental burden, and even
> more it takes us in wrong directions by placing our true concerns beyond our
> reach, involving us in institutional efforts to reach the issue which we ourselves
> have displaced.

This is ideological distortion of not just our experience but that of the
politicians also. United Nations peace efforts, for example, are restricted to
the realm of international politics so that the *internal* politics of states are
largely ignored. And yet such separation of geographical scales of analysis
are a crucial weakness in all peace-keeping efforts. It seems that the
holism of our approach cannot be applied to peace except by a few
elements of protest movements.

Finally we must stress that this model does not posit three processes
operating at three scales but just one process which is manifest at three
scales. In general this process takes the following form – the needs of
accumulation are experienced locally (for example, closure of a hospital)
and justified nationally (for example, to promote national efficiency) for
the ultimate benefits organized globally (for example, by multi-national
corporations paying less tax). This is a single process in which ideology
separates experience from reality. There is but one system – the world-
economy.

2. World-economy, nation-state and locality

This model represents our particular organization of political geography
summarized by the sub-title of this book – world-economy, nation-state
and locality. Hence we follow the established pattern of using three scales
of analysis but treat them in a more analytical manner than other studies.
Even though each of the following chapters concentrates largely on
activities at one of the three scales they do not constitute separate studies
of each scale. For instance imperialism is a concept associated with the
global scale but we will argue that it cannot be understood without
consideration of forces operating within states. Alternatively political
parties operate at the national scale but we will argue that they cannot be
understood without consideration of the global scale. In every chapter
discussion will range across scales depending on the particular
requirements for explanation.

Each chapter follows a similar format. We begin by reviewing past
approaches which are evaluated as different 'heritages' in political

geography. Some of this heritage is then dismissed as either no longer relevant or even misleading and false. Other parts of our heritage are built upon and developed. And finally some new elements are added to political geography in the application of world-systems logic to the subject-matter. In short we dismiss, develop and generate political geography ideas.

Chapters 2 and 3 are devoted to geopolitics and imperialism respectively. In the former case we identify a largely national-orientated ideological heritage and in the second case a contrasting revolutionary heritage. Both heritages are largely dismissed on the grounds of committing the error of developmentalism. We develop ideas on state-building and political cycles in our presentation of a dynamic model of politics in the world-economy. The particular new elements derived from our world-systems logic concern the role of the USSR in geopolitics and the geographies of imperialism.

In Chapter 4 we deal with the classic trilogy of political geography – territory, state and nation. Their heritages are dealt with separately but all involve biological analogies and explanations which are dismissed. We develop ideas on territoriality as a political strategy, the state as a mechanism of control and the nation as a vehicle for political consensus. Reinterpretations and new ideas from our world-system logic involve the spatial structure of the state, a theory of *states* in the world-economy, and a materialist theory of nationalism.

Chapter 5 stays at the same scale in its treatment of electoral geography. The heritage of these studies involves a very restricted geographical coverage, biased towards core states, due to the liberal theory of elections which has been employed. We develop what are sometimes termed 'realist' ideas about elections and political parties. We employ world-systems logic to interpret party ideologies and the operation of parties in *all* parts of the world. Although electoral geography is one of the major growth areas in modern political geography, we will argue that it is in particular need of a major rethink.

In the final chapter the ecological heritage of urban studies is described and its political implications exposed. When we come to dismiss this past, however, we find that it leads to querying much more modern work which treat the 'city' as a separate, operating system. We do not accept the existence of such an entity, hence our use of the term locality to refer to local areas of experience both rural and urban. The main area we develop is the study of neighbourhood effects which we treat more generally as socialization into local political cultures. No new ideas are derived in this chapter and we concentrate on illustrating past themes in new contexts.

The end-result is a political geography which attempts to rethink our studies in world-economy terms. There is some new wine in old bottles but also some old wine in new bottles. Although none of this wine is as yet sufficiently matured, it is hoped that it will not taste too bitter for the discerning reader.

Chapter 2

GEOPOLITICS REVISITED

THE IDEOLOGICAL HERITAGE

Mackinder's Heartland Theory

1. Political background: from Liberal to Conservative
2. Spatial structure: land power versus sea power

German geopolitics

1. Political background: Nazi connections
2. Spatial structure: global pan-regions

Containment and deterrence: The American world model

1. Containing the 'fortress': dominoes and Finlands in the Rimland
2. Counter-balancing the Heartland: nuclear deterrence
3. Cohen's model of geostrategic and geopolitical regions

BRINGING HISTORY BACK IN

Rokkan's geopolitical map of Europe

1. Spatial structure: two geopolitical distances
2. Critique: political space versus political economy

Modelski's long cycles of global politics

1. The symmetry of global politics
2. Critique: the poverty of mechanisms of change

A dynamic model of hegemony and rivalry

1. Political distortion of the world-market
2. The rise and fall of hegemonic states: paired Kondratieffs
3. Hegemony and rivalry in the logistic wave

CURRENT AND FUTURE STRUCTURES OF GEOPOLITICS

The world-systems interpretation of the USSR

1. Vodka-Cola: the transideological enterprise
2. Semi-periphery: socialism as a development strategy
3. World power: socialism as an anti-systemic force

Alternative geopolitics of the future

1. The armageddon scenario: return to mini-systems
2. The new hegemony scenario: the Japanese century
3. The socialist scenario: transformation of the world-economy

Chapter 2

GEOPOLITICS REVISITED

One thing that most political geographers have agreed about for the last couple of generations is the need to rethink geopolitics. The most common result of such musings has been the virtual abandonment of geopolitics. The problem with this solution is that by cutting out geopolitics we virtually cut off political geography from its distinguished heritage of 'founding fathers' such as Friedrich Ratzel in Germany, Sir Halford Mackinder in Britain and Isaiah Bowman in the USA. That political geographers have been willing to take such an extreme step is testimony to the profound impact that German geopolitics of the 1930s and 1940s had on political geography in particular and geography in general. The term 'geopolitics' became an embarrassment to be distinguished from 'respectable' political geography. Saul Cohen has been a major exception among political geographers in keeping global thinking alive in political geography and we follow his example in this chapter. Geopolitics is too useful a concept and too important a subject for geographers to abandon.

One researcher cannot maintain a viable research tradition, however. The legacy of Mackinder and others has been developed outside geography in the field of international relations. According to Hollist and Rosenau (1981) Mackinder is part of the heritage of the 'realist' school of international relations which consists of 'interpretive' studies of international power relations between states. These 'traditional' studies have been challenged in recent years by the 'behavioural' school which deals with quantitative analysis of inter-state relations. They have attempted to devise 'objective laws' of international relations to supplant the subjective models of the traditional realists. Hollist and Rosenau (1981) report that this academic conflict has been turned into a triangular contest with the advent of the world-systems perspective in international relations.

Political geography was largely by-passed by the quantitative revolution in geography so that it did not experience a quantitative-behavioural school equivalent to that found in international relations. In a sense, therefore, we are attempting to 'bounce' political geography from realist position to world-systems approach by missing out the intermediate quantitative stage. This is rather ironic in that it was in a review of one of the products of the behavioural school – Bruce Russett's (1967) *International Regions and the International System* – that Brian Berry (1969) made his derogatory and oft-quoted remark that political geography was a 'moribund backwater'. No matter, as far as we are concerned here this means that we can go ahead and develop our world-systems ideas without the intellectual encumbrances that surround international relations researchers. Unlike Berry, we will have little time for quantitative international relations studies as currently conceived because of the narrow context within which they are produced. The world-systems approach provides us with a more complete framework of analysis. This does not mean that we ignore the behavioural school's work but simply that we interpret it within a broader context which tends to ask different and deeper questions.

The world-systems approach brings to the fore many issues avoided or at least seen as tangential by other approaches. The organization of this chapter is based upon three such issues. First we deal with the issue of national exceptionalism (Agnew 1982). One of the features of geopolitics is that each researcher's theory invariably fits the particular needs of the researcher's country. Such models are therefore partial views of reality and so are ideological in terms of our political geography framework. Our first section discusses this ideological heritage. Concern for such current policy needs has led to a neglect of history and in the second section we assess two attempts by political scientists to use a time-span equivalent to that of the world-systems approach. In this section we confront the issue of whether there can be separate studies of 'international politics' and 'international economies'. In Chase-Dunn's (1982) phrase, are there two logics or one? We will derive a model of the rise and fall of state hegemonies to illustrate the single political-economy logic of the world-economy. This model forms the basis for our discussion of imperialism but this is such an important theme in the world-systems approach that we allocate the whole of the next chapter to it. To conclude this chapter we return to current concerns of geopolitics and USA–USSR rivalry. In many ways this is the real test of our rethinking geopolitics. The way in which the world-systems approach deals with the Soviet bloc is one of its most distinctive and intriguing features undermining as it does most of the assumptions of traditional geopolitics.

Before we enter our discussions of geopolitics and imperialism we need to define each term. Although not usually discussed in the same context both terms do relate to political activity at an inter-state scale. Current usage distinguishes geopolitics as concerned with rivalry between 'major powers'(core and rising semi-periphery states) and imperialism as domination by strong states (in the core) of weak states (in the periphery). Politically geopolitics describes a *rivalry* relation whereas imperialism describes a *dominance* relation. Spatially they are currently reflected in 'east–west' and 'north–south' spatial patterns respectively. Although there have been previous definitions, and these are dealt with below, we will employ these current uses of the terms here. The interesting question for political geography is the relation between the two concepts in their politics and spatial structure. In world-systems analysis geopolitics is about rivalry (currently East versus West) in the core for domination of the periphery by imperialism (currently North over South).

THE IDEOLOGICAL HERITAGE

The starting point for almost all discussions of geopolitics is Sir Halford Mackinder's Heartland Theory. Despite its neglect in geography it remains probably the most well-known geographical model throughout the world. Although first propounded in 1904 it continues to inform debate on foreign policy – Walters (1974: 27) goes as far as saying 'the Heartland theory stands as the first premise of Western military thought'. This remarkable achievement of longevity is the subject matter of this section.

Everybody carries around a world model in their heads. The model is frequently brought into operation to make sense of and evaluate the great quantities of information we receive daily about different parts of the world. The basic principle of most world models is that they are state-centric. That is to say they treat the state as the basic unit of the world-order. First, the world is viewed from the specific perspective of a person's home state and, second, other states are ordered along dimensions in relation to the home state such as friendly/unfriendly, strong/weak, rich/poor and even good/bad. Of course such evaluations do not arise spontaneously among people but they are learnt as part of becoming a citizen of a particular state. World models are outward expressions of national popular sentiments. But they are not restricted to such manifestations. Most of geopolitics has involved producing world models to inform public opinion and influence a country's foreign policy. The models we hold in our head consist of bits of theories from long-dead propagandists that most people have never heard of. An important task for political geography is to reveal these theories and evaluate their validity. Since it is an ideological heritage that we describe here we will organize it along national lines starting with Mackinder's original British view followed by the 'notorious' German geopolitics and concluding with American 'Cold War' containment ideas.

MACKINDER'S HEARTLAND THEORY

Mackinder's world model was presented on three occasions covering nearly forty years. The original thesis was presented in 1904 as 'The Geographical Pivot of History', the ideas were refined and presented after the First World War (1919) in *Democratic Ideals and Reality* where 'Pivot Area' becomes Heartland and then in 1943 Mackinder at the age of eighty-two provided a final version of his ideas. Despite this long period covering two world wars the idea of an Asiatic 'fortress' remains the centrepiece of his models and is largely responsible for its popularity since 1945. Most discussion of Mackinder concentrates on his 1919 work but here we will be particularly concerned with the origins of his ideas just after the turn of the century. For further details see Parker (1982).

1. Political background: from Liberal to Conservative

Mackinder developed his world strategic views at a crucial period in the world-economy when Britain was losing her political and economic leadership. In the nineteenth century Britain had been the champion of a liberal world-economy which she could dominate. The rise of USA and Germany in the final quarter of the century dramatically changed the situation. Mackinder had been a leading member of the Liberal Party – the party of free trade – but about 1903 he began to revise his views. Britain's role was changing and he no longer believed that simple accumulation of capital in London would be sufficient to meet the challenge of Germany's massive growth in heavy industry. He converted to a protectionist position which involved changing political parties – the Conservatives were the party of 'tariff reform'. This new position emphasized the need to maintain British industry to face the German challenge. These concerns with current power rivalries are directly expressed in his famous world model (Semmel 1960).

2. The spatial structure: land power versus sea power

Mackinder's original presentation of his model is a very broad conception of world history. Basically he identifies central Asia as the pivot-area of history from which horsemen have dominated Asian and European history because of their superior mobility. With the age of maritime exploration from 1492, however, we enter the Columbian era when the balance of power swung decisively to the coastal powers notably Britain. Mackinder now considered this era to be coming to an end. In the 'post-Columbian' era new transport technology, particularly the railways, would redress the balance back in favour of land-based power and the pivot-area would reassert itself. The pivot-area was defined in terms of a zone not accessible to sea-power and was surrounded by an inner crescent in mainland Europe and Asia and an outer crescent in the islands and continents beyond Eurasia (Figure 2a).

What had this to do with current (1904) power politics? Well at its simplest this model can be interpreted as a historical-geographical rationalization for the traditional British policy of maintaining a balance of power in Europe so that no one continental power could threaten Britain. In this case the policy implications are to prevent Germany allying with Russia to control the pivot-area and so to command the resources to overthrow the British Empire. Mackinder's message in 1904 was that Britain is more vulnerable than before to the rise of a continental power.

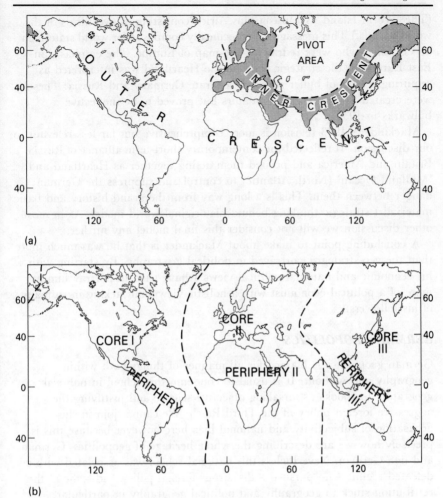

2. Alternative geopolitical models (a) Mackinder's original model (b) A model of pan-regions

British foreign policy needs revision to accord with the new post-Columbian situation to supplement a revised trade policy.

In his 1919 revision of this world model he redefines central Asia as the 'Heartland' which is larger than the original 'pivot area'. This is based on a reassessment of the penetrative capabilities of sea powers. Nevertheless the same basic structure remains and the fear of German control of the Heartland is still central. In fact he is much more explicit in his advice as given in his famous dictum:

> Who rules East Europe commands the Heartland
> Who rules the Heartland commands the World-Island
> Who rules the World-Island commands the World.

(The 'World-Island' is Eurasia plus Africa consisting of two thirds of the world's lands.) This message was specifically composed for world statesmen at Versailles who were redrawing the map of Europe. The emphasis on East Europe as the strategic route to the Heartland was interpreted as requiring a strip of buffer states to separate Germany and Russia. These were created by the peace negotiators but proved to be ineffective bulwarks in 1939.

Mackinder's 1943 revision is more comprehensive but far less relevant to our discussion. It reflected the contemporary short-term alliance of Russia, Britain and America and posited them acting together as Heartland and 'Midland Ocean' (North Atlantic) to control and suppress the German danger between them. This is a long way from the grand history and basic materialist strategic thinking behind his original world model. As in most other discussion we will not consider this final model any further.

A concluding point to make about Mackinder is that he was much more than the geo-strategist portrayed in political geography. By starting with his economic and national political views I have tried to portray him as more of a political economist with a holistic viewpoint lacking in so many of his followers.

GERMAN GEOPOLITICS

German geopolitics is blamed for all manner of things both within geography and without. It is usual to condemn this school in political geography textbooks as forsaking objective science and justifying the aggressive foreign policy of the Third Reich. We cannot join in this accusation of subjectivity and national bias here however because this is precisely how we are describing the whole heritage of geopolitics, German and non-German. Nevertheless this national school was associated with a defeated regime who pursued a disastrous foreign policy and some of the retribution stuck to geography and political geography in particular.

1. Political background: Nazi connections

The story starts in 1924 with the setting up of the Institute of Geopolitics in Munich under Karl Haushofer with its monthly magazine *Geopolitik*. Literally thousands of articles were published on geostrategy over the next couple of decades in this journal. However, this was not simply an academic exercise. Haushofer had direct contact with the top of the Nazi hierarchy through Rudolf Hess, Hitler's deputy, and following Hitler's rise to power, Haushofer became one of the most prominent academics in his country. There is some dispute on the degree to which he was able to influence German foreign policy but there is no doubt that geopolitics achieved a degree of recognition never achieved before or since. Haushofer became notorious in the Second World War when his work was publicized in the USA as a guide to Hitler's plans. But in all probability his role was over-estimated during the war. In any case all states have training programmes in military strategy and geopolitical frameworks not necessarily all that dissimilar to Haushaufer's Munich Institute. The important point from our viewpoint is to see what sort of world model he devised.

2. Spatial structure: global pan-regions

Haushaufer drew his ideas from Ratzel and Mackinder. From the former he adapted the ideas of *lebensraum* (living space) and the resulting need for large regions of political unity. From the latter he borrowed the heartland theory as a key to understanding Germany's position in the world. He saw landpower as superior to seapower so that a German–Russian alliance was an integral part of his model. His promotion of such an arrangement in the face of ideological differences between nazism and communism was vindicated with the Russian–German Pact of 1939. However, he does not seem to have advocated invasion of Russia. Rather accommodation with this essentially Asian power was seen as necessary to give Germany space to carve out its own 'pan-region'. This idea derived from Ratzel and was evolved into a world model of three pan-regions based upon Germany, Japan and USA (Figure 2b). This is an interesting geographical organization in that it involves functional regions around each core state cross-cutting environmental-resource regions which straddle the earth latitudinally. Hence each pan-region would have a share of the world's arctic, temperate and tropical environments. As political-economy concepts they involve three regions with the potential for economic self-sufficiency or autarky. If fully evolved such a model would consist of three separate world-systems each with its own core – Europe, Japan and Anglo America – and periphery – Africa and India, East and South-east Asia, and Latin America respectively. Such a world model of co-existence is no better or worse than other models and may not be too far from the mark with the current demise of the USA dominance of the world-economy.

CONTAINMENT AND DETERRENCE: THE AMERICAN WORLD MODEL

German geopolitics accommodated USA not as the dominant power but as one member of a set of three dominant powers. Their world model can be interpreted as a sort of Monroe Doctrine × 3. With the defeat of Germany the USA emerged as the strongest world power and its interests were far greater than the hemispheric region allocated in the German plan. USA required a global strategy and a world model to base it on. This meant a return to Mackinder-type thinking. Although the original thesis had warned of the strategic superiority of land-power in the twentieth century, Mackinder's final (1943) work had been much less pessimistic from a sea-power viewpoint. This position was more fully developed by Nicholas

Spykman who directly perceived post-war American needs as neutralizing
the power of the Heartland. As a counter to the Mackinder thesis he
argued that the key area was the 'inner crescent', which he renamed the
'Rimland' and control of the latter could neutralize the power of the
Heartland. All was not lost therefore for the sea-power in twentieth-
century geopolitics. By the end of the war it was clear that in effect the
Heartland could be equated with the USSR. Germany's failure to defeat
Russia had enhanced Mackinder's reputation. From this point onwards
there existed a general world model which we can call the
Heartland–Rimland thesis involving land power (the USSR) versus sea-
power (the USA) separated by a contact zone (the Rimland). To be sure
there were minor variations in terms of definitions and emphases but this
three-tier structure originally derived from Mackinder's 1904 paper
persisted into the post-1945 era. It survived a barrage of criticisms –
Mackinder's initial emphasis on railways seemed pretty antiquated in the
age of inter-continental ballistic missiles – but in a sense it does not matter
whether the model is an accurate representation of reality; what does
matter is that enough people believed it to the true. Therefore the
Heartland–Rimland thesis could become an ideological tool of US foreign
policy makers.

The application of Mackinder's ideas so many years after they were first
propounded is not due to his being some sort of prophetic genius. It
relates, instead, to the fact that he provided a simple spatial structure
which precisely suited the needs of US foreign policy after 1945. The
world was reduced to two 'super powers' with the onset of the Cold War
and the Heartland–Rimland thesis provided an easy way of
conceptualizing the new situation. The original hydrology basis of 'pivot
area' and Mackinder's concern for German expansion were conveniently
forgotten and we were left with a model in which the enemy, the USSR,
had control of the 'fortress',the Heartland, and policy was formulated
accordingly.

1. Containing the 'fortress': dominoes and Finlands in the Rimland

If the USSR is a fortress then the way to deal with a fortress is to
surround it and seal it in. In policy jargon this is known as containment
with the ring of post-war anti-Soviet alliances in the Rimland as the seal –
NATO in Europe, CENTO in West Asia and SEATO in East Asia.
Where the seal came unstuck intervention was necessary and the Rimland
contains the majority of major and minor conflicts in the post-1945 era –
Berlin, Korea, the Middle East and Vietnam are the major conflicts. All of
this activity is premised on preventing Soviet domination of the 'World-
Island'. In its wake it has spawned more limited but equally simple spatial
models to deal with particular sectors of the Rimland. The classic analogy
is domino theory whereby the 'fall' of one country will inevitably lead to
the defeat of US interests in adjacent countries: the loss of Kampuchia

puts Thailand and Malaysia at risk, and so on. O'Sullivan (1982) has demolished this idea of countries lined up like dominoes to be toppled by Communists or held up by US support. The main feature of the theory is that it conveniently avoids all discussion of the *internal* conflicts of the countries and therefore prevents the emergence of alternative theories of unrest to externally inspired communist agitation. In Western Europe Domino theory has been replaced by the notion of 'Finlandization'. This admits that there will be no Soviet military take-over but the USSR influence will nevertheless be extended by insidious control of the domestic politics of the countries involved. Finland is supposed to be the 'model' for this process. Again this simple theory has been demolished in recent political geography (Liebowitz 1983). Quite simply the world is more complicated than these simple spatial analogies allow for. Nevertheless such ideas have lain behind US foreign policy and 'dominoes' are reappearing in the 1980s in central America.

2. Counter-balancing the Heartland: nuclear deterrence

Whereas containment policy emphasizes the Rimland the second policy that reflects the three-tier world model concentrates more on the implications of a Soviet Heartland. Walters (1974) makes a very cogent argument that the policy of nuclear deterrence would never have developed but for the Heartland theory. Quite simply, once it is accepted that the USSR have the superior geopolitical position then nuclear weapons become the necessary salvation of the West. A nuclear arsenal will act as a counterbalance to Russia's basic strategic advantage. *Despite* the Heartland theory, a new balance of power can be created on the basis of the nuclear deterrent and the World-Island can be saved. Hence perhaps the most momentous foreign policy decision of all time – to generate what was to become the nuclear arms race – is based upon a geographical theory which nearly all geographers and political scientists reject. Nevertheless it should not be thought that these ideas are diminishing in importance. The renewal of the Cold War and the rise of conservative politics in domestic affairs has been paralleled by a new belligerent neo-conservative foreign policy lobby (Ajami 1978) where Mackinder again becomes the prophetic genius to stop the Germans . . . . er, sorry the Russians. In recent years this has been most forcibly argued by Gray (1977) who claims to remind us once again of the 'lessons of geopolitics'. Some ideas, it seems, never go away – as long as they continue to have an ideological utility.

3. Cohen's model of geostrategic and geopolitical regions

Saul Cohen is the only geographer working in this field who has attempted a complete revision of the Heartland–Rimland thesis. His basic purpose is to question the policy of containment with its implication that the whole Eurasian littoral is a potential battleground. He exposes, once again, the poverty of Heartland–Rimland theory. For instance he points out that by viewing the situation as land-power versus sea-power a containment policy can only be seen as locking the stable door after the horse has bolted, given current Soviet naval strength in all oceans. His revision of strategic thinking consists, therefore, of providing a much more militarily flexible and geographically sensitive model. His movement away from the Heartland–Rimland thesis comes in two stages and we will deal with each in turn chronologically.

In his *Geography and Politics in a World Divided* Cohen (1973) offers a hierarchical and regional world model. This is based on exposing the 'unity myth' which he believes has misled previous geopoliticians. According to Cohen there is not a strategic unity of space but rather there are separate arenas in a fundamentally divided world. He brings forward the traditional geographical concept of the region to describe this division. A hierarchy of two types of region are identified depending on whether they are global or regional in scope. Geostrategic regions are functionally defined and express the inter-relations of a large part of the world. Geopolitical regions are subdivisions of the above and they tend to be relatively homogeneous in terms of one or more of culture, economics and politics.

Cohen's (1973) use of these concepts to produce a world model is shown in Figure 3. He defines just two geostrategic regions each dominated by one of the two major powers and termed 'the Trade-Dependent Maritime World' and 'the Eurasian Continental World'. Hence his initial spatial structure is similar to the old geopolitical models. However, he goes a step further and divides each geostrategic region into five and two geopolitical regions respectively. In addition South Asia is recognized as a potential geostrategic region. Between the two existing geostrategic regions

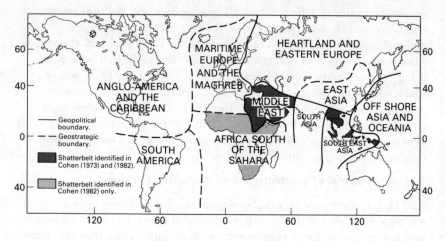

3.   Cohen's geostrategic regions and their geopolitical subdivisions

there are two distinctive geopolitical regions which are termed shatterbelts – the Middle East and South-east Asia. Unlike other geopolitical regions these two are characterized by a lack of political unity; they are fragmented with both geostrategic regions having 'footholds' in the region. They are of strategic importance to both great powers and it is here where 'containment' must be practised. Essentially Cohen is saying that not all parts of the Rimland are equally important and policy must be sensitive to this fact. Selective containment rather than blanket containment is the policy in line with his geographical 'realities'.

In a revision of his model Cohen (1982) has further emphasized the divisions of the world strategic system. He has modified some of the details of his initial spatial structure – notably the designation of Africa south of the Sahara as a third shatter belt (Figure 3) – but the major change is one of emphasis on 'second order' or regional centres of power. In the original model geopolitical regions were the basis of multiple power nodes and this comes to the fore in the revised model. Three geopolitical regions have developed new world powers – Japan, China and Europe – to join the USA and the USSR. Other geopolitical regions have developed second-order powers which dominate their region, such as India, Brazil and Nigeria. Cohen assesses twenty-seven states as second-order powers and beyond these he defines third-, fourth- and fifth-order states. Definitions are largely based on the scope for influence beyond the states' boundaries. The end result is a multiple-node world with many overlapping areas of influence which is much more dynamic than the old bi-polar model. The key difference is the greater inter-connectedness between regions and between countries on different rungs of the hierarchy. The influence of both the old major powers has declined to be taken over in part by the rise of the new regional powers. This is a far cry from the simplicity of the Heartland–Rimland thesis and is returning towards the traditional complexity of regional geography models.

There is one crucial aspect in which Cohen is similar to the Heartland–Rimland devotees. Like them he is attempting to inform his own country's foreign policy. Cohen's revised model is explicitly intended to counteract the calls for a renewal of containment policy in the wake of the election of conservative Ronald Reagan to the presidency, for instance. Cohen's is very much an American view of the world and as such continues our ideological heritage.

The purpose of this section has not been to 'expose' these ideological biases since they are not particularly well hidden. Smith (1984) for instance, has recently shown that Bowman's rhetoric against German geopolitics in the Second World War rings a little hollow today when we remember his own contribution to America's war effort. However, our point is not to be anti-American, or anti-German or anti-British but to recognize generally the national bias that has permeated all geopolitical strategic thinking (O'Loughlin 1984). As Agnew (1982) so aptly puts it – one country's containment is another country's expansion. There are other world models we could have considered – Kubalkova and Cruickshank (1981) in addition deal with Russian, Chinese and third world models for instance – but they all suffer from the same ideological affliction. The models we have looked at are important in the context of this discussion because they derive directly from traditional political geography. We must come to terms with Mackinder and geopolitics not by ignoring them but by understanding these ideas in their historical and national contexts. Only in this way can we go beyond our distinguished yet notorious heritage.

BRINGING HISTORY BACK IN

Well, where do we go from here? There is an important aspect of Cohen's work which was not mentioned above. Part of his attempt to distance himself from the Mackinder tradition involved dismissing the utility of a historical approach to political geography. Whereas Mackinder employed the broad brush of history to set up his model Cohen provides detailed assessments of the current situation with little or no reference back to the past. His use of history merely consists of providing examples to illustrate his concepts – in the nineteenth century, for instance, the British empire was a geostrategic region whereas American continental expansion produced a geopolitical region. But there is no attempt to find continuities in the development to the current situation. In fact this is explicitly excluded as potentially misleading. Hence in one sense our world-systems approach is closer to Mackinder with his identification of 1492 as the beginning of the modern world. Our way forward is not to return to Mackinder, however, but to evaluate work by modern political scientists who share our large time perspective at an international scale. There are two relevant areas of study – comparative politics which attempts to find similarities across states and international politics which concentrates on inter-state relations. In this section we take one example from each field – Stein Rokkan's geopolitical map of Europe and George Modelski's cycles of world politics. Both are specifically chosen because they complement the approach we have adopted and illustrate the limitations of a purely 'political' approach.

ROKKAN'S GEOPOLITICAL MAP OF EUROPE

It would be incorrect to give the impression that Mackinder's style of geopolitics is the only legacy of traditional political geography at the international level. Derwent Whittlesey (1939), for instance, maintained the environmental emphasis of traditional geography but used it for comparative political analyses. His studies of core-areas of states and

especially his discussion of the unusual cases of Italy and Germany are
mentioned by Rokkan (1975: 583) as direct inspirations for the basis of his
geopolitical map of Europe. Hence despite his training in political
philosophy and political sociology Rokkan came to see himself following in
the geographical tradition in social science (Rokkan 1980: 163).

Rokkan's starting point was to explore three paradoxes which he
identified in comparative politics. This first paradox is that theories of
development have concentrated on new countries whereas most of the
information pertaining to development is available for the 'old' countries of
Europe. Rokkan set himself the task of codifying the political processes in
state formation in Europe as a necessary and preliminary task for
understanding other regions. Within this task he confronted the other two
paradoxes: first that initially strong states did not form in the most
economically advanced parts of Europe and second that the development
of the territorial division of Europe into states coincided with the rise of a
world network of trading links which undermined established boundaries.
Part of Rokkan's response to these paradoxes was to construct what he
termed a geopolitical map of Europe. Its purpose is to provide
a framework for comparative studies of political variation within Europe.

1. *Spatial structure: two geopolitical distances*

All of Rokkan's work is based upon Talcott Parson's specification of the
social system. This model emphasizes the functions required for any
society to maintain its existence. Rokkan identifies several roles covering
economic, military, judicial and religious functions. As we move from
simple local societies to modern complex societies these roles become
highly differentiated (Figure 4). However, these distinct processes of

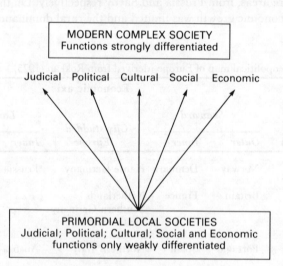

4. Differentiation between primordial local societies and modern complex societies

development need not operate in unison and Rokkan considers the uneven pattern of these developments to be a key feature of European state formation.

To provide a parsimonious description of such a complex pattern of processes two dimensions are emphasized which are termed 'geopolitical distances'. The first is a north–south dimension measured by 'geopolitical' distance north of Rome. This describes cultural differentiation with Rome as focus of Empire and Papacy. The second is an east–west dimension measured westwards and eastwards from the central band of trading cities of medieval Europe stretching from Northern Italy to the Baltic. This describes economic differentiation across Europe. These two dimensions can now be used as 'centre-culture' and 'centre-economic' axes to tabulate European states. The resulting geopolitical map is in Table 3.

The lynchpin of this map is the east–west dimension about city-state Europe. From Florence to Hamburg a set of trading centres existed with no one centre able to dominate and control the trading system. But neither did they form the basis of the modern state system. Instead they contributed to the fragmentation of central Europe which lasted into the nineteenth century. Only two defensive alliances – the Swiss cantons and the Dutch provinces – at strategically crucial locations developed to form modern states. In contrast on the seaward side medium-sized states emerged in the middle ages. These were not strong enough to control city-state Europe but commanded the necessary resources based upon a balance of urban and rural economies to build a modern state machinery both civil and military. Nevertheless it was not until Napoleon that city-state Europe was finally conquered. When the Rhinelands and northern Italy were finally united into modern Germany and Italy the force came from outside these economic core areas, from Prussia and Savoy respectively. On the landward side urban economic growth was limited and the rural dominance was

Table 3   A geopolitical map of Europe (derived from Rokkan (1975))

	Economic axis				
	Seaward		*City-studded Europe*	*Landward*	
Cultural axis	*Outer*	*Inner*		*Inner*	*Outer*
Protestant	Norway	Denmark	Hanse Germany	Prussia	Sweden
Mixed	Britain	France	Netherlands Southern Germany Switzerland		
Catholic	Portugal	Spain	Northern Italy	Austria	Poland Hungary

unable to sustain strong medium-size states. Large units resulted so that 'empire-Europe' only became divided into modern states in the twentieth century with the aftermath of the First World War.

The north–south dimension is most clearly represented by the religious cleavage between Catholics and Protestants. But Rokkan sees it as much more than religious. Whereas east–west reflects differential state formation, north–south reflects differential nation formation. The rise of the Protestant religion became an important element in national development in northern Europe by defining national churches and legitimizing national languages. In contrast in Catholic Europe the universal claims of the church were maintained to hinder national developments. This was especially the case in the 'crusading' counter-Reformation empires of Iberia and Austria fighting the threat of Islam. In neither cases was a modern nation formed according to Rokkan.

There are many other aspects of this model that are not mentioned here: we cannot do full justice to Rokkan's ideas in this short space. Nevertheless the basic elements of the geopolitics are clear enough and we are now in a position to attempt an assessment.

2. *Critique: political space versus political economy*

Let us start by making a simple geographical comment on the geopolitical map and build up our argument from there. Despite its actual location on the Baltic Sea, Poland becomes part of the south because of its Catholicism. In this case geopolitical distance from Rome is very different from actual distance. This is legitimate in a conceptual map but it does raise questions about whether the map is being distorted to fit the theory. It is not enough to identify Poland in the Catholic 'South', the question is why is this northern European state Catholic in the first place? Put another way why are geopolitical distance and actual distance so far apart in this case? The answer lies in the nature of the counter-Reformation and its relation to the emerging world-economy. In Wallerstein's schema Poland is not 'south' but part of a new periphery based around the Baltic trade. In this peripheralization process it is the eastern European cities and their largely Protestant merchant class who decline as the trade becomes taken over by 'foreign' merchants, largely Dutch. The decline of the towns and local merchants leaves Catholic landowning control in the periphery which results in the counter-Reformation. Hence the key geopolitical distance is not a cultural one from Rome but an economic one in terms of relations with the rising core of the world-economy (Wallerstein 1980a).

This brings us to a second criticism of the geopolitical map. Rokkan's concentration on state formation leads to an emphasis on the medium states of the west which completely neglects the rise of the Dutch state. One of his paradoxes is the failure of city-state Europe to capitalize on the emerging new world but this is certainly not the case for Holland at the very top of the old trading-city routes. The Dutch may not have developed all the bureaucratic-military machinery of the absolute states but they nevertheless came to dominate the world-economy in the mid-seventeenth century. For a short period they were, in our terms, the strongest state in the world-economy (Wallerstein 1980a).

It is of course, true that other parts of city-state Europe did not maintain their position in the development of the European system. Northern Italy in particular suffered a major relative decline. In the world-systems approach this does not constitute an unusual occurrence. Northern Italy is the first example of the decline of an area into semi-peripheral status in the modern world-economy. Wallerstein, in fact, uses the case of Venice to illustrate such decline and relates it to high-cost inflexible economic arrangements compared with the dynamic growth areas of north-west Europe (Wallerstein 1979).

Of course the major difference between Rokkan's geopolitical map and the world-systems approach is in the limitation of his concern to Europe. The rise of Atlantic trade contributes to the advantages of western European states only as an exogeneous feature in this model. Hence whereas he misinterprets the eastern European periphery he largely ignores the American periphery. This has implications beyond the geographical scope of the model. Rokkan is not concerned with the crisis of feudalism and its particular geographical expression which Wallerstein uses to explain the initial lead of Iberian states in establishing the world-economy. For Rokkan Spain and Portugal are counter-Reformation crusading states in the south. Spain's defeat of the Moslems in Iberia is considered more important than their establishment of an American empire. In world-systems terms the war with the Moslems represents the final stages of a long-running conflict between two world-empires (Christendom and Islam) – the crusades – whereas the expansion into America represents the very beginning of the establishment of a world-economy – the first imperialism.

So far this critique of Rokkan's geopolitical map has merely provided alternative interpretations of the facts that he sets out. But our criticisms are ultimately much more fundamental than whether Rokkan's grid or Wallerstein's three-tier structure are the most accurate spatial representation. As an application of Parson's social system Rokkan stands in the centre of the modern social science tradition. Wallerstein's three challenges to that tradition can therefore be identified in Rokkan's work. The myth of universal laws is to be found in his treatment of feudal states and mercantile states as essentially common entities. We consider the origins of the modern state in some detail in Chapter 4 but here we can note that by crossing the transition from feudalism to capitalism Rokkan imputes similar motives to state-builders which are unwarranted. The poverty of disciplines is expressed in his concentration on political processes at the expense of the economic foundations. He uses just one sub-system of Parson's schema – the integration system – and treats it as a largely separate mechanism. Finally Rokkan's model represents a severe case of the error of developmentalism with states as his prime units of analysis. His emphasis is on explaining diversity between European states rather than the unity of the single system that was emerging – a competitive state system as an integral and essential feature of the new world-economy.

MODELSKI'S LONG CYCLES OF GLOBAL POLITICS

When we move from Rokkan's comparative politics to Modelski's international politics some of the criticisms made above are overcome: Modelski is concerned with the global political system in which the extra-European arena is central to the argument and the emphasis is upon a system of states rather than the ordering of individual states.

Modelski's model is also of interest because it was developed specifically to counter Wallerstein's approach. Like some other critics, Modelski has argued that Wallerstein (1974b) under-valued the importance of political processes in the original statement of his world-economy framework. Hence Modelski's model is an attempt to correct the balance. The fact that Modelski and others are mistaken in their interpretation of the world-economy as neglecting politics is testified by much subsequent writings of Wallerstein and his associates. If Modelski's criticism were correct this book could not, of course, be written. These origins of Modelski's model, however, are much less important to us than the final product which provides a serious alternative 'political' framework for our geopolitics.

1. The symmetry of global politics

There are many superficial similarities between Modelski's global cycles and the framework we are using. Modelski's global system begins about 1500 and then proceeds to develop in a cyclical manner. Modelski (1978: 218) creates a new type of cycle of just over a hundred years in length – so that we are currently experiencing the fifth such cycle. Each cycle is associated with a world power which is defined as a state which engages in over half the 'order-keeping' function of the global political system. Four such world powers have existed – Portugal, Netherlands, Britain and the USA. These have dominated 'their centuries' – Portugal the sixteenth, Netherlands the seventeenth, Britain the eighteenth and the nineteenth and currently the USA in the twentieth. Britain is unique in dominating two global cycles.

The details of these global cycles is shown in Table 4. In each case the rise and fall of the world power is indicated through definite steps. A cycle starts with a weak global organizational structure of severe political competition which degenerates into global war. Such wars have a wide geographical range and have global pay-offs – the winner is able to order

Table 4 Long cycles of global politics

Cycles	World powers	World wars	Legitimating treaties	Key institutions	Landmarks of decline
I	Portugal	Italian Wars (1494–1517)	Treaty of Tordesillas	Global network of bases	Spanish annexation (1580)
II	Netherlands	Spanish Wars (1579–1609)	Twelve year truce with Spain (1609)	'Mare librum'	The English Revolution
III	Britain	French Wars (1688–1713)	Treaty of Utrecht (1713)	Command of the sea	Independence of USA
IV	Britain	French Wars (1792–1815)	Paris and Vienna (1814, 1815)	Free trade	Imperialism
V	USA	German Wars (1914–45)	Versailles and Potsdam (1919, 1945)	United Nations	Vietnam War

the resulting political system. This phase ends with a legitimizing treaty which formally sets up the new world order centred on the new world power. No world power can maintain its control so that a decline phase sets in. Initially the world order becomes bi-polar and then multi-polar before the system becomes weakly organized again, is ripe for the rise of a new world power, and the cycle starts again. Even more so than with Rokkan's geopolitical map, we can be impressed by the symmetrical order Modelski finds in international politics.

2. Critique: the poverty of mechanisms of change

Whereas the geographical scope of Rokkan's model was less than the world-economy, Modelski's model is larger than the world-economy. His international political system is global right from its inception. This is not just a matter of geographical definition: it relates to how the role of Portugal is interpreted. For Modelski, by taking over the trading network in the Indian Ocean the Portuguese became the centre of a global system and hence a world power. In contrast Wallerstein places most of the Portuguese activity in the external arena outside the world-economy; Spanish American colonization is far more important in that it creates a new periphery. For Modelski Spain only operated on the fringes of his system and never developed a 'world outlook'. Here we come to the crux of the difference between the two approaches since the notion of a world outlook in the global sense is totally unnecessary for Wallerstein. His world system was originally a European world-economy and only became global in scope about 1900.

Why is a world outlook an important criteria for Modelski? The mechanisms for change in his system are two-fold. First there is what Modelski (1978: 224) terms 'the urge to make global order'. Once the possibilities of a global order became known an innate will for power has become expressed as an urge to shape world order. Only a few people may have such a world outlook but they respond to the inarticulated needs of the many. Second the nature of international politics as a system means that structures run down and have to be reconstructed. All systems suffer a loss of order and survive by cyclical development. Table 4 describes a particular expression of this general process. It is on the basis of these two mechanisms that change has occurred in Modelski's global system.

Clearly here we have uncovered the weak point of the model. For all its symmetry, its mechanisms of change are inherently disappointing. We can trace this back to Modelski's starting point that the global political system must be functionally distinguished from the world-economy. This is not to say that he necessarily underestimates the importance of economic processes – Modelski's politics are about who gets what in the world system – but he treats the two processes as distinct. In our terminology this is a classic illustration of the poverty of disciplines. As we have argued in Chapter 1 the state system and the economic system are integral parts of a single process of development incorporated in the concept of the world-economy. There are not two logics but one. The world-economy could not operate except within the political framework provided by a competitive state system. It is a necessary, though not sufficient, definition of a capitalist world-economy (Chase-Dunn 1982). The implication of this is that the mechanisms of change are not economic or political but both. Instead of Modelski's political framework we need a political-economy framework for bringing history back into our geopolitics.

A DYNAMIC MODEL OF HEGEMONY AND RIVALRY

In the world-systems approach we have a system of cycles which represents a far superior mechanism of change than in Modelski's politics. The processes we described in the last chapter operate to produce change that is essentially economic in nature. The basic argument is summed up in the phrase 'anarchy of production'. But this is only part of the process. This materialistic mechanism is much broader than economics. Political mechanisms are an integral part of the overall process of restructuring the world-economy that occurs within these cycles. It is this political element that is described here.

1. Political distortion of the world market

Political activity has always been an integral part of the world-economy. State policies are important processes in the changes observed in the world-economy. Since they are neither independent processes nor mere reflections of economic necessities (economism) it follows that there is some choice available. If there were no choice there would be no need for public institutions such as the state. Public agencies have the role of distorting market forces in favour of those private groups controlling the agency. There has never been a 'pure' world-economy even in periods where free-trade has dominated. The power of a public agency and hence its ability to organise the market depends upon the strength of its backers and their material resources. Strong states may promote a 'free market' while less strong states may favour explicit distortion of the market through protectionism, for instance. In this way states can act as a medium through which a first set of production processes upon which the world-economy operates are translated into a second set of distribution processes and patterns. Since these intermediate processes tend to favour the already-strong it follows that political activity will often increase the economic polarization of the market (that is helping the core at the expense of the periphery).

The power of a state to organize the market to its own ends is not just a property of that state's resources. The fact that we are dealing with a world-economy and not a world-empire (that is there is a multiplicity of states) means relative positions are more important than measures of absolute power. These state positions are relative not only to other states however, but also to the gross availability of material resources within the world-economy. The cyclical nature of material growth means that opportunities for operating various state policies vary systematically over time. This is not just a matter of different economic environments being suited to alternative state strategies. At any particular conjunction, specifically successful policies can only work for a limited number of agencies. Quite simply every successful state eliminates opportunities for other states. There will always be constraints in terms of the total world resources available for redistribution via state activities. Given the 'correct' policies it is *not* possible for all semi-periphery states and the periphery to become core-like. Although this is not a zero-sum game in a static sense since the available production is always changing in a cyclical fashion, nevertheless we do have here a sort of 'dynamic zero sum game'.

2. The rise and fall of hegemonic states: paired Kondratieffs

If state activity is an integral part of the operation of the world-economy we should be able to model it within our temporal and spatial framework. Just such a model has been proposed by Wallerstein and his associates (Research Working Group 1979). They postulate political activity occurring over a time-period covering two Kondratieff waves. This activity centres around brief hegemonic interludes when one state dominates the world-economy. Hegemony builds up in three stages. Initially the state gains primacy in production efficiency over its rivals. This enables its merchants to develop a commercial supremacy which finally leads on to financial dominance. When productive, commercial and financial activities of one state are more efficient than all rivals, that state's hegemony occurs. This favoured situation is brief, however, as rivals emulate the technical achievements and the hegemonic state's lead over its rivals declines first in production, then commerce and finally finance.

The rise and fall of hegemonic power relates to 'paired-Kondratieffs' as follows. If we start with a first growth phase, A-1, we find geopolitical rivalry as core states compete for succession to leadership. On hindsight, however, we can see new techological advances are concentrated in one country so that increased productive efficiency gives this state a long-term advantage. A-1 is associated with the stage of *ascending hegemony*. In B-1 overall decline of the world-economy leaves less opportunities for expansion but the ascending power now derives commercial supremacy and is able to protect its interests relative to its rivals. By this stage it is clear which state is to be new hegemonic power. B-1 is associated with the stage of *hegemonic victory*. With renewed growth of the world-economy we reach A-2, the stage of *hegemonic maturity*. By this time the financial centre of the world-economy has moved to the hegemonic state which is now supreme in production, commerce and finance (that is, 'true' hegemony). Since the hegemonic power can successfully compete with all its rivals it now favours 'opening' the world-economy. These are periods of free-trade.

Finally *declining hegemony* occurs during B-2 when productive efficiency is no longer sufficient to dominate rivals. This is a period of acute competition as new powers try to obtain a larger share of a declining market. There are periods of protectionism and formal imperialism as each rival attempts to preserve its own portion of the periphery.

According to Wallerstein's research group the four Kondratieff cycles from the industrial revolution can be interpreted as two 'paired Kondratieffs' (Table 5). The first pair covering the nineteenth century correspond to the rise and fall of British hegemony and the second pair describe a similar sequence of events for USA in the twentieth century. There is no need to consider this table in great detail except to note how several familiar episodes neatly fit the model.

In terms of our discussion of state involvement in the operation of the world-economy phases A-2 and B-2 are particularly important. In A-2 the hegemonic power imposes policies of open trade on the system to reap the rewards of its own efficiency. In the mid-nineteenth century Britain proclaimed 'free trade' backed up by gunboats and a century later a new world-policeman, this time with aircraft carriers, was going through the whole process of liberalising trade once again. These policies certainly contributed to the massive growth of the world-economy in the A-2 phases and were imposed through a mixture of negotiation, bargaining and bullying. Options for non-hegemonic powers were highly constrained and they largely went along with the hegemonic leadership.

All this changes with the onset of the B-2 phase, however. As productive efficiencies spread, economic leadership deserts the hegemonic power. These are key periods because of the opportunities available for other core and semi-periphery states that declining hegemony provides. The imposition of free trade is no longer taken for granted as various states work out new strategies for the new circumstances. In the late nineteenth century Britain entered the depression as hegemonic power and came out behind Germany and USA in terms of productive efficiency. B-2 phases are clearly fundamental periods of restructuring in the world-economy in which geopolitical processes play an important role. We are currently living through just such a phase.

3. Hegemony and rivalry in the logistic wave

What about the period before 1790? Wallerstein and his associates extend their model back to the very beginning of the world-economy. This involves identifying paired-Kondratieffs in the sixteenth, seventeenth and eighteenth centuries. The first two coincide with Hapsburg and Dutch hegemony respectively but the third pair cover a period of English–French rivalry with no clear hegemonic victory. Unfortunately the use of Kondratieff cycles for this early period must remain highly tentative. As we have previously indicated we prefer to stay on much firmer ground by employing the early world-economy logistic curve. The A-phase involved

Table 5 A dynamic model of hegemony and rivalry

	Great Britain		USA	
	1790/8		1890/6	
A_1 Ascending Hegemony	Rivalry with France (Napoleonic Wars) Productive efficiency: industrial revolution		Rivalry with Germany Productive efficiency: mass production techniques	
	1815/25		1913/20	
B_1 Hegemonic Victory	Commercial victory in Latin America and control of India: workshop of the world		Commercial victory in the final collapse of British free trade system and decisive military defeat of Germany	
	1844/51		1940/5	
A_2 Hegemonic maturity	Era of Free Trade: London becomes financial centre of the world-economy		Liberal economic system of Bretton Woods based upon the dollar: New York new financial centre of the world	
	1870/75		1967/73	
B_2 Declining Hegemony	Classical age of imperialism as European powers and USA rival Britain. 'New' industrial revolution emerging outside Britain		Reversal to protectionist practices to counteract Japan and European rivals	
	1890/96			

the establishment of the world-economy and the geopolitical rivalry was largely concerned with preventing it being transformed into a world-empire. With the consolidation in phase B we come to a hegemonic episode based upon Dutch efficiencies in production, commerce and finance. At this time (*c.* 1650) we find mercantilist policies being devised by England and France to upset the liberal trade regime imposed by the Dutch. This seventeenth-century sequence of events has many similarities with those for the paired-Kondratieffs in the nineteenth and twentieth centuries. This accounts for the attempt by Wallerstein and associates to apply their model to this period. However Dutch hegemony is very short and much less decisive than the later British and American versions. This will become apparent when we compare the 'old' and 'new' imperialisms in the next chapter. The whole of the long B-phase is probably best interpreted generally as a competitive period finally centred upon English–French rivalry but with important contributions from Holland, Prussia, Sweden and N.E. America. The rivalry was finally settled by the advantage adhering to England in the wake of the industrial revolution. In the meantime the general lack of hegemonic control meant that groups in Sweden and Prussia and even N.E. America could carve out important niches for themselves in the world-economy. The first two cases illustrate early examples of the use of powerful state machineries to control part of the world-economy for private ends. In the America case semi-peripheral status was achieved without control of a state-machinery although the eventual need for such a machinery led to the War of Independence and subsequently the Federal Constitution.

CURRENT AND FUTURE STRUCTURES OF GEOPOLITICS

The need for a viable historical perspective does not lessen our interests in current geopolites. To say that we have recently moved from an A-2 phase to a B-2 phase signalling the decline of American hegemony is informative, of course, but only takes our argument so far. The problem is that parallels across history can provide frameworks for analysis but they cannot cope with all the particular features of a situation. Nevertheless the world-systems approach does supply the principles and concepts for describing the current structure including some of its more unique attributes.

The similarities between the American position in the twentieth century and Britain in the nineteenth century are very real as our model, and that of Modelski, emphasize. But there are important differences as well. British hegemony went relatively unchallenged in the mid-nineteenth century. In contrast USA has been viewed as just one of two 'superpowers' since 1945 with the USSR providing political, though not economic, challenge. There was no equivalent rivalry during British hegemony. This final section of the chapter is concerned with this 'novel' feature of current geopolitics. An even more 'novel' feature is the massive destructive capabilities of the two super powers which can take any survivors back to a world of multiple mini-systems. It is this latter scenario which makes understanding of the current 'novel' features of 'our' geopolitics so very important.

THE WORLD-SYSTEMS INTERPRETATION OF THE USSR

We have seen that the traditional approaches to geopolitics treat the USSR as a land-power threat to the traditional dominance of sea powers. To balance the picture we will start our discussion by giving the Soviet view of its world position. In contrast to the expansionary motives assumed in western strategy, the USSR interprets its position as essentially defensive. This viewpoint is based upon two invasions since its inception in 1917, first US and Western European support for white Russians in the Civil War of 1918–21 and second the German invasion of 1941–44. Hence the Soviet Union is the protector of the socialist world surrounded by a hostile capitalism. One country's containment is indeed another country's expansion!

For our argument here the most relevant part of the Soviet model is the notion of *two* world-systems operating contemporaneously, a capitalist one and a socialist one. This notion stems from Stalin's attempt to build socialism in one country between the world wars and was expanded with the institution of COMECON after the Second World War as a 'co-operative division of labour' in Eastern Europe in contrast to the capitalist competitive division in the West. An attempt has been made by Szymanski (1982) to integrate this orthodox Marxist position with Wallerstein's framework. He claims that there are indeed two separate world-systems and economic transactions between them constitute luxury trade rather than essential trade. In this sense the two systems co-exist in the way other contemporaneous systems, Roman and Chinese world-empires for instance, have done before. This conception of two separate economic systems that compete politically is, of course, the mirror image of American geopolitics. We will show that both positions provide less insight than a world-systems interpretation of a single world-economy.

1. Vodka Cola: the transideological enterprise

Charles Levinson (1980) has provided a wealth of evidence to expose what he terms 'the ideological facade' of both US and USSR geopolitics. The following selection of some of the information he has compiled will give an indication of the basis of his argument. He shows that the largest forty multinational corporations all have co-operative agreements with one or more of the eight Eastern European states with communist regimes – thirty-four of them with USSR itself. He lists 151 corporations from fifteen different countries which have offices in Moscow. There are 108 multinational corporations from thirteen countries listed as operating in Bucharest alone. In the other direction 170 acknowledged multinational joint ventures by the USSR in nineteen 'Western' countries are tabled. It is not surprising therefore that by 1977 one third of USSR imports and one quarter of USSR exports were with Western countries. Levinson's conclusion is that although it is international politics which makes the news it is these crucial economic transactions which steer international politics. Hence detente *followed* trade and not vice versa. This is what Levinson calls the 'overworld' of economic dealings which have seen USSR and Eastern Europe become inexorably integrated into the world-economy. It is epitomized by the Pepsi Cola Corporation's deal to sell cola drink in

Russia and to market Vodka in the West – hence the title of Levinson's book *Vodka Cola*.

Gunder Frank (1977) has provided further evidence for the same process which he terms *trans-ideological enterprise*. He charts the massive rise in east–west trade especially since the death of Stalin in 1954 and discusses the various bartering arrangements and other agreements which have made this growth possible. The motives for all this activity are very traditional. For the corporations there is an extension of the geographical range of their profit-making. This is particularly important at a time of world-wide recession. The Eastern European states provide a source of relatively cheap, yet skilled, disciplined and healthy labour. And of course there is the vast raw material potential of the Soviet Union. For the latter the motive is equally straightforward. Co-operation with Western corporations was the only solution to a technology lag which the Soviet Union has suffered in the wake of rise of electronic industries in the West. Increasing integration into the world-economy is the price USSR has to pay for keeping up with its ideological competitors.

2. The semi-periphery interpretation: socialism as development strategy

Wallerstein interprets all this evidence as placing the Soviet Union and its Eastern European allies in the semi-periphery. Gunder Frank (1977) shows that the Soviet Union lies in an intermediate position between 'west' and 'south'. For instance 'East–South' trade is used to pay for 'East–West' trade in numerous multilateral arrangements. In short USSR exploits the South but is itself exploited by the West in terms of trade arrangements. (This process of unequal exchange in trade is explained in the next chapter under informal imperialism.) This places the Soviet regime economically on a par with other non-socialist semi-peripheral countries such as Brazil or Iran. Although it can be argued that *within* COMECON trade is not capitalistic – prices are not set by the world market – it is influenced by world market prices. Furthermore this production is for exchange, and ultimate use of production is grossly distorted by the world-economy as a whole through its aggressive inter-state system. With our single political economy logic the current situation of the USSR and its allies cannot be interpreted as anything other than as an integral part of the world-economy.

If the Soviet Union represents an example of an aggressive upward-moving semi-periphery state where does this leave its socialist rhetoric? According to Brucan (1981) Eastern Europe provides a model for development strategy rather than socialism. From the very beginning with Lenin's New Economic Policy of 1921 the essence of Soviet policy has been 'catching up' and this involved all-out mobilization of national potential. The original heavy industry 'import substitution' phase of protectionism or autarky has given way to an export orientation in the 1970s which Frank and Levinson have charted (Koves 1981). In fact the original ideology of the revolution had to be developed to invent the intermediate state of 'socialism' between capitalism and communism to cover the period when USSR was 'developing the forces of production'. All this seems very much like mercantilism in new clothing (Frank 1977; Wallerstein 1982 and Chase-Dunn 1982). USA, Germany and Japan have in their turn been aggressive, upwardly mobile, semi-peripheral states who have used political means (protectionism, public investment in infra-structure and other support) to improve their competitive position in the world-economy. Soviet 'socialism' seems to be a classic case of a modern semi-periphery strategy.

3. World power: socialism as an anti-systemic force

But of course, the USSR is more than just another rising semi-periphery state. The establishment of the Soviet state in 1917 was the culmination of a revolutionary movement whose internationalism was stemmed but who nevertheless represented, and still represents, an ideological challenge to the capitalism of the world-economy. With the revolution initially limited to Russia, Stalin had no option but to build 'socialism in one country' – to catch up before the new state was destroyed. From this point onwards the logic of the world-system placed the USSR in a 'Catch 22' situation. In order to survive the state needed to compete with other states but this competition involved playing the world-economy game by capitalist rules. This has come to a head in the current recession. There have always been policy conflicts within the Soviet bloc between fundamentalists who emphasize their socialist credentials and the technocrats emphasizing efficiency. This 'red versus expert' conflict has been recently resolved in the latter's favour under the pressures of the current world recession. This can be seen throughout Eastern Europe and is particularly obvious in post-Mao China.

The fact that the world-revolutionary movement – Wallerstein terms them anti-systemic forces – is currently in the vice of the world-economy does not lessen the unique nature of the USSR challenge to US hegemony. Never before has a semi-peripheral state had the world-wide impact that the Soviet state has had. Unlike other semi-periphery states the USSR is *not* a regional power in Cohen's term but is truly a political super power of global proportions. During its period of hegemony the USA has been challenged by the USSR on all continents. This is because the socialist ideology of the USSR has been more compatible with peripheral liberation movements than the USA's liberalism. Nearly all national movements in the second half of the twentieth century have employed socialist rhetoric even if they have been unable to practise fully these ideas. The result has been that the challenge to the USA's hegemony has been on two fronts – political and ideological by the USSR, and with the downturn of the current Kondratieff wave, economic by Europe and Japan. These two challenges lead to alternative future geopolitical scenarios.

ALTERNATIVE GEOPOLITICS OF THE FUTURE

It is not our purpose in this study to be prophetic but nevertheless discussion of geopolitics does awaken in all of us a curiosity concerning the future. Stanley Brunn (1981) has provided ten scenarios for the twenty–first century in which different geographical themes are explored. Here we concentrate on just three scenarios, each of which follows part of our previous discussions. We shall start with the most pessimistic and conclude with the most optimistic scenario.

1. The armageddon scenario: return to mini-systems

Brunn's final scenario includes nuclear war in which complete annihilation of the human race is 'more than a remote possibility'. The stockpiling of missiles by both super powers to achieve 'mutually assured destruction' (MAD) has horrendous implications. Currently there are the equivalent of five tons of TNT in nuclear explosive power per capita in the world. As Short (1982: 92) points out, never has an acronym been so appropriate as MAD. Short follows Thompson's (1980) argument that there is a 'logic of exterminism' in the continued build-up of nuclear capability by both sides deriving from mutual distrust. Despite the economic linkages discussed above, ideological competition between super powers remains and is potentially so very dangerous.

The geography of the armageddon scenario has been thoroughly explored by William Bunge (1982) in his *Nuclear War Atlas*. From Mackinder's strategy based on the railway age we swiftly move into the satellite age in Bunge's geopolitics. In this new geopolitics the two-dimensional strategic thinking of the past gives way to three-dimensional thinking – for both super powers the enemy is in the sky *above*. This simplifies the strategic map – we are all vulnerable, military and civilian, as the world becomes one large 'shatter belt', to use Cohen's terminology. The actual pattern of nuclear strikes will not be random, however. Each aggressor will attack the enemy's cities first to reduce their organizational capacity. Bunge uses Christaller's central place theory to illustrate this point. Cities will be successively eliminated down the central place hierarchy. Government, finance, production, distribution, all aspects of 'urban culture' will disappear. Bunge believes that the size of nuclear stockpiles indicates the targeting of cities as small as 25,000. Very few central place functions will survive. In Bunge's words 'the nation is not only decimated it is decapitated'. Openshaw and Steadman (1982) have simulated this scenario for Britain under a moderate nuclear attack (only 200 one megaton bombs) and predict as many as 43 million deaths out of a population of 55 million. Geographically this represents the destruction of the entire British urban system and the territorial disintegration of the

British state (Taylor and Johnston 1984). This is nothing less than the destruction of civilization and the return of 'barbarism'. In world-systems terms the capitalist mode of production will be eliminated and survivors will rebuild their lives in new mini-systems based upon the reciprocal-lineage mode. This is perhaps optimistic since it assumes that blast survivors will not fall victim to the nuclear winter which dust and smoke will bring to all corners of the world. In this case the armageddon scenario will truly mean the end of our species.

2. The new hegemony scenario: the Japanese century

If by some chance we avoid armageddon, the simplest scenario to predict is one that follows the logic of our paired-Kondratieff model of hegemony and rivalry. The beginning of such a scenario can be found in Mary Kaldor's (1979) *The Disintegrating West*. The declining hegemony of USA is ushering in a new era of rivalry which Kaldor terms 'west versus west'. The existence of just such a new situation was signalled by the American trade deficit in 1971 and by the Nixon administration's response which Kaldor refers to as 'parochial policy', that is, international liberal economic policy sacrificed for short-term national ends. Hence the trade deficit was overturned but at the price of exposing America's fragile leadership of the liberal world order. Kaldor traces European reactions to this decline of the USA back to nineteenth-century ideologies. The pro-American 'Atlanticists' retain the ideology of the mid-nineteenth-century free trade liberals whereas the emerging 'Gaullist' European position mimics the 'new mercantilism' of the late nineteenth century – European parochial policy to combat American parochial policy (Kaldor 1979: 23). Bergesen and Schoenberg (1980) take this parallel with the late nineteenth century even further. The current decline of non-alignment among peripheral states is interpreted as a new, albeit 'looser', imperialism based upon arms sales dependence. In their words: 'It is like the end of the nineteenth century all over again, only new actors' (Bergesen and Schoenberg 1980: 266).

The replacement of American hegemony by a new era of rivalry is now generally accepted – President Nixon referred to it as 'multi-polarity'. Five 'poles' are usually identified: the USA, the USSR, Western Europe, Japan and China. But the really interesting question is what follows. In the paired-Kondratieff model one of these rivals should emerge to form a new hegemony. This will be based not upon military prowess but on economic efficiency, initially in production. This rules out the USSR and China. According to Kaldor (1979: 20) 'a historic reversal in the direction of uneven development' has occurred with the massive penetration of the American market by European and especially Japanese manufactured products. As Japanese economic supremacy moves from production to commerce and finally to finance we should be looking for changes in

Japanese trade policy from their special brand of 'inscrutable' mercantilism to a new liberalism. In this scenario the twenty-first century will be the Japanese century.

3. The socialist scenario: transformation of the world-economy

The prediction of a 'Japanese century' using Kondratieff waves can be made without recourse to a world-systems perspective. In an alternative approach, capitalism can be viewed as a self-adjusting system where technological advances are regularly brought forward (every fifty years) to resolve production problems. Hall (1981) points out that the geography of these technological salvations has changed over time so that Japan may well be the home of the next 'adjustment' in capitalism. This interpretation of Kondratieff waves is the opposite of Wallerstein's approach. Whereas the Japanese prediction is acceptable, the notion that this is part of a self-adjusting system is not. For Wallerstein the cycles of the world-economy are accompanied by cumulative trends resulting from regular restructuring of the system which only temporarily resolve crises of capitalism. These reorganizations include several economic processes, notably increasing the labour market (proletarianization), and related political processes. Wallerstein's (1980c) point is that each restructuring brings such trends closer to their asymtote of 100 per cent. For instance geographical expansion can no longer contribute to resolving a crisis since the world-economy became global in scope around 1900. For Wallerstein this is an option that has been used up. Other options will become more difficult to use as they approach their asymtote so that rather than being self-adjusting, the system is coming to its end. In Wallerstein's (1980c, 179) words: 'We are living in the historic transition from capitalism to socialism.'

The politics of the world-economy are fundamental to this transition. There is nothing inevitable about future change; it has to be fought for and won. Wallerstein (1980c) emphasizes the role of anti-systemic forces. We have already noted that two of the five poles of the current era of rivalry have anti-systemic regimes and that their emergence has 'spoilt' American enjoyment of their hegemony relative to the much less troublesome world of British hegemony a century earlier. Although anti-systemic regimes are inevitably compromised by their membership of the world-system, Wallerstein emphasizes their mobilization of populations against capitalism which produces an upward spiral effect of opposition. Hence over the last 150 years there has been an upward trend in anti-systemic politics which is one of the cumulative trends which will eventually undermine the world-economy. In the current rivalry phase it is not only traditional inter-state competition which is important therefore, but the great amount of internal unrest in the wake of social security cut-backs in the core and direct wage reductions elsewhere. Urban riots in the core, economic and political crises in the semi-periphery, for instance in Poland, Iran, Nigeria, Brazil to mention one country from each of the four continents, and impoverishment within peripheral countries are equally as important as the rise of Japan. It is not only the economics of the world-economy that is being restructured, the politics are also being gradually transformed. As the various options run out politics will come to dominate economics again in the world-system as it becomes necessary to replace the anarchy of production by the planning of production. This scenario constitutes the world-systems approach to the traditional crisis of capitalism and the transformation to socialism. For Wallerstein the process will take another 100–150 years to complete and we cannot yet envisage what the new system will look like any more than the European upper class of 1450 could predict the capitalist world-economy. We can, however, suggest that any attainment of a more egalitarian system will depend upon geopolitics giving way to imperialism as the key relation in the future dynamics of the world-economy as the locus of change moves 'south'.

Chapter 3

GEOGRAPHY OF IMPERIALISMS

THE REVOLUTIONARY HERITAGE

The rise and fall of the classical theory

1. Imperialism as geopolitics
2. The Hobson–Lenin paradigm
3. Despatching imperialism to history

A world-systems interpretation of imperialism

1. Cycles of imperialism
2. Four sub-relations of imperialism
3. A new geography of revolution

FORMAL IMPERIALISM: THE CREATION OF EMPIRES

Two cycles of formal imperialism

1. The cumulative number of colonies
2. Establishment: creation, reorganization and transfer
3. De-colonization: geographical contagion and contrasting ideologies

The geography of formal imperialism

1. Core: the imperial states
2. Periphery: the political arenas

The economics of formal imperialism

1. The Sugar islands of the Caribbean
2. 'Islands of development' in Africa

INFORMAL IMPERIALISM: POLITICS, TRADE AND PRODUCTION

Trade policy and the world-economy

1. Free trade and the hegemonic state
2. Protectionism and the semi-periphery
3. The choice for the periphery

The mechanism of unequal exchange

1. Free labour and subsistence wages
2. Social imperialism in the core
3. Division: social imperialism versus subsistence wages

Chapter 3

GEOGRAPHY OF IMPERIALISMS

Despite its obvious political and geographical characteristics, the topic of imperialism is a neglected theme in political geography. This is not just a problem of political geography, however, but is more to do with the nature of modern social science as a whole. It relates directly to what is referred to in Chapter 1 as the poverty of disciplines. The term 'imperialism' is a classic political-economy concept which cannot be properly defined in either political or economic categories alone (Barratt Brown 1974: 19). Hence the neglect of imperialism has spread far beyond political geography. One of the most cogent criticisms of the whole 'modernization' and 'development' schools of modern social science, for instance, is that they seem to conveniently 'forget' or at least 'ignore' the contribution of imperialism to the modern world situation.

The geographical extent of European political control in the periphery is shown in Figure 5. All areas that were at some time under core control are shown and can be seen to include almost all the periphery. The major exception is China but even here the leading core states delimited their 'spheres of influence'. In geographical terms the result of this political control was a world organized as one huge functional region for the core

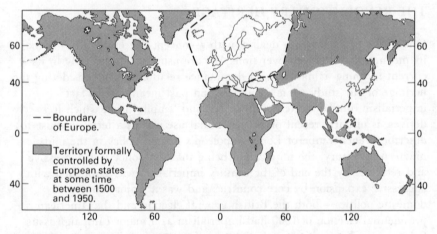

5. The geographical extent of European political control of the periphery

states. This has been, and we shall argue remains, the dominant spatial organization of the twentieth century. And yet until recently this subject was considered so unimportant that it was largely left to historians to debate it outside the social sciences.

In our world-systems approach, of course, imperialism is much more than a problem of history. 'Bringing history back in' means opening up the issues of imperialism once again. One of the achievements of the new neo-Marxist perspectives on social science is the rediscovery of the revolutionary heritage of imperialism. Of course the concept has not been neglected just because it is difficult to fit into the modern disciplines of political science and economics; imperialism has been neglected because it is part of a classical revolutionary theory which modern social science was designed to circumvent. We cannot understand imperialism, in a world-systems or any other framework, without first understanding its revolutionary heritage. The first section of this chapter describes this heritage and the subsequent interpretations of historians who could safely label these issues as concerns of the past.

The remainder of this chapter is primarily descriptive in nature. The neglect of our theme means that we must start our political geography studies at a stage where ordering of information is our dominant concern. This is achieved by using the dynamic model of hegemony and rivalry presented in the previous chapter. These descriptions are divided into two sections, the first dealing with formal imperialism and the second with informal imperialism. Both imperialisms are characterized by the dominance relation between core and periphery, the distinction between them being that the former involves political control of periphery territory in addition to economic exploitation.

THE REVOLUTIONARY HERITAGE

One of the problems with dealing with a concept like imperialism is that its meaning has changed over time. We are using it in this study in its current meaning as indicating a dominance relation but in considering the heritage of our study we must understand past meanings. In fact imperialism, unlike the terms 'imperial' and 'empire' from which it derives, is of fairly recent origin. Its initial use was as a term of abuse to describe French Emperor Louis Napoleon's foreign policy in the mid-nineteenth century, the implication being that the policy was aggressive and reckless. By the end of the century imperialism was associated with aggressive expansion by core countries and was a major concern of domestic politics – both the British general election and the American presidential election of 1900 had imperialism as a major campaign issue for instance. From this contemporary debate one contribution stands out as being of continuing significance – J. A. Hobson's (1902) *Imperialism: A Study*, written in the aftermath of the British imperial war in South Africa. As a polemic against imperialism this was to become a source for Lenin's theory and we consider these surprising links between English liberalism and Russian Marxism in our outline of the revolutionary theory below. This is followed by a description of how the subject matter became despatched into history before we consider the development of new theory which has become part of the world-systems approach.

THE RISE AND FALL OF THE CLASSICAL THEORY

Imperialism had a central role to play in the theories of the generation of Marxists after Marx and Engels. Whereas Marx did not use the term 'imperialism' and made no general study of the effects of capitalism in the periphery, for Lenin and his associates imperialism had become the essence of the capitalism of their time. Hence when we refer to the classical theory of imperialism it is to Lenin not Marx that we refer. However, we must be careful not to equate the classical Marxist concept of imperialism with the modern concept. The classical concept was both broader and more akin to our geopolitics than is often realized. The various meanings of the concept will become clear as we look at the different theories.

1 Imperialism as geopolitics

Lenin's famous pamphlet on imperialism was written during the First World War as part of an on-going debate in Marxist circles on the meaning of the war. It was avowedly polemic and popular and represents a position that subsequently became orthodox Marxism rather than an original contribution (Brewer 1980: ch. 5). That is to say he draws upon work of other authors, reorders some ideas, changes the emphases to suit his debating position but adds little to the argument. Lenin particularly draws on the work of an Austrian Marxist Hilferding and the British liberal writer Hobson.

According to Brewer (1980) Hilferding is the real founder of the Marxist theory of imperialism. He used the term imperialism to mean inter-core rivalry which incorporated dominance over the periphery but which did not make this its primary characteristic. Rather he emphasized the rise of finance capital in a new monopoly era when industrial and financial capital are fused into one system. He was particularly impressed by the power of the banks and their relations to industry and the state in pre-1914 Germany. He concluded that finance capital needed strong state support in terms of economic protection and obtaining territories for investment, markets and raw materials. But he remained concerned largely with the internal developments of core countries rather than the 'spillover' effects into the periphery. These ideas are developed in Bukharin's (1972)

Imperialism and the World Economy of 1917 in which the idea of imperialism as the geopolitics of a particular stage of capitalism – Bukharin's finance monopoly capitalism – is proposed. Lenin takes this argument one step further and defines imperialism as a stage of capitalism, the 'highest', in fact. By this he meant that the competitive capitalism that Marx had described in the mid-nineteenth century had been replaced by a monopoly capitalism. This was the final stage of capitalism because the contradictions of the system were reflected in inter-state rivalries which had produced a world war as the beginning of the revolution. For Lenin the First World War represented the death throes of capitalism.

2   The Hobson–Lenin paradigm

The other major source for Lenin's ideas was, as we have indicated, Hobson's non-Marxist anti-imperialism. For Hobson the 'taproot' of imperialism was surplus capital generated in the core looking for investment outlets in the periphery. Hobson collected data on overseas investment, areas and populations of colonies and dates of acquisitious and concluded that 1870 was a vital turning point in European history. Lenin reproduced this information in his own pamphlet and Wallerstein (1980b) feels it is reasonable to talk of the Hobson–Lenin paradigm. This has three basic positions: (1) Within states there are different interests between different sectors of capital; (2) a monopoly, finance sector was emerging as the dominant interest which could steer the state into imperial ventures for its own interests but against the interests of the other sectors and (3) despite much popular support these ventures were against the real interests of the working classes in these countries. Wallerstein terms this a paradigm because of its influence in setting the agenda for all subsequent studies of imperialism. In this sense whether we agree with Hobson and Lenin's theses or not, we remain a 'prisoner' of their ideas as long as they continue to be the starting point of discussions on imperialism.

Wallerstein (1980b) emphasizes the similarities between Hobson and Lenin on imperialism. This is important because their association has given Lenin's revolutionary theory a respectability in Western thought which it might not otherwise have received. But there are, of course, fundamental differences between the two men. As an English liberal, Hobson's anti-imperialism pointed towards reformist solutions of free trade and raising domestic consumption. Lenin's theory was intended as a contribution to overthrowing the capitalist system. By understanding the stage that capitalism had reached, revolutionary forces could seize the opportunity that the world war offered and create a new system. This was not a prediction but a statement of the theoretical rationale for revolutionary strategy and practice. In the end the practice was only partially successful, producing a successful revolution in Russia alone. But the theory remained to be refined and updated by sympathizers and criticized and dismissed by opponents. The best way of achieving the latter is to take the subject off the political agenda. This was done by despatching the topic to history where the final stage of capitalism becomes converted into the harmless 'age of imperialism'.

3 Despatching imperialism to history

After the First World War these 'classical' theories of imperialism became used as raw material in debates on the causes of the First World War and/ or growth of European empires. They became simplified as 'single-cause' theories, as economic determinism, to be refuted by careful, scholarly historical research. This begins with Schumpeter's (1951) assertion in 1919 that imperialism, far from being the highest stage of capitalism, is essentially anti-capitalist and reflects the militarism of the pre-capitalist European nobility. Schumpeter therefore dismisses economic motives and brings social and political causes to the fore. Subsequent historical interpretations have emphasized narrowly political causes. These are the 'balance of power' theories (Foeken 1982) which sees imperialism as a vehicle of European diplomacy in the late-nineteenth-century rivalry between Germany, France and Britain. This is most fully developed by Mansergh (1949) and represents the antithesis of the classicial theory emphasizing as it does the decisions of a few political leaders at the expense of any general political-economy process.

Since the Second World War there has been a reaction against such narrow historical interpretations. In a series of studies Robinson and Gallagher have attempted to rethink the whole debate. Their critique is of particular relevance to our study on two counts. First they challenge the whole idea of an 'age of imperialism' in the late nineteenth century (Gallagher and Robinson 1953). They emphasize the continuity of policy throughout the nineteenth century and do not accept that 1870 represents a fundamental watershed in modern history. After all India, 'the jewel in Britain's imperial crown', was obtained before the age of imperialism and continued to be by far the most important imperial possession throughout the age of imperialism. Second they queried whether the causes of European expansion could be found solely in processes – economic or political or both – operating in the core (Robinson, Gallagher and Denny 1961). As studies of imperialism began appearing from the periphery it became clear that the timing, nature and form of dominance relations were often conditioned by local circumstances in the periphery. Robinson (1973) has elaborated this into a theory of collaboration whereby certain peripheral elites interact with core states to help produce imperialism. This explains why European powers could control so much of the periphery with relatively little military involvement. Clearly British control of India would have been impossible without collaboration. In short the classical debate was hopelessly Euro-centric. Hence we can say that Robinson and Gallagher were steering the temporal and spatial co-ordinates of the debate in the direction of the framework adopted for this study.

A WORLD-SYSTEMS INTERPRETATION OF IMPERIALISM

Robinson and Gallagher help us to break out of the Hobson–Lenin paradigm but they do not chart a new theory. By extending the debate beyond the 'age of imperialism' they leave the way open for other historians to commit what we have termed the myth of universal law whereby imperialism is a general political process based on motives of expansion and conquest. Lichtheim (1971), for instance, considers the 'imperialism' of the Roman Empire and other world-empires alongside modern imperialism. Within our world-systems framework – the time limit is quite explicit – imperialism is a dominance relation in the world-economy and therefore is not found prior to the sixteenth century. Previous political expansions are based on fundamentally different political-economy processes and require a separate term to describe them.

Of course, if we can extend Robinson and Gallagher's concern for the nineteenth century backwards to the origins of our system we can also bring the concept forward to the present. It was not just historians who were taking note of new studies of the periphery in the period since the Second World War. As we pointed out in Chapter 1, dependency theory was developed and extended to become the world-systems approach. In political terms de-colonization put imperialism back on the agenda with concepts such as Ghanaian leader Kwame Nkumah's concept of 'Neo-Colonialism' as another stage of capitalism. The time was ripe for a second set of revolutionary theories to emerge to inform and direct the periphery in their relations with the core (Blaut 1975). Here we briefly decribe the world-systems theory of imperialism.

Wallerstein (1980b) follows Robinson and Gallagher in breaking out of the Hobson–Lenin paradigm. In world-systems terms this paradigm is a classic example of the error of developmentalism taking as it does countries as units of change and identifying stages through which they pass. But we go beyond Robinson and Gallagher's theses by transcending their dichotomies of continuity versus discontinuity and core versus periphery.

1 Cycles of imperialism

The continuity–discontinuity debate is subsumed under our cyclical property of the world-economy. Imperialist activity will vary with the political opportunities afforded to states during the uneven growth of the world-economy. Our paired-Kondratieff model in the last section illustrates how formal imperialism is part of an unfolding logic interacting with periods of hegemony when informal imperialism is prominent. Hence imperialism is a relation that has occurred throughout the history of the world-economy. But this continuity does not preclude identification of particular phases when different strategies prevailed. Hence the very real differences between mid-nineteenth-century British hegemony and the late-nineteenth-century 'age of imperialism' are incorporated but without any suggestion of a particular 'stage' in a linear sequence.

2   Four sub-relations of imperialism

In a similar manner the world-systems approach can incorporate both sets of arguments in the core-versus-periphery debate on causes of imperialism. We will use part of Johan Galtung's (1971) 'structural theory of imperialism' to model a range of 'sub-relations' through which the overarching dominance relation of imperialism operates. We will simplify our argument to just two types of state, core (C) and periphery (P), and two classes in each state, dominant (A) and dominated (B). This provides for four groups in the world-economy: core/dominant class (C_A), periphery/dominant class (P_A), core/dominated class (C_B) and periphery/dominated class (P_B). From this we can derive four important relations: *collaboration*, $C_A - P_A$, whereby the dominant classes of both areas combine to organize their joint domination of the periphery; *social-imperialism*, $C_A - C_B$, in which the dominated class in the core is 'bought off' by welfare policy as the price for social peace 'at home'; *repression*, $P_A - P_B$, to maintain exploitation of the periphery by coercion as necessary; and *division*, $C_B - P_B$, so that there is a separation of interests between dominated classes, that is, the classic strategy of divide and rule. In our approach therefore, Robinson's (1973) collaboration is just one sub-relation of a broader set of relations of imperialism.

3   A new geography of revolution

Finally we should note how this new theory diverges fundamentally from the classical Marxist theory. This is partly expressed in the different definitions of imperialism with the latter theory incorporating much more than core–periphery relations. But it is much more than a matter of definitions. Brewer (1980) shows that the classical theory's relative neglect of the periphery was no accident but a reflection of a theory of revolution which expected transformation to occur in the core where the forces of production, and hence the contractions of capitalism, were most developed. Indeed in the classical view penetration of the periphery by core countries could be seen as beneficial since 'progressive' capitalism would free the area from the shackles of feudalism just as it had done earlier in Europe. As we have seen the neo-Marxist view interprets such penetration in a completely different manner with capitalism in the periphery never having a progressive liberating role but rather being regressive from the beginning – what Frank terms the development of underdevelopment. The so-called progressive elements of capitalism, therefore, are geographically restricted to the transformation from feudalism to capitalism in the core. From the world-systems perpective this results in a geographical re-alignment of revolutionary forces in terms of core versus periphery with the latter becoming a major locus of future revolt and change. The new theories of imperialism define, in effect, a new geography of revolution as indicated in the transformation of the world-economy scenario briefly described at the end of the previous chapter.

FORMAL IMPERIALISM: THE CREATION OF EMPIRES

The formal political control of parts of the periphery has been a feature of the world-economy since its inception. From the early Spanish and Portuguese Empires through to the attempt by Italy in the 1930s to forge an African empire, formal imperialism has been a common strategy of core domination over the periphery. Of course, this process must not be confused with the concept of the world-empire as an entity with its own division of labour. Even the British Empire, on which the sun really did not set for over a century, was not a world-empire in our terms but rather a successful core state with a large colonial appendage. In this section we describe the rise and fall of such 'appendages' within the framework of the dynamic model of hegemony and rivalry described in the previous chapter. This description is organized into three parts. First we look at imperialism at the system scale to delineate the overall pattern of the process. Second we consider the imperialist activities of the core states who created the overall pattern. Finally we turn to the periphery and briefly consider the political arenas where this dominance relation was imposed.

THE TWO CYCLES OF FORMAL IMPERIALISM

If we wish to describe formal imperialism the first question that arises is how to measure it. Obviously figures for population, land area or 'wealth' under core political control would make ideal indices for monitoring imperialism but such data is simply not available over the long time period we employ here. Instead we follow Bergesen and Schoenberg (1980) and use the presence of a colonial governor to indicate the imposition of sovereignty of a core state over territory in the periphery. These personages may have very many different titles (for example, high commissioner, commandant, chief political resident) but all have jurisdictions signalling core control of particular parts of the periphery. Obviously the size of such territorial jurisdictions vary widely in terms of population, land area and wealth but the presence of governors does provide a constant unit of measure over five hundred years. As Bergesen and Schoenberg (1980: 232) admit there is 'no clear cut way to measure colonialism' but this direct measure of political control does provide a reasonably sensitive index of formal imperialist activity at the world-scale.

Bergesen and Schoenberg obtain their data from a comprehensive catalogue of colonial governors compiled by Henige (1970). He identifies

412 colonial jurisdictions and provides a listing of governors for all such territories from their establishment to de-colonization. Bergensen and Schoenberg identify two clear 'waves of colonial expansion and contraction' from this data. We will rework the data here to order it in terms of our time metric and to identify more than just the period of colonial control in a territory. Our analysis differs from that of Bergesen and Schoenberg in two respects, therefore. First the data is classified in terms of time periods compatible with our space–time matrix. The metric we have used is a simple 50-year sequence from 1500 to 1800 and a 25-year sequence from 1800 to 1975. This provides for some detail in addition to the long A- and B-phases in the original logistic wave plus an approximation to the A- and B-phases of the subsequent Kondratieff waves. Second we record more than merely establishment and disestablishment of colonies. From the record of governorships we can also trace reorganizations of existing colonized territory and transfer of sovereignty of territory between core states. Both of these are useful indices in that they are related to phases of stagnation (and hence the need to reorganize) and core rivalry (expressed as capturing rival colonies). In the analyses that follow the establishment of colonies is divided into three categories: creation of colony, reorganization of territory and transfer of sovereignty.

1 The cumulative number of colonies

We can start by replicating Bergesen and Schoenberg's study. By cumulating the number of colonies created and subtracting the number of de-colonizations, the total amount of colonial activity can be found for each time period. The results of this exercise are shown in Figure 6 which reproduces Bergesen and Schoenberg's two long waves of colonial expansion and contraction. There is a long first wave peaking at the conclusion of the logistic B phase and contracting in the A-phase of the first Kondratieff cycle. This largely defines the rise and fall of European empires in the 'New World' of America. The second wave rises through the nineteenth century to peak at the end of the 'age of imperialism' and then declines rapidly into the mid-twentieth century. This largely defines the rise and fall of European empires in the 'Old World' of Asia and Africa. Hence the two waves incorporate two geographically distinct phases of imperialism. This simple space–time pattern provides the framework in which we investigate formal imperialism more fully.

2 Establishment: creation, reorganization and transfer

The 411 colonies identified by Henige (1970) have been classified into three types as indicated above. All three categories are shown in Figure 7 and we will describe each pattern in turn.

Where governors are imposed on a territory for the first time we refer to the creation of a colony. Since this is one political strategy of restructuring during economic stagnation we expect colony creation to be associated

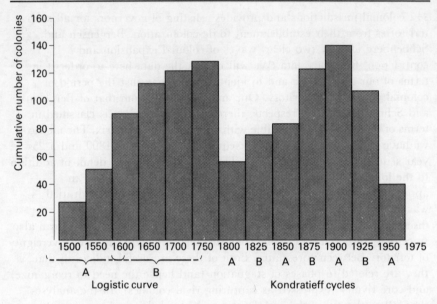

6. The two long waves of colonial expansion and contraction

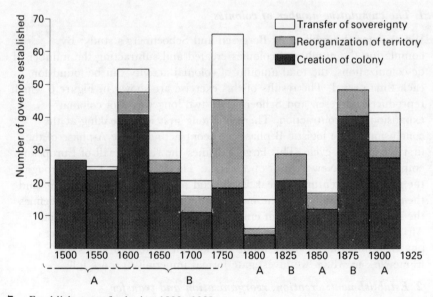

7. Establishment of colonies, 1500–1925

with B-phases of our waves. This is generally born out by Figure 7. The major exception is the imperialist activities of Spain and Portugal in the original A-phase in the emerging world-economy. This followed the Treaty of Tordisellas when the Pope divided the non-European world between these two leading states. This curtailed the usual rivalry associated with colony creation and it seems that the world-economy was not yet developed sufficiently to enable informal imperialism to operate outside Europe. With the onset of the seventeenth-century stagnation phase colonial creation expanded with the entry into the non-European arena of north-west European states. From this first peak of colony creation, the process slows down until a minor increase during the period of British–French rivalry at the end of the logistic B-phase. During the Kondratieff cycles colony creation goes up and down with the A- and B-phases but the most notable feature is the 'age of imperialism' clearly marked by the late-nineteenth-century peak. Hence we incorporate both the continuity and the discontinuity arguments by viewing colonial activity as a cyclical process.

Reorganization of territory should be particularly sensitive to periods of stagnation. Such periods involve pressures on states to cut back public expenditure and in the time-scale we are dealing with here this is reflected in attempts to make colonies more 'efficient'. Hence the reorganizations shown in Figure 7 are generally associated with B-phases. The major peak here is at the end of the logistic B-phase when the relative decline of Spain and Portugal meant that their colonies were becoming acute burdens to the state exchequers.

Transfers of sovereignty is a direct measure of inter-state rivalry in the periphery. This is mainly a feature of the logistic B-phase when this type of activity was relatively common. With the onset of the Kondratieff cycles such 'capture' is quite rare and is concentrated into just two periods, both A-phases. What these actually represent is the sharing out of the colonial spoils after two global wars. The first relates to the defeat of France and the confirmation of British hegemony. The second relates to the defeat of Germany and the confirmation of USA hegemony. In both cases the losing powers were deprived of colonies.

3 De-colonization: geographical contagion and contrasting ideologies

The pattern of de-colonization is a much simpler one (Figure 8). There have been two major periods of decolonization and these are directly responsible for the troughs in Figure 6 and hence generate the two-wave pattern.

Although both peaks occur in A-phases they do not correspond to equivalent phases in our paired-Kondratieff model: the second A-2 phase of American hegemony is a period of major de-colonization but the first A-2 phase of British hegemony is clearly not such a period. The first de-colonization period occurred earlier during an A-1 phase of emerging hegemony. This is best interpreted as the conclusion of the agricultural capitalism of the logistic curve. The de-colonization involved the termination of Spanish and Portuguese colonies in Latin America and by this time the colonizing powers had long since declined themselves to semi-peripheral status. For the competing core powers in this period of

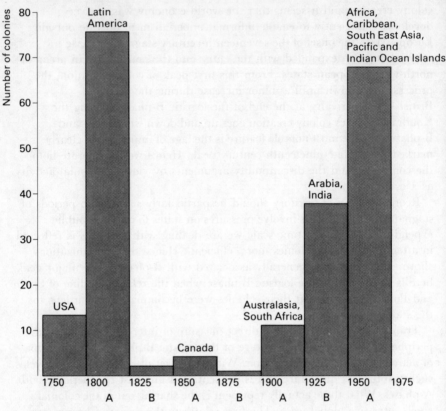

8. Decolonization, 1500–1925

emerging British hegemony there were obvious advantages to freeing these
anachronistic colonies. This was particularly recognized by George
Canning the British Foreign Secretary in his often-quoted statement of
1824 that a free South America would be 'ours' (that is, British). This de-
colonization did set the conditions for British 'informal imperialism' in
Latin America in the mid-nineteenth century which is discussed in the
next section.

One feature of the de-colonization process that must be mentioned is its
geographical contagion. De-colonization is not a random process but is
spatially clustered at different periods. The de-colonization of the Americas,
for instance, did not affect existing colonies in the Old World. This spatial
contagion shows the importance for de-colonization of processes operating in
the periphery. The American War of Independence served as an example for
Latin America in the first de-colonization phase and Indian independence
led the way for the rest of the periphery in the second de-colonization period.
At a regional level political concessions in one colony led to cumulative
pressures throughout the region. In this sense the independence awarded to

Nkrumah's Ghana in 1957 triggered off the de-colonization of the whole
continent in the same way that Bolivar's Venezuelan revolt of 1820 led the
way in Latin America.

One final point may be added to this interpretation. The rhetoric of the
colonial revolutionary leaders in the two periods was very different. The
'freedom' sought in Latin America was proclaimed in a liberal ideology
imitating the American Revolution to the north whereas a century and a
half later the ideology is socialist, mildly at first in India, but much more
vociferous in Ghana and many subsequent wars of national liberation. It is
for this reason, of course, that the first de-colonization (Latin America)
was more easily re-aligned in the world-economy under British liberal
leadership than the second de-colonization with its numerous challenges to
American liberal leadership. In broad terms we can note that the first de-
colonization period is a liberal revolution at the end of agricultural
capitalism whereas the second period encompasses socialist-inspired
revolutions at the end of industrial capitalism and which have been much
more anti-systemic in nature.

THE GEOGRAPHY OF FORMAL IMPERIALISM

Imperialism is a dominance relation between core and periphery. Our
discussion so far has stayed at the system level and we have not
investigated the geography of this relation or 'who was "dominating" who
where?' We answer this question below by dealing first with the core and
then with the periphery.

1 Core: the imperial states

Who were these colonizing states? In fact they have been surprisingly few
in number. In the whole history of the world-economy there have been
just twelve formal imperialist states and only five of these can be said
to be major colonizers. Figure 9 shows the colonial activity of these
states in graphs using the same format as Figure 7. Seven graphs are
shown, separate ones for Spain, Portugal, Netherlands, France and
Britain/England and combined ones for the early and late 'minor'
colonizing states respectively. In the former case these consist of the Baltic
states of Denmark, Sweden and Brandenburg/Prussia and the 'late-comers'
are Belgium, Germany, Italy, Japan and USA. These graphs show the
individual patterns of colonial activity of the states that created the total
picture we looked at above.

In the logistic A-phase before 1600 all colonial establishment was by
Spain and Portugal. The onset of the B-phase brings Netherlands, France,
England and the Baltic states into the fray. This is complemented by a
sharp reduction in colony creation by both Spain and Portugal – the
location of the core of the world-economy had moved northwards and this
is directly reflected in the new colonial activity. As the B-phase progresses

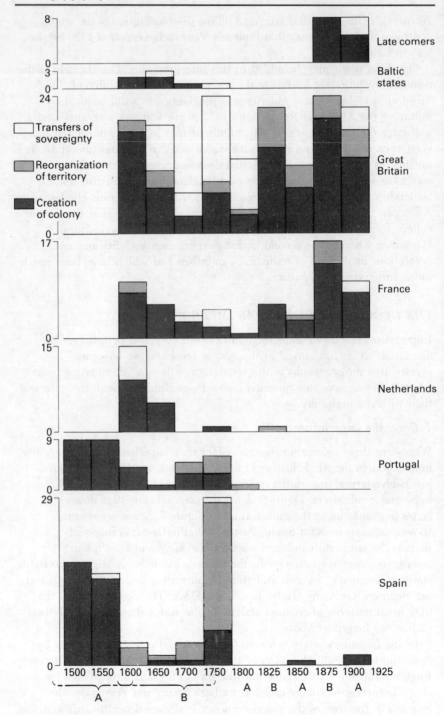

9. Establishment of colonies by imperial states, 1500–1925

all of these new states continue their colonial activities but at a reduced scale except for England/Britain for whom colony-capture is as important or more important than colony creation. As we move into the Kondratieff cycles the Netherlands almost totally cease establishment of colonies so that in the mid-nineteenth century all colonial creation is either British or French. In the classical 'age of imperialism' these two old-stagers are joined by the five late comers.

Figure 9 enables us to define four periods of colonial activity by imperial states:

1 The first non-competitive era occurs in the logistic A-phase when only Spain and Portugal were imperial states.
2 The first competitive era occurs in the logistic B-phase when eight states were involved in imperialist expansion.
3 The second non-competitive era of the mid-nineteenth century coincides with the rise and consolidation of British hegemony. In this period there are only two states involved in imperial expansion, Britain and France.
4 The second competitive era is the 'age of imperialism' and coincides with the decline of British hegemony. In this period seven states were involved in imperial expansion. We shall use this division of core-state activity in our discussion of peripheral arenas.

2 Periphery: the political arenas

Fifteen separate 'arenas' can be identified in which colonial activity occurred in the periphery. The first arena we can term Iberian America and includes Spanish and Portuguese possessions in America obtained in the first non-competitive era. The other fourteen arenas are shown in Figures 10, 11 and 12 covering the other three periods of colonial activity. The arenas have been allocated to these periods on the basis of when they attracted most attention of imperial states. We shall describe each period and its arenas in turn.

The dominant arena of the first competitive era was the Caribbean (Figure 10). This was initially for locational reasons in plundering the Spanish empire but subsequently the major role of the Greater Caribbean (Maryland to North-east Brazil) was plantation agriculture supplying sugar and tobacco to the core. Of secondary importance were the Northern America colonies who did not develop a staple crop and effectively prevented themselves becoming peripheralized. This was to be the location of the first major peripheral revolt, of course. The other important arena for this period were the African ports which formed the final apex of the famous Atlantic triangular trade. It is this trade and the surplus value to be derived from it that underlay the colonial competition of this era. The final two arenas were much less important and related to the Indies trade which Wallerstein doubts was integral to the world-economy until after 1750.

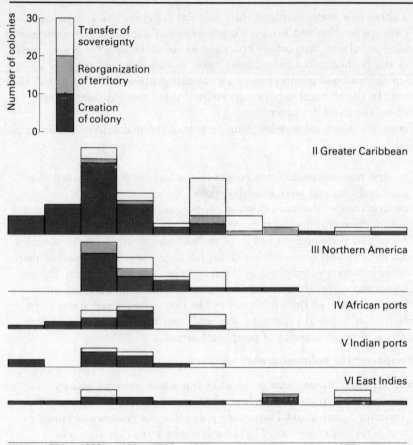

10. Establishment of colonies: arenas of the first competitive era

In the second non-competitive era colonial activity was much reduced but four arenas did emerge as active in the mid-nineteenth century (Figure 11). There was no competition among core states within these arenas which were consequently divided between France and Britain. Although without the authority of the Papal Bull legitimizing the earlier Spain–Portugal share-out, Britain and France managed to continue some colonial activity while avoiding each other's ambitions. Indian Ocean Islands (including Madagascar) and Indo-China were 'conceded' by Britain as French arenas and the latter left India and Australasia to the British.

This peaceful arrangement was shattered in the next competitive period during a series of 'scrambles' the most famous being that for Africa although similar pre-emptive staking out of claims occurred in the Mediterranean arena, Pacific Islands and for Chinese ports (Figure 12).

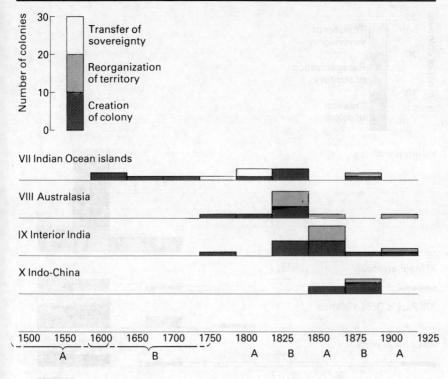

11. Establishment of colonies: arenas of the second non-competitive era

With the collapse of the Ottoman Empire there was a final share-out of Arabia after the First World War. The brief take-over of this last arena completes the pattern of formal core control of periphery as depicted by Figure 5 at the beginning of this chapter.

THE ECONOMICS OF FORMAL IMPERIALISM

The pattern of formal imperialism is now clear. In two major cycles over four hundred years a small group of core states took political control in fifteen separate arenas covering nearly all of the periphery. But why did this dominance relation of imperialism take this political form? Many non-Marxist critics of imperialism, Hobson for instance, have argued that formal imperialism is uneconomic for the core states concerned, benefiting only that small group directly involved in the imperial ventures. As we have seen this line of argument leads on to the notion of economic dominance by large monopoly or finance capital and the identification of imperialism as a 'stage' or 'age'. But formal imperialism existed as a major aspect of the world-economy for over four hundred years starting with the activities of state-licensed charter companies. The problem with such strict economic evaluations of formal imperialism is that they have emphasized

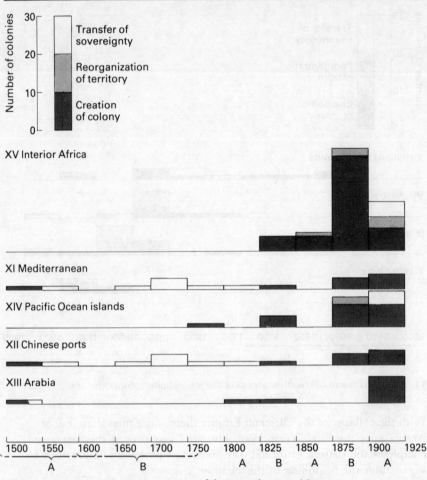

12. Establishment of colonies: arenas of the second competitive era

trade and the search for new markets for core production. But, as
Wallerstein (1983: 38–9) points out, this explanation just does not accord
with the historical facts: 'by and large it was the capitalist world that
sought out the products of the external arena and not the other way
round'. In fact non-capitalist societies did not need products from the core
states and such 'needs' had to be 'created' *after* political take-overs.
Certainly the search for markets cannot explain the massive imperialist
effort on the part of core states over several centuries. Instead Wallerstein
suggests that the search for low-cost labour forces is a much better
explanation. This switches emphasis from exchange to production.
Incorporation of new zones into the periphery invariably led to new
production processes based upon the lowest labour costs. From the original
production of bullion in the Spanish colonies in the sixteenth century to
the current production of uranium from Namibia, the largest remaining

colony, formal imperialism has been the prime means of ensuring the transformation of external arenas into the world-economy's division of labour. We will illustrate this process using the two 'classic' imperialisms of the first and second competitive eras respectively – the Caribbean and Africa.

1. The sugar islands of the Caribbean

The original Spanish colonization of the Americas largely by-passed the islands of the West Indies. Some larger islands were secured but their main function was only to protect the trade generated on the mainland. As can be seen on Figure 10 all this changed in the logistic B-phase. In the period 1620–70 twenty-five colonies were created in the 'greater' Caribbean by the Netherlands, France and England. In addition England captured three colonies from Spain, and the Netherlands captured three from Portugal. This zone from north-east Brazil to south-east North America was converted after this 'scramble' into 'plantation America' based on the production of tobacco and especially sugar. These two crops represented new 'tastes' of core consumers which provided a buoyant market even in a stagnation era (Wallerstein 1980a).

Sugar production was labour-intensive and ecologically damaging. Soil exhaustion had led to production migrating westward from Mediterranean islands, to Atlantic islands and to north-east Brazil in the late sixteenth century. From there the Dutch introduced it to Barbados, the English to Jamaica and the French to St Domingue. By the late seventeenth century it had overtaken contraband as the main function of the Caribbean islands. Its labour demands were first met by indentured labour but by 1700 African slaves were the dominant source. Caribbean sugar became the major product of the Atlantic trade based upon African slaves. Sugar production was so profitable that even semi-peripheral states joined in the business in the seventeenth century with Denmark, Sweden and Brandenburg/Prussia all obtaining their sugar islands. With highly organized production based on cheap labour, the sugar plantations have sometimes been viewed as the precursors of the organization that was to become the factory system in the industrial revolution in the core. Clearly, in the Caribbean incorporation into the periphery was a process which directly increased the total *production* of the world-economy.

2. 'Islands of development' in Africa

At the other end of the slave trade the European states only secured 'stations' on the West African coast (Figure 10) where they exported slaves received from local slave-trading states. Originally this trade was only a luxury exchange with an external arena. By 1700 however Wallerstein (1980a) considers it to have become integral to the restructured division of labour occurring during the logistic B-phase. However, as West Africa becomes integrated into the world-economy the production of slaves becomes a relatively inefficient use of this particular sector. Hence British abolition of the slave trade in 1807 reflects long-term economic self-interest underlying the moral issue. Gradual creeping peripheralization of West Africa throughout the nineteenth century is accelerated by the famous 'scramble for Africa' in the age of imperialism (Figure 12). In the final quarter of the nineteenth century colonies were being created in Africa at the rate of one a year. This enabled the continent to be fully integrated into the world-economy as a new periphery.

The spatial structure of this process was very simple and consisted of just three major zones (Wallerstein 1976b). First there were the zones producing for the world market. Every colony had one or more of these and the colonial administrators ensured that a new infra-structure, including ports and railways, was developed to facilitate the flow of commodities to the world market. This produced the pattern which economic geographers have termed 'islands of development'. These 'islands' were of three types. In west Africa peasant agricultural production was common – the Asante cocoa-growing region is a good example. In central Africa company concessions for forest or mineral production were more typical such as the concessionary companies in the Congo which devastated the area in what was little more than plunder. In east Africa and south Africa production based on white settler populations was also found. In all three cases production was geared towards a small number of products for consumption in the core.

Surrounding each 'development island' was a zone of production for the local market. These were largely peasant farming areas producing food for the labour attracted to the first zone. The remainder of Africa became and still is a large zone of subsistence agriculture which is integrated into the world-economy through its export of labour to the first zone. One of the key processes set in motion by the colonial administrators was a taxation policy which often forced peasants outside the two market zones into becoming wage labourers to provide for their new need for money. Labour migration continues today with the massive flows of labour from the Sahel to the coast in west Africa and from central Africa to south Africa. Every island of development has its own particular pattern of source areas for labour. This international migration incorporates all the advantages to capital of alien labour. It is cheap; it has few rights; the cost of reproduction is elsewhere; and it can be disposed of easily as necessary in recession. Zone 3, the labour zone, is at the very edge of the world-economy – the periphery of the periphery.

It is ironic but not surprising that huge tracts of Africa are merely producers of cheap labour for the world-economy. This is where Africa entered the story and although the legal status of this labour has changed, it is the same basic process which relegates most of Africa to the very bottom of the world order. This has continued despite the granting of independence to nearly all of Africa in the post-Second World War era.

The migration goes on unabated although now it is between independent states instead of between colonies. Formal imperialism may have been an effective strategy for setting up this situation but it is clearly not a necessary criterion for its continuation: imperialism is dead; long live imperialism!

INFORMAL IMPERIALISM: POLITICS, TRADE AND PRODUCTION

In his *The Geography of Empire* Keith Buchanan (1972) does not discuss the formal imperialisms of the past but concentrates solely on the contemporary dominance of USA in the world-economy. In what he terms 'the new shape of empire', he points out that the decolonization process has provided formal independence for colonies from a single imperial state but it has not provided independence from the imperial system as a whole (Buchanan 1972: 57). In world-economy terms what we have is a change of strategy by core states from formal to informal imperialism. This is not a new phenomenon. In our model of hegemonies and rivalries the former were associated with informal imperialism. Hence we expect the rise of each hegemonic power to lead to a period of informal imperialism similar to that described by Buchanan for American hegemony. In fact this is exactly what we find. There have been only three hegemonic powers in the history of the world-economy and each is associated with one of the three classic examples of informal imperialism. First in the mid-seventeenth century Dutch hegemony was based, in large part, on the Baltic trade whereby eastern Europe remained politically independent while becoming peripheralized. Dutch merchants dominated the trade but there was no Dutch political control. Second in the mid-nineteenth century Britain employed the 'imperialism of free trade' when Latin American became known as Britain's 'informal empire'. Finally mid-twentieth-century. American hegemony has been associated with de-colonization to be replaced by neo-colonialism – political independence of the periphery tempered by economic dependence.

Informal imperialism is a much more subtle political strategy than formal imperialism. For this reason it is much less amenable to the descriptive, cataloguing approach employed in the last section. Buchanan (1972) produces numerous interesting maps on topics such as US support for indigenous armies and police to control their own populations – which he terms 'Vietnamization' – but he is unable to capture the basic mechanism of informal imperialism through this empirical approach. Here we develop our argument in two stages. In the first place we show that informal imperialism is no less 'political' despite its emphasis on 'economic' processes. This involves a discussion of trade policy not as a part of economic theory but as alternative state policies within different sectors of the world-economy. But political intervention in the world market cannot change the structural constraints of the world-economy. In the final part of the chapter we describe the basic mechanism of unequal exchange which generates and maintains uneven development throughout our world.

TRADE POLICY AND THE WORLD-ECONOMY

The mainstream of economic thought traces its origins back to Adam Smith's *Wealth of Nations* written in 1776. This book criticized the policy of mercantilism as generally practised at that time and instead advocated a policy of laissez-faire. Ever since Smith free trade has been a basic principle of all orthodox economics. In the early nineteenth century Ricardo added the idea of comparative advantage to the theory. This claimed that with each state specializing on what it could best produce, free trade would generate an international trade equilibrium to everyone's mutual advantage. Free trade was therefore the best policy for all states and any political interference in the flow of commodities in or out of a country was neither in the interests of that particular country nor of the system as a whole.

There are two related paradoxes in this orthodox economics. The first is that it simply does not work out in practice. In the three cases which we have identified as informal imperialism the peripheral states did not gain from the openness of their national economies – Eastern Europe still lags behind Western Europe, Latin America is still a collection of periphery or semi-periphery states and Africa and Asia are part of a 'South' periphery in which mass poverty is increasing during the current recession. As we shall see, states that have 'caught up' have employed very different policies. This leads on to the second paradox concerning free trade which is that most politicians in most countries at most times have realized that it does not work. Although they have not always had theoretical arguments to back up their less than orthodox economics, most politicians have found that the interests of the groups they represent are best served by some political influence on trade rather than simply leaving it all to the 'hidden hand' of the market. I suppose we can ask, who is right – 'economic theorists' or 'practical politicians'? The answer is that they both are . . . sometimes, it all depends on the world-economy location of the state in question.

1. Free trade and the hegemonic state

We can interpret the orthodox economic advocacy of free trade as a reflection of the structural advantage of core powers, in particular hegemonic core powers, in the world-economy. As the most efficient producers of commodities such states can promote free trade in the knowledge that their producers can beat other producers in any open economic competition. The market favours efficient producers and the efficient producers are concentrated in the hegemonic state by definition. In such a situation it is in the interests of the rising hegemonic power to present free trade as 'natural' and political control as 'interference'. But, of course, there is nothing natural about free trade, the world market, or any other man-made institution. 'All organization is bias' is Schattschneider's (1960) point as we have discussed in Chapter 1 and orthodox economics represents a classic case of attempting to organize non-hegemonic interests off the political agenda. The question we ask of any institution, however, is 'what is the organization of bias in this institution?' (Bachrach and Baratz 1962: 952). In the case of the world market it is clear that the bias is in favour of core states and hegemonic core states in particular. The whole history of the world-economy is testimony to this fact. The purpose of inter-state politics is either to maintain this bias or to attempt to change it. The former political strategy is the free trade one which is associated with informal imperialism. This is neither more nor less 'political' than protectionism, mercantilism or formal imperialism which attempt to change the status quo. The former is political non-decision-making, the latter political decision-making in Bachrach and Baratz's (1962) terms. Of course politics is so much easier when the system is on your side.

2. Protectionism and the semi-periphery

The practical politicians who have generally failed to adhere to the orthodox prescriptions for trade have not been without their economic champions, of course. The most famous is the mid-nineteenth century German economist Friedrich List and the world-systems approach is much closer to his analysis than Adam Smith's. For List there was no 'naturally' best trade policy; rather tariffs were a matter of 'time, place and degree of development' (Isaacs 1948: 307). List even admitted that had he been an Englishman he would have probably not doubted the principles of Adam Smith (Frank 1978: 98). But List realized that free trade was not a good policy for the infant industries of his own country, Germany. Hence he advocated a customs union – the famous Zollverein – with a tariff around the German states under Prussian leadership. List rationalized his unorthodox position by arguing that there are three stages of development, each of which requires different policies. For the least advanced countries free trade was sensible to promote agriculture. At a certain stage, however, such policy must give way to protectionism to promote industry. Finally when the latter policy has succeeded in advancing the country to 'wealth and power' then free trade is necessary to maintain supremacy (Isaacs 1948). In world-systems terms List's theory can be translated into policies for periphery, semi-periphery and core countries respectively. Since the Germany of his time was semi-peripheral, he advocated protectionism. In fact we can identify protectionism or, more generally, mercantilism as the strategy of the semi-periphery. Both modern champions of free trade –

Britain and the USA – were major advocates of mercantilist policies *before* their hegemonic period – Britain against the Dutch, the USA against Britain. In fact US Secretary of State Alexander Hamilton's famous *Report on Manufactures* in 1791 remains a classic statement on the need to develop a semi-peripheral strategy as defined here (Frank 1978: 98–9).

3. The choice for the periphery

Friedrich List advocated free trade as the tariff policy of the periphery. In fact there has been and continues to be disputes within peripheral countries on the best policy. Gundar Frank has described this for mid-nineteenth century Latin America as a contest between the 'American' party and the 'European' party. The former wanted protection of local production and represented the local industrialists. The latter were liberals who favoured free trade and were supported by landed-interests who wished to export their products to the core and receive back better and cheaper industrial goods than could be produced locally. Generally speaking the 'European party' won the political contest and free trade triumphed. It is in this sense that Frank talks of local capital in allegiance with metropolitan capital under-developing their own country. This is the collaboration relation in informal imperialism epitomized by nineteenth-century Latin American liberals. In contrast in the USA the 'American party' (notably Republican protectionism) was triumphant and the country did not become under-developed.

Frank's political choices for Latin America a century ago can be identified in the other two classic cases of informal imperialism. Of course his terminology is no longer appropriate – we shall rename his positions peripheral strategy (the European party) and semi-peripheral strategy (the American party). In eastern Europe we have already noted that the counter-Reformation represents the triumph of Catholic landed-interests over local urban interests. In our new terms the landed interest of eastern Europe adopted a peripheral strategy and opened up their economy to the Dutch.

The current pattern of informal imperialism provides modern political leaders in the periphery with the same basic choice. In any particular state which strategy is adopted will vary with the internal balance of political forces and their relation to core interests. This has been somewhat obscured, however, by the same ideological facade which confuses the geopolitics described in the last chapter. In Africa, for instance, Young (1982) distinguishes between states in terms of the self-ascribed ideology of their governments. The two most common categories are 'populist socialism' and 'African capitalism'. In our framework these represent semi-periphery and periphery strategies respectively. Ghana provides a good example of a country where both options have been used. Nkrumah's development policy of using cocoa-export revenues to build-up the urban-industrial sector is a typical semi-peripheral approach which only officially become 'socialism' towards the end of his regime. Nkrumah's great rival Busia, on the other hand, led a government which adopted a liberal trade policy to the advantage of the landed-interests behind the cocoa exports, what we would term a peripheral policy. Hence the overthrow of Nkrumah was not a defeat for socialism, and the overthrow of Busia was not a defeat for capitalism. In world-systems terms, in the case of Ghana both semi-peripheral and peripheral strategies failed politically and economically. Success in the world-economy depends on much more than politicians, however charismatic.

THE MECHANISM OF UNEQUAL EXCHANGE

The above argument can be summarized as saying that core states, especially hegemonic core states have a *structural* advantage in the world-economy. By 'structural' we mean that the advantage is built into the whole operation of the world-economy. This is more than a mere cumulative advantage – the system relies on this inequality as part of its functioning. Hence there are no solutions to overcoming world inequalities within the world-economy but there are state strategies which can aid one state at the expense of the others. Wallerstein (1979) uses Tawney's tadpole philosophy to illustrate this. Although a few tadpoles will survive to become adult frogs most will perish not because of their individual failings but because they are part of an ecology which limits the total numbers of frogs. Similarly if all countries adopt 'perfect' policies for their own economic advance, this does not mean all will rise to membership of the core. To have a core you need a periphery and without both there would be no world-economy. In this situation it is easier to maintain a core position than to rise upwards.

But what is the mechanism which maintains the core-periphery structure? The exact process has changed over the history of the world-economy and here we will concentrate upon the period of industrial capitalism. Our discussion is based loosely on Emmanuel's (1972) concept of unequal *exchange* in which we will emphasize the political process. Emmanuel's work is an attempt to explain the massive modern inequalities of the world-economy. Whereas before the mid-nineteenth century wages were not very different across the various sectors of the world-economy, currently wage differences are very large. Why this change in the intensity of the core–periphery structure? The answer to this question provides us with the basic mechanism of informal imperialism.

1. Free labour and subsistence wages

Emmanuel's starting point is the concept of a labour market. The rise of the world-economy produced 'free' labour initially in the core countries where men and women were able to work for whom they pleased. But this freedom was a very hollow one when there were insufficient jobs or when

wages were set by employers. In fact 'free' labourers were no better off
than their predecessors in feudal Europe and their lack of security might
mean that they were worse off. The labour market operated initially on an
individual basis with the result that the more powerful party to the
agreements – the employer – could force the lowest wages on the worker.
In this situation subsistence wages were the norm with wage levels
reflecting the price of bread which would form up to half a labourer's
expenditure. The purpose of wages was to sustain and reproduce the
worker and no more. In classical economics subsistence wages were just as
'natural' as free trade but, unlike the latter, this part of our economics
heritage has not remained orthodox, at least in the core countries. Quite
simply economists were not able to keep wages off the political agenda.

2. Social imperialism in the core

Wages could rise above subsistence levels under certain circumstances. For
instance relative scarcity of labour would tip the balance of negotiations in
favour of labour. Hence in the mid-nineteenth century the highest wages
were not in the European core but in the new settler colonies – notably
Australia – with their labour shortages. Marx also mentioned a 'historical
and moral element' beyond the market and it is this idea that Emmanuel
develops. Marx had used this concept to cover such things as differences
in climate and in consumption habits which lead to different levels of
subsistence wage. Emmanuel adds a political dimension. Where workers
combine they can negotiate from a position of strength in the labour
market and obtain more than subsistence wages. This was recognized by
politicians, of course, who legislated against unions – in England the
Combination Acts of the early nineteenth century. Thompson (1968)
argues that after 1832 in England a working-class politics emerged to
challenge the state. Although initially unsuccessful, in the mid-nineteenth-
century period of economic growth, unions consolidated their position and
made economic gains for their members. Subsistence wages were no longer
'natural', the issue of wage level was negotiable. Although originally
restricted to skilled workmen, Lenin's labour aristocracy, unionism
gradually spread to other workers. With the extension of the voting
franchise, governments began to make further concessions to workers
culminating in the establishment of the welfare state in the mid-twentieth
century. This process was also going along in different ways but essentially
the same direction in other countries. But only in core countries. Political
pressure to increase the well-being of the dominated class has only been
successful in core and a few semi-peripheral countries. The end result has
been a high-wage core and a low-wage periphery, reflecting both the
'social imperialism' and 'division' relations described previously.

3. Division: social imperialism versus subsistence wages

Hence modern massive material inequalities at the world scale reflect relatively successful political pressure from the dominated class in the core and lack of any such success in the periphery. But how does this contrast help maintain the current structure of core and periphery? This is where unequal exchange comes in. Every transaction between core and periphery is priced in a world market that incorporates these inequalities in its operation. Hence peripheral goods are· 'cheap' and core goods are 'expensive'. When a German consumer buys Ghanaian cocoa low Ghanaian wages are incorporated into the price. When a Ghanaian buys a German car high German wages are incorporated into the price. This is not a matter of different technology levels, although these are interweaved with unequal exchange, but the essential difference is in social relations at each location – the relative strength of the German worker compared to his Ghanaian equivalent. For 1966, for instance, it has been estimated that the peripheral countries trade of $35 billion would have been 'worth' $57 billion if produced under high-wage conditions (Frank 1978: 107). The short fall of $22 billion is the result of unequal exchange. Needless to say this is very much greater than all aid programmes put together. It is the difference between social imperialism and subsistence wages.

We have now reached the crux of our argument. The interweaving of class conflict at a state scale and the core–periphery conflict at the global scale through the process of unequal exchange produces the uneven development so characteristic of our world. And the beauty of this process is that it goes on day after day unrevealed. Unlike free trade and subsistence wages which have been victims of political action, the world market remains off the political agenda. It cannot be otherwise in a world divided into many states where each has its own separate politics. Unequal exchange is an integrated mixture of inter-state and intra-state issues which conventional international politics cannot deal with. The world market appears to be based upon the impersonal forces of supply and demand which determine prices. The only issues that arise are the terms of trade or the balance of prices between core and periphery goods. The fact that these terms do not reflect the hidden hand of the market but are defined by centuries of imperialisms producing global differentials in labour costs is conveniently forgotten. This non-decision-making represents a major political achievement of the dominant interests of the modern world-economy.

Chapter 4

TERRITORY, STATE AND NATION

TERRITORY AND TERRITORIALITY

Elements of spatial structure

1. Core-areas
2. Capital cities
3. Frontiers and boundaries

Sack's theory of human territoriality

1. Territorial behaviour
2. Functions and strategies of territoriality

THEORIES OF THE STATE

Hartshorne's theory of territorial intergration

1. Centrifugal forces: physical features and social diversity
2. Centripetal forces: state-idea and federalism
3. Critique: developmentalism and vertical integration

Marxist theories of the state

1. Miliband versus pluralist theory
2. Poulantzas versus instrumentalism
3. Derivationists versus relative autonomy
4. Hegemony and ideological state apparatus

The state in the world-economy

1. Relative autonomy and the multiplicity of states
2. Derivation of world government
3. The variety of state forms: a space–time introduction

NATION AND NATIONALISM

The doctrine of nationalism

1. The core doctrine
2. The special secondary theories

Nationalism in practice

1. A typology of nationalisms
2. National self-determination: plebiscites
3. National determinism: Jovan Cvijic's language maps of Macedonia

Nairn's theory of nationalism

1. Nationalism and uneven development
2. Nationalism and 'mass society'
3. Nationalism and intellectuals

TERRITORY, STATE AND NATION

The heyday of political geography was the inter-war years of 1918 to 1939. Geographers were advising at the Peace Conference in Versailles in 1919 and in subsequent years Mackinder, Hausofer, Bowman and others became important figures beyond the confines of academic geography. The retreat from this geopolitics in geography was rapid after 1945. Political geography as a whole was devalued in geography and geopolitics was downgraded within political geography. This change of emphasis in scale of analysis is most clearly seen in the chapter on 'Political geography' in the semi-centennial publication of the Association of American Geographers in 1954 entitled *American Geography: Inventory and Prospect*. In this chapter Hartshorne (1954) makes the now familiar lament of political geography's 'underdevelopment' within the wider discipline. Most instructive is his discussion of methods in political geography. Broad international themes are replaced by emphasis on 'area studies', 'political division of the world' and above all the 'political region'. This was not new, Hartshorne was able to draw on previous and current studies, but it confirmed a political geography in which world strategic views were conspicuous by their absence.

Hartshorne's assessment was a co-operative product emanating from a 'Committee on Political Geography' including six other prominent geographers. It has been largely substantiated by subsequent textbooks in the 1960s and early 1970s. 'Political region' has been interpreted as the modern nation-state for purposes of organizing the subject matter in these texts. Three basic concepts have emerged from this approach – territory, state and nation – which are the subject matter of this chapter. We can think of these as the basic trilogy of traditional political geography freed from its geopolitics heritage.

The chapter is organized into three sections, each devoted to one concept of the trilogy. The discussion within each section follows broadly similar lines. The history and etymology of the concept is our starting point. We then review the traditional political geography studies of the concept and assess them from a world-systems perspective. Finally we attempt to integrate each concept into our new approach. Hence the traditional trilogy is not dismissed – it is revised, reformed and reintegrated into our political geography.

TERRITORY AND TERRITORIALITY

Jean Gottmann (1973: 16) has described the origins of the concept of
territory. It derives from the Latin for 'land' (terra) and 'belonging to'
(torium) and was originally applied to a city's surrounding district over
which it had jurisdiction. Its initial application was to the city-states of
classical Greece and it reappeared to describe the jurisdictions of medieval
Italian cities. It was never applied to the whole Roman Empire or
mediaeval Christendom with their universal pretentions: 'territory' implies
a division of political power. In modern usage application to cities has
become obsolete to be replaced by application to modern states. A
territory is the land belonging to a ruler or state. This meaning has
been traced back to 1494, approximately to the birth of the world-
economy.

The modern meaning of territory is closely tied up with the legal
concept of sovereignty. In fact this is a way in which it can be
distinguished from the city-scale definition. Sovereignty implies that there
is one final and absolute authority in a political community (Hinsley
1966: 26). This concept was not evolved in the classical Greek world – city
territories were *not* sovereign. Instead Hinsley traces the concept back to
the Roman Empire and the emperor's *imperium* over the Empire. This is a
personal political domination with no explicit territorial link given the
empire's universal claims. It is this concept that was passed on to
mediaeval Europe as Roman Law and is retained in modern language
when a king or queen is referred to as the sovereign of a country. But
mediaeval Europe under feudalism was a hierarchical system of power and
authority not a territorial one. The relations of lord and subject were
personal ones of protection and service and were not territorially based. It
is the bringing together of territory and sovereignty which provides the
basis of the modern inter-state system. This emerged in the century after
1494 and was finalized by the Treaties of Westphalia of 1648. This is
usually interpreted as the first treaty defining modern international law. It
recognized that each state was sovereign in its own territory: that is,
interference in the internal affairs of a country was the first offence of
international law. The result was a formal recognition of a Europe
parcelled up into some three hundred sovereign units. This was the
original territorial basis of the modern inter-state system – the first 'world
political map'.

This first mosaic of sovereignties was a direct result of the strife
resulting from the religious wars in Europe in the wake of the Reformation
and counter-Reformation. The crucial political issue of the day was order
and stability, or rather the lack of it, and the territorial state emerged as
the solution to the problem of security (Herz: 1957). The legal concept of
sovereignty was backed up by a 'hard shell' of defences which made it

relatively impenetrable to foreign armies so that it became the ultimate unit of protection. Herz (1957) provides a technical explanation for this development – the gunpowder revolution in warfare which made individual city ramparts obsolete. The original 'hard shell' of the walled city was replaced by the sovereign state and new defences based upon much larger resources. Such new warfare required a firm territorial basis, not the personal hierarchy of the mediaeval period.

Herz's explanation is a good one in that it incorporates an important dimension in the origins of modern state formation. But it is only a partial explanation. Tilly (1975) introduces other factors in the 'survival' of these states and the inter-state system. Security provides a stability in which a territory's resources can be mobilized more completely. The territorial state is associated with the rise of absolute monarchs in Europe with their centralized bureaucracies, taxation and large armies. In a world-systems perspective, however, we need to go beyond these 'political' factors. We follow Gottmann (1973) in identifying two basic functions of the territorial state – security and opportunity. The former relates to the origins of the inter-state system as we have seen, the latter to the emerging world market.

The rise of a world-economy provided different opportunities to entrepreneurs in different locations. In the agricultural world-economy described by Wallerstein (1974a, 1980a) the major groups contesting for advantage in the new world market were the agricultural landed interest on the one hand and the urban merchants on the other. According to Smith (1978) this conflict is directly related to the rise of the modern state with the landed aristocracy giving up their mediaeval rights in return for the sovereign's support against the new rising urban class. But this initial alliance between landed interests and the new managers of the state apparatus soon had to give way to a more flexible 'politics'. In a competitive state system security requires more than recognition of sovereignty. It requires keeping up with neighbouring states in economic terms. Hence the emergence of *mercantilism* which we have briefly discussed in previous chapters. Mercantilism was simply the transfer to the territorial state of the commercial policies of the trading city (Isaacs 1948: 47–8). The scale of territorial restrictions on trade was enhanced to become a major arm of state-making. Mercantilism was based on the premise that each state had to grab as much of the world market as it could by building its industry and commerce at the expense of other states. The power of the state ultimately depended on the success of its mercantilism. The exact nature of different states' policies in the world market reflected the balance of power between the landed and merchant interests. The former succeeded overwhelmingly in eastern Europe to produce its peripheralisation as we have seen, in the rest of Europe the balance varied with merchants most successful in the two most successful states of the Netherlands and England. In all cases this commercial policy beyond the confines of cities was the product of the new territorial state and the inter-state system. Security and sovereignty, opportunity and mercantilism were all premised on the territorial state.

ELEMENTS OF SPATIAL STRUCTURE

One of the most valid criticisms of traditional political geography has been of the lack of coherence in the way the different elements are put together (Cox 1979). Claval (1984), for instance, claims that it was the unco-ordinated nature of the sub-discipline rather than the embarrassment of geopolitics that was the root cause of its decline since 1945. There have been attempts to move beyond a cataloging of topics and we shall discuss some of them in the section on the state. Here we will present the basic political-geography ideas on spatial aspects of the territorial state. We will deal with core areas, capital cities and boundaries. These three topics are undoubtedly the most universally discussed in traditional political geography and we consider their relevance to our own project.

1. Core-areas

The subject of core-area has created confusion in political geography because of inconsistency in definition. Burghardt (1969) identifies three distinct concepts:

1. nuclear core as a germinal area around which accretions of territory have produced the modern territorial state;
2. original core as a germinal area but which failed to obtain accretions of territory; and
3. contemporary core as the current area of greatest political and economic importance in a state. In this discussion we will omit consideration of (3) and concentrate upon the historical evolution of territories. The contemporary core will be considered in the next section.

The historically oriented core-area concept originates with the 'father' of political geography Friedrich Ratzel. The modern use of the concept, however, derives largely from Whittlesey (1939) and the application of his ideas to the development of European state system by Pounds and Ball (1964). They begin by defining two categories of state, 'arbitrary' and 'organic', the latter term obviously reflecting Ratzel's influence. In fact no organic analogy is intended; rather a distinction is made in the way in which territory is allocated to a state. In the arbitrary category the territory is allocated on some preconceived geographical frame as the result of a political settlement whereas in the organic case the territory evolves slowly by accretions around a core-area. It is the latter process which Pounds and Ball attempt to delineate for Europe.

Pounds and Ball (1964) argue that in order to become the germinal area of a modern state, core-areas must have some initial 'considerable' advantage over neighbouring areas. To become a viable core-area a district must have been capable of generating an economic surplus at an early date. This would provide the resources first to defend itself against conquest and second to expand its domination over less well-endowed neighbours. In feudal Europe this involved fertile soil for agricultural production plus nodal location for trade in materials not available locally. This environmental argument is illustrated by describing the development of the expansion of the authority of French kings from 987 when they merely controlled the area around Paris. France is described as the 'prototype'. Fifteen more core-areas of modern European states are then identified (Figure 13). Burghardt (1969) criticizes this part of the study because it confuses nuclear and original cores. The core-areas Pounds and Ball identify for Poland and Hungary, for instance, never became the basis

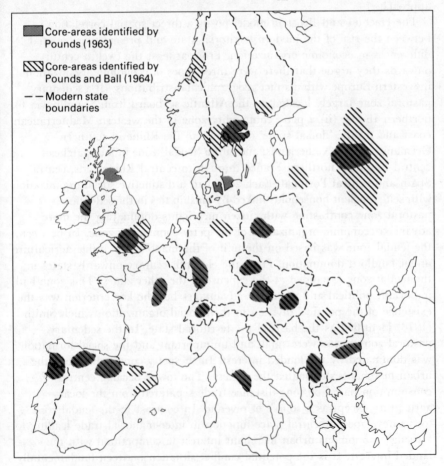

13. Core-areas of European states

of a process of accretion although they are the historic cores of modern states.

A more serious criticism is that the identification of core-areas is on a 'post-diction' basis. Since we know which states exist today then identification of their core-areas does not mean that we have an adequate explanation of the processes operating in the past. Pounds and Ball's fifteen core-areas are not the only possible districts with the necessary geographical characteristics to become the germinal areas of modern states. Of course it takes much more than geographical conditions to produce a modern state as Tilly (1975) emphasizes. We need to specify what the nature of the society that existed in these core-areas was so that the process underlying its political success can be understood. This has recently been attempted by Hechter and Brustein (1980) and we will present their explanation of core-areas as an improvement on the original model and one which can be made compatible with the world-systems approach.

The Hechter and Brustein model posits a direct spatial correlation between the rise of the modern territorial state and pre-existing regional differences in economic organization. From at least the twelfth century onwards they argue that there were three types of economic organization in western Europe with distinct geographical distributions: (i) a sedentary pastoral zone largely located on the Atlantic seaboard from Scandinavia to northern Iberia; (ii) a petty commodity zone in the western Mediterranean coast and up the 'dorsal spine' of Europe to the Rhine in southern Germany and the Netherlands; and (iii) a 'feudal' zone in four patches— central England, northern France through to central Rhinelands, central Spain and central Portugal. Each zone had a distinctive social organization with self-sufficient households linked by kinship ties in the sedentary pastoral zone contrasting with citizen merchants dominating the more advanced economic organization of the petty-commodity zone. In between, the feudal zone was based on the unit of the manor with arable agriculture under landlord domination. From the eleventh century onwards states in the feudal zone expanded at the expense of the other zones. This zone had important political and economic advantages but the key criterion was the existence of the political division in their social organization which Smith (1978) identified as the basis of the territorial state. In the sedentary pastoral zone towns were small and unimportant and the social formation was dominated by the landed interest. In the petty commodity zone the urban merchants dominated the society. The towns became centres of consumption based on long-distance trade separated from the local agriculture except as a source of revenue. In contrast in the feudal zone towns developed a central place function in inter-manorial trade leading to a rising autonomous urban merchant interest in competition with the landed interest. It is the potential conflict situation between fundamentally different interests which the territorial state evolves to contain. In the

petty commodity zone and the sedentary pastoral zone the existing
political monopolies did not require the existence of the new territorial
state. Hence successful core-areas, in the sense of nuclear cores, tended to
occur in the feudal zone.

Hechter and Brustein (1980) only consider western Europe so that their
identification of core-areas is not exactly the same as Pounds and Ball
(1964). Generally speaking the two sets of core-areas coincide with major
differences only in Iberia, Italy and the Netherlands. This is a problem of
lack of clarity in exactly how these historical cores are to be identified. No
matter, the crucial point is that four of the five initially strongest territorial
states in the world-economy, Portugal, Spain, France and England, all
emerged from core-areas in the feudal zone. As such this model can be
added to Rokkan's geopolitical map of Europe as an explanation of why it
was the seaward countries – and these four in particular – that led the
way in establishing the new inter-state system even though it was 'city-
state' Europe which seemed to be more economically advanced. But more
important, these social conditions based upon conflict of interest produced
the first modern states which could forge a world-economy with themselves
as part of a much larger core.

We have introduced the Hechter and Brustein model as an improvement
of the original geographical model. There are clearly many refinements
required before a fully developed theory of core-area is available. We need
to link it, for instance, with Wallerstein's use of the crisis of feudalism as a
generator of the economic expansion of Europe. Nevertheless it is an
improvement over the previous model. This is most clear in the way in
which it is grounded in the *specific* social formation of Europe at a particular
time. The Pounds and Ball model, in contrast, provides a *general* definition of
core-area which enables it to be used in other contexts in which different
processes operate.

Pounds (1963) and de Blij (1967) have extended the geographical core-
area concept beyond Europe. These analyses are criticized by Burghardt
(1969) for confusing the historical concept with the modern notion of a
core-area. From our perspective they not only confuse political processes
over time, they confuse political processes across the spatial structure of
the world-economy. Most of the core areas of modern non-European states
consist of the original zones through which the territory was incorporated
into the world-economy. As such the vast majority are coastal or else are
associated with raw materials which attracted European penetration. They
are therefore the opposite of the initial European core-area. Instead of a
process generating a strong territorial state as a unit of security and
opportunity, in the non-European case core-areas are the vulnerable areas
which provide opportunities for external interests. To equate European
core-areas with the development of territorial states in other parts of the
world is a typical error of the developmentalism described previously.
Most peripheral states began their history as colonial appendices of

imperial states as we have seen and this constitutes another example of the neglect of imperialism as a factor in the making of our world. Modern non-European territorial states are not repeating the political processes that generated the European state. In the world-systems approach we identify two sets of broad mechanisms, one for the core and one for the periphery. The core-area model as the germinal area of the modern state is a very early process that contributed to the development of core processes in the world-economy and which have not been repeated in the periphery.

2. Capital cities

One of the features of core-areas is that they usually have the capital city of the state located within them. Paris and London are obvious examples of this. This has led some political geographers to identify 'natural' and 'artificial' capital cities with the former represented by those in core-areas. As Spate (1942) pointed out long ago, any such distinction is to misunderstand the nature of politics in our society. London is no more 'natural' than Canberra; they are both the result of man-made decisions, albeit over very different time horizons. Spate rightly dismisses this old dichotomy but retreats into case studies as his own approach to capital cities. Whereas case studies are invaluable for understanding the nature of capital cities they are not sufficient for a full appreciation of the role of these localities in the territorial state. They are, after all, the control centre of the territory, the locus of political decision-making, the symbolic centre of the state and often very much more. As well as the complexity that Spate identifies, which leads him to emphasize their differences, there are important similarities which we will draw upon here.

Many European observers have remarked that Washington DC is an unusual capital in that it is not one of the largest cities in its country. Lowenthal (1958) even calls it an 'anti-capital' reflecting as it does initial American 'anti-metropolitan' revolutionary politics. Henrikson (1983) has reviewed this literature and concludes, not surprisingly, that it manifests a Euro-centric bias. Like Spate before him, Henrikson can find no justification for treating Paris and London as 'ideal models' which the rest of the world should follow. Instead Henrikson identifies two models of the capital city: the European concept of the capital as the opinion-forming centre of the state dominant in political, cultural and economic spheres and the American concept of a responsive centre which specializes in politics. Fifer (1981) for instance refers to Washington DC as 'a company town'. Henrikson is more poetic – 'a small, cozy town, global in scope'.

These two concepts do not cover all cases, however. In a famous paper Mark Jefferson (1939) described a 'Law of the Primate City' in which he propounded the 'law' that a country's capital city is always 'disproportionately large'. This law 'fits' the European concept but is obviously at variance with the American concept. The reason why it is still quoted is because it fits so many countries in the periphery. In most Latin

American, African and Asian states the capital city is truly primate – Buenos Aires, Lima, Dar es Salaam, Dakar, Djakata and Manila, to name just two from each continent. This should not be read as meaning that they employ a 'European concept' in the definition of their capital since their position is so very different. In the same way as we dismiss the European core-area model for peripheral states we also avoid using the 'European concept' to cover most peripheral capital cities.

We can reconcile these problems of definition and add to our analysis of capital cities by employing the world-systems approach. There are three types of capital city – one the result of core processes, one the result of peripheral processes and a third reflecting semi-peripheral political strategies. We will describe each type in turn.

The capital cities resulting from core processes are what Henrikson terms the European concept. The rise of the classic examples of this type are part of the initial economic processes that led to Europe becoming the core of the world-economy. The mercantilist competition of the logistic wave involved the development of vastly increased political involvement centred on the historic capital city. The new bureaucracies were located there and these cities grew rapidly to dominate their territories. They became the political control centres that were attempting to steer the emerging world-economy in directions beneficial to their particular territory.

In contrast in the periphery new cities emerged or particular old cities grew where they were useful to the exploitative core-periphery relation. Most commonly these were ports directly linked to the core. They were the product of peripheral processes and have often been likened to 'plug holes' sucking out, as it were, the wealth of the periphery. In formal imperialism political control was directly associated with this process so that these 'parasitic cities' became 'colonial capitals'. Many of them retained their political status following independence and they remain the most extreme examples of Jefferson's primate cities.

But not all colonial administrative centres have remained as capital cities. Some governments have recognized the imperialist basis of their inherited capital city and have relocated their 'control centre' elsewhere. This is part of a conscious semi-peripheral strategy to break the core–periphery links symbolized and practised through the old capital. Often it is expressed as a 'nationalist' reaction as capitals are moved from the coast inland to the old 'core' of a pre-world-economy social formation. A good example of this can be found in the relocation of the Russian capital. In the original incorporation of Russia into the world-economy, the capital was moved from Moscow to a virgin site on the Baltic Sea where St Petersburg was built as 'a window on the west'. After the revolution the capital returned to Moscow as the new Soviet regime retreated from this outward stance in its attempt to break with the peripheralizing processes of the past. Other similar examples of relocation are from Istanbul to Ankara in the centre of Turkey's territory, from Karachi inland to Islamabad in Pakistan, inland from Rio de Janeiro to central Brazil in Brazilia and currently Nigeria is moving its capital from the colonial port of Lagos inland to a new site at Abuja in central Nigeria. In all cases we can interpret the relocation as part of a semi-peripheral strategy which is attempting to lessen peripheral processes operating in the country.

The semi-periphery strategy tends to produce what Henrikson terms the American concept of a capital city, in effect a political 'company town'. The case of Washington DC is also the result of an attempt to prevent peripheralization in the creation of the United States of America. It represents the dominance of 'national politics' over the needs of the world-economy and has been the model for other federal capitals, some of which we have already mentioned. As a compromise between the sectional interests of North and South its closest parallels are the cases of Ottawa (between French (Quebec) and English (Ontario) Canada) and Canberra (between the two largest cities in Australia, Sydney and Melbourne). Washington DC, Ottawa and Canberra all represent part of a strategy for mobilizing a new territory for competition in the world-economy.

In summary therefore we can identify three types of capital city reflecting world-economy processes: the initial core processes in Europe and the peripheral processes in Latin America, Africa and Asia, both of which generate 'primate cities', and capital cities which have developed as part of a conscious semi-peripheral strategy which tend to be located in past and current semi-peripheral states.

3. Frontiers and boundaries

Frontiers and boundaries have probably been the most popular topic in political geography. However, as long ago as 1963 Pounds (1963: 93–4) noted a decline of interest in this subject matter. This reflects the lessening of boundary disputes in the areas where political geography was largely practised – Europe and North America. This contrasts with the first half of the twentieth century in Europe when boundary issues were central to international politics. Furthermore many of the early political geographers of this century (for example, Sir Thomas Holdrich) were themselves boundary drawers and surveyors in the imperial division of the periphery. Hence concern for boundaries has waxed and waned with the changing interests of the core countries. Of course, boundary issues continue to be a vital ingredient of politics beyond Europe and North America. Good reviews of the early work on boundaries are available in Minghi (1963), Jones (1959) and Prescott (1965). Here we shall reinterpret some of this vast quantity of material in world-systems terms.

The usual starting point in this subject-area is to distinguish frontiers from boundaries. This is necessary since the terms are commonly used interchangeably. Kristof (1959) uses the etymology of each term to derive their essential difference. Frontier comes from the notion of 'in front' as the 'spearhead of civilization'. Boundary comes from 'bounds' implying territorial limits. Frontier is therefore outward-orientated and boundary inward-orientated. Whereas a boundary is a definite line of separation, a frontier is a zone of contact.

These definitions fit very neatly into our world-systems framework. A frontier zone is the area between two social systems or entities. In the case of world-empires this can be between other world-empires or their juxtaposition with outside mini-systems. Classic cases are the frontiers of China and Rome. Although in each case they built walls between their 'civilization' and barbarians, the walls were part of a wider frontier zone. In Roman Britain, for instance, Hadrian's Wall was just part of the fortifications of the highland military zone or frontier which separated the civilian south and east from the non-Roman north and west. With the rise of the world-economy a frontier emerged between this system and the systems it was surplanting. The history of imperialism is about pushing forward the frontiers of this new world-system. It produced the 'classic' frontier in the American west, but also other similar frontiers in Australia, South Africa, North Africa, north-west India and Asiatic Russia. The frontier ended with the closing of the world-system at the beginning of this century. We now live in a world with one system so that there are no longer any frontiers – they are now phenomena of history.

Frontiers everywhere have been replaced by boundaries. Boundaries are a necessary component of the sovereignty of territories. Sovereignty must be bounded: a world of sovereign states is a world divided by boundaries. Boundaries therefore are an essential element of the modern world-economy. But of course the process of boundary making is very different in the various sections of the world-economy. Jones (1959) identifies five types of boundary concepts – 'natural', 'national', 'contractual', 'geometrical' and 'power-political'. These categories are not exclusive to one another: from our perspective, for instance, we would identify all boundaries as reflecting the power-politics of their respective producers. Nevertheless these are useful concepts which, as Jones is able to show, reflect the different ideas of the state in the evolving world-economy. The idea of 'natural' boundaries are products of the strength of the French state in eighteenth-century Europe and its use of the new rationalist philosophy to claim a larger 'natural' territory (Pounds 1951, 1954). In contrast the idea of 'national' boundaries is the Germanic reaction to French expansionist ideas. We will consider this reaction further in our discussion of 'nation' below. These two ideas are rationalizations of particular power-political positions in the core and semi-periphery of the world-economy. In the periphery, also, two types of boundary emerged. In non-competitive arenas in the nineteenth century, such as·India and Indo-China, the boundaries reflect the expansion of one core state at the expense of weak pre-capitalist social formations. This is where frontiers are extended and then converted to boundaries. The limits are finally achieved when two powers begin to approach one another's peripheral territory. This may lead to the formation of a buffer state in the periphery as in the cases of Afghanistan between Russia and British India and Thailand between French Indo-China and British India. In competitive arenas the boundaries are usually far more arbitrary as they reflect contractual arrangements between competitors. It is in these areas that 'clear' international boundaries are necessary to prevent disputes. Hence such boundaries commonly follow physical features such as rivers or else are simply geometrical lines usually of longitude or latitude. Examples of such 'contractual' boundaries are, of course, the USA's western boundaries to north and south along the 49th parallel and the Rio Grande respectively. The most competitive arena of all, Africa in the late nineteenth century, has the most 'contractual international boundaries'. Here the concepts of 'natural' or 'national' boundaries had no relevance as ethnic groups and river basins were divided up in complete contrast to the boundary processes then evolving in the core. Once again, we find contrasting processes in core and periphery which are the hallmark of the world-systems approach.

SACK'S THEORY OF HUMAN TERRITORIALITY

So far we have only related elements of the spatial structure of the state to our overall framework. The discussion has remained as unco-ordinated as the material it has been based upon. We hope to overcome this general criticism when we integrate these themes into our subsequent treatments of state and nation. Before we do this however we present a recent study of territoriality which breaks new ground in trying to derive an abstract theory.

The concept of territoriality entered political geography in the form of analogies with animal behaviour (Wagner 1969, Soja 1971). Parallels were drawn between territories and hierarchies of robins, sticklebacks and deer and human social and political arrangements. The most famous development of these ideas is that of popular writer Robert Ardrey (1966) in his *Territorial Imperative*. He insists that the universal requirements of identity, security and stimulation are met by instinctive territorial behaviour in species as different as robins and human beings. Unfortunately this type of speculative argument has resulted in a neglect of the study of territoriality in geography. Sack has rectified this situation in a theory which emphasizes territorial behaviour in human beings as a conscious decision-making strategy.

1. Territorial behaviour

Sack's theory (1981, 1983) is based upon the identification of two basic forms of spatial relation – action by contact and territoriality. Most of geographical analysis has been concerned with action by contact, both direct and indirect, as in all spatial interaction theories dealing with flows of people, commodities and ideas. The key concept of this spatial relation is distance decay. In contrast there is a spatial relation of territoriality based on the key concept of territory. This is the attempt to affect, influence or control actions by enforcing control over a specific geographical area. This behaviour is territoriality and the area is the territory.

Sack gives a simple example to illustrate these alternative forms of controlling action. Assuming that the children of a household have entered a writer's study and damaged material, what action should be taken? One solution is to coerce the children to behave properly – a good spanking. A heart-to-heart talk on good behaviour might suffice. Both of these are examples of action by contact, painful and less painful. A different approach would be to make the study 'out of bounds' to prevent future access to the material by the children. This latter solution is the territorial one and the study becomes defined as a territory. The only contact with the children is the need to communicate the new household rule. Note that all territoriality relies upon initial action by contact in this need to communicate.

2. Functions and strategies of territoriality

Sack (1981, 1983) develops his theory as an abstract matrix combining a set of functions of territoriality with a range of strategies which incorporate specific combinations of functions. This is presented in a 'neutral' manner so that it can be applied to alternative theories of power and over a full range of historical examples. In Table 6 we have selected those parts of this theory that are most relevant to our study of territory as defined by sovereign states. As we shall see Sack's theoretical definition of territory and our concrete political treatment are wholly compatible. What we present here, therefore, is a partial description of the theory as it can be applied to sovereign states in our world-systems framework. We shall begin by outlining the four functions of territoriality in Table 6 before discussing their different combinations in nine different strategies.

A. The most important function of territoriality as implied in its definition, is the enforcing control over access to the territory. Territory explicitly involves an 'in-group' and an 'out-group'. In inter-state relations this is termed citizenship. All states control flows across their territorial boundaries on the basis of distinguishing between their own citizens and 'foreigners'.

B. A much more subtle function of territoriality is its role in reifying power. Unlike physical features such as rivers and roads, power is an intangible concept until it impinges on behaviour. In the modern world

Table 6 Some Functions and Strategies of Territoriality

Types of strategy	Functions of territoriality			
	A. Enforcing control	B. Reifying power	C. Displacing social relations	D. Containing events
1. Territorial definition of social relations	X	X		X
2. Efficient span of control	X			X
3. Mismatch of territory and process	X	X	X	X
4. Territoriality as an end and not means	X	X	XX	
5. Inequality by differential access	X			
6. Divide and rule	XX	X	X	X
7. Social conflict obscured	X		X	
8. Obscuration by geographical scale	X		X	
9. Territorial secession	X	XX		X

X = *important function*; XX = *very important function*.

one way in which power is made explicit and real is through its direct link to the territory of the modern state. It is for this reason that much political action from defining boundaries to siting capital cities has been considered 'natural'.

C. Territoriality has a vital function in displacing attention from the social relation of dominance. Dominance becomes transformed into neutral enforcement of the 'law of the land' so that the social relation is displaced to a territorial rule. All modern states rely upon most citizens obeying their laws as a member of a territorial community, the nation-state.

D. Territoriality acts as a container of events. The territory becomes an object to which other attributes are assigned. In peace this will involve all the territory being subject to particular outside pressures such as International Monetary Funds demands for welfare cuts to pay off debts. The IMF will assess a country as a container of a set of potential resources. In wartime the territory is a container of enemy personnel. In the twentieth century this has led to civilian populations being targets of air-raids. The application of this concept in the nuclear age leads to genocide or even speciecide as we have seen.

Table 6 shows how different combinations of these four functions can be used to produce types of strategy. We will briefly consider each.

1. The territorial definition of social relations is a combination of A, B, and C. The state's territory is the container for defining citizenship which may be used to provide preferential access to resources in the territory. This is reified through mystical justification by nationalism. The ultimate losers of this strategy are stateless refugees.

2. An efficient span of control relates to enforcing the containment of events. As a state increases in size its boundary extends and control may become more difficult. One of the explanations for the 'fall' of all world-empires is that they over-extended their span of control. In the world-economy the Spanish and Portuguese empires seem to have become a classic example of this process when both states declined to semi-peripheral status and became little more than conveyor belts for wealth from 'their' periphery to the core in north-west Europe.

3. Mismatch of territory and process will occur in some of the boundary drawing exercises described previously. This combines all four functions and is perhaps best illustrated in the definition of African colonial boundaries and their continued use by the independent states. Territory is the basis of a new control attempting to reify power with a new nationalism by displacing traditional ethnic social relations.

4. Territory appears as an end rather than a means in the modern state system through nationalism. The territorial function of displacing social relations is vital here as 'class differences' are overwhelmed by national consensus. We consider this further below.

5. Territoriality in involving control of access can become a strategy of generating inequality. The best example of this is the process of social imperialism described in the last chapter whereby welfare provisions for all citizens of a core state have multiplied the inequalities between core and periphery.

6. Divide and rule is in many ways the basic strategy underlying the world-economy's need for an inter-state system. By dividing up opposition into separate territories in which power is reified capital interests have been able to contain revolts to specific territories and avoid a world-wide revolution.

7. Social conflict is obscured when enforcing control and displacing social conflict are combined. The result is a situation where conflict occurs between territories in place of the original generating social conflict. An example of this is the classical Marxist interpretation of the First World War where conflict between industrial and banking groups culminated in a war of 'nations'.

8. Obscuration by geographical scale again involves A and C but this time is concerned with a double use of territory. This is the allocation of political power to a scale of operation at which it is relatively powerless. This is essentially the argument proposed in Chapter 1 for our political interpretation of three scales in political geography. Political power is limited to the scale of ideology, sovereign territories, while the scale of reality, of basic change, is the world-economy.

9. Territorial secession is in many ways the reverse of the functions we have described. They are turned and used to generate partition of the territory. In this sense it is related to strategy 3 but concentrates more on the breaking of the reification of power of the territorial state. Palestine, Cyprus, Northern Ireland, Lebanon, Korea, Vietnam and, of course, Germany are or have been examples of such successful strategies on one side or the other.

This whole section on territory has been plagued by the need to keep insisting that there is nothing 'natural' about the processes we study in political geography. 'Organic states', 'natural' capital cities, 'natural' boundaries, 'instinctive' territoriality are all equally myths. The first importance of Sack's work is that it is a beginning in defining new theories of conscious decision-making which exorcise once and for all dangerous natural analogies in political geography. Second, and more important, is the fact that we are provided with a framework that allows us to go beyond Herz's simple security definition of the territorial state and expand on Gottmann's addition of opportunity. Using just Herz's concept we are led to argue that technological developments have made the territorial state obsolete; with this more sophisticated theory we can see that there is much more to the state than a shell. Other uses of territoriality will ensure the survival of this phenomenon as long as the world-economy survives.

THEORIES OF THE STATE

The notion of sovereignty assumes the existence of the state. The territoriality we described above only operates through the medium of the state. But this is a two-way relationship. At the simplest level the state is defined by its possession of sovereignty. This distinguishes it from all other forms of human organization. As Laski (1935: 21–2) points out this sovereignty amounts to nothing less than supreme coercive power within a territory – the state 'gives orders to all and receives orders from none' inside its recognized boundaries. Invasion by a foreign power or internal insurgency aiming at creating a new state are both violations of a state's sovereignty. If not defeated the state no longer has a monopoly of coercion in its territory and faces extinction. The division of Poland between Germany and the USSR in 1939 is an example of extinction by external violation of sovereignty.

It is important to distinguish between state and government at the outset of this discussion. Again using Laski (1935: 23), government can be interpreted as the major agent of the state and exists to carry out the day-to-day business of the state. Governments are short-term mechanisms for administering the long-term purposes of the state. Hence every state is served by a continual succession of governments. But governments only represent the state, they cannot replace it. A government is not a sovereign body: opposition to the government is a vital activity at the very heart of liberal democracy; opposition to the state is treason. Governments may try and define themselves as the state and hence condemn their opponents as 'traitors' but this is a very dangerous game. If this strategy fails the state may find itself challenged within its boundaries by what McColl (1969) terms the *insurgent state* with its own core-area, territory and claims to sovereignty. In this case the fall of the government can precipitate overthrow of the state as happened, for instance, in Vietnam in 1975.

It has been suggested that this distinction between state and government is not of practical interest because all state action must involve some specific government action acting in its name (Laski 1935: 25). The important point, however, is that this distinction is a theoretical one and it is at this level that this chapter is pitched. One of the major problems of political science and political geography is that they have considered government action without understanding the wider context in which it occurs. That framework can only be provided by developing a theory of the state separate from the particular actions of particular governments. That is the purpose of this section; we return to consideration of governments in the next chapter.

Quentin Skinner (1978: 352–8) has described the origins of the modern concept of the state and once again we find that a basic concept in our modern world first appears at the same time as the emergence of the world-economy itself. The word state comes from the Latin *status* and its mediaeval usage related to either the 'state' or condition of a ruler or the 'state' of the realm. The idea of a public power separate from ruler and ruled which is the supreme political authority in a given territory does not occur at this mediaeval period or earlier periods. The modern concept develops from this mediaeval usage in the sixteenth century first in France and then in England. Skinner (1978) argues that this is because these two countries provided early examples of the properties that make up the modern state – a centralized regime based on a bureaucracy operating within well-established boundaries. By the end of the sixteenth century Skinner claims that the modern concept of the state is well-established in these two countries and modern political analysis focusing on the nature of the state can be said to begin from this time onwards.

This 'analysis' has led to several 'theories of the state' some of which have been implicitly or explicitly incorporated into political geography. In recent years some geographers (Johnston 1980a) have criticized traditional political geography for its dearth of theory and in particular its failure to consider the issue of how to theorize the state. The problem is not that political geography has had no theory of the state – it is impossible to study any phenomena without an implicit theory of its nature – but rather that the theory being used has not been adequately presented so that the full implications are not expressed. In this section we describe the traditional theory of the state in political geography and then attempt to uncover its hidden assumptions. By revealing its biases we move directly into Marxist theories of the state where such state-bias is modelled explicitly. Finally we describe the limitations of Marxist theories when set within our world-systems approach: we move from a theory of the state towards a theory of the state*s*.

One final point needs to be made at this stage. It might be expected that we start this section with a precise definition of the state and then pursue our studies on this basis. Unfortunately, but inevitably, the definition of state varies with the different theories we discuss. Hence just as with territory, we will define the term state in several ways as we develop our argument. To begin with Skinner's 'modern concept' described above is sufficient for discussing traditional political geography theories.

HARTSHORNE'S THEORY OF TERRITORIAL INTEGRATION

The basic elements of a geographical theory of the state were developed in the early 1950s by Gottmann (1951, 1952), Hartshorne (1950) and Jones (1954). Gottmann analysed the political partition of the world and concluded that it was based upon two main factors – movement which causes instability and iconography which causes stability. In this approach movement includes all exchanges throughout the world whether of people, commodities or ideas. Iconography is a system of symbols in which people believe, encompassing elements of national feeling from the state flag to the culture transmitted through the state's schools. These two forces oppose one another and the world map at any one time is the balance achieved between stability and instability. Hartshorne's (1950) 'functional approach to political geography' developed this idea of two opposing forces more fully.

For Hartshorne the fundamental purpose of the state is to bind together its various social and territorial segments into an effective whole. This integration function can be carried out 'vertically' for social groups and 'horizontally' for territorial groups. Vertical integration is not the concern of political geography except where it is related to territorial differences according to Hartshorne. He produces, therefore, what we may term a theory of territorial integration.

Territorial integration depends upon two sets of forces – centrifugal forces pulling the state apart and centripetal forces binding it together. Gottmann's movement and iconography are important examples of centrifugal and centripetal forces respectively. Hartshorne's approach now involves a listing of both types of forces and a discussion of their operations. We will briefly describe each set of forces in turn.

1. Centrifugal forces: physical features and social diversity

The centrifugal forces typically emphasized by political geography are the physical characteristics of a state's territory. The size and shape of a country may be important, for instance. De Blij (1967: 42–5) discusses such issues in some detail but it seems that physical factors vary greatly in their importance as centrifugal forces. Although the physical separation of Pakistan into east and west is obviously relevant to the ultimate disintegration of the original state into a new Pakistan in the west and Bangladesh in the east, this contrasts with the ease with which the USA has been able to integrate its forty-ninth and fiftieth states, Alaska and Hawaii respectively. Similarly land-locked states in Africa suffer serious problems of dependence threatening their viability, whereas this seems much less important to land-locked Switzerland and Austria. Obviously these contrasts reflect, once again, differences between core processes and periphery processes in the world-economy in which these spatial characteristics have different importance. Hence Hartshorne is correct to warn us to be wary about placing too much weight on such factors *per se* since they are all less important as centrifugal forces than what he terms the diversity of the character of the population of a state. This diversity may be expressed in many ways. Language, ethnic and religious differences are the most common cause of territorial conflict in states but other features such as political philosophy, education and levels of living varying by region may be disruptive. Short (1982) considers the latter diversity – regional inequality in material well-being – to be the most salient centrifugal force in the modern world. We will return to this point when we discuss materialist theories of nationalism in the next section.

2. *Centripetal forces: state-idea and federalism*

All of the above features have been associated in different states with civil wars and sometimes partition. But partition does not always result and there are, in any case, many states that have never experienced a civil war based on territorial divisions. What binds states together, therefore? Hartshorne identifies one basic centripetal force of overwhelming importance – the state idea. Every state has a *raison d'être*, a reason for existence, and it is the strength of this 'idea' which counteracts the centripetal forces. In the modern world this state-idea, like Gottmann's iconography, is closely associated with nationalism and we will consider it as such in the next section. We can note here that it is easier to define when it is lacking – for instance it has been said of both the Central African federation and the Caribbean federation that they failed to hold together because each lacked a widely held 'state-idea' (Dikshit 1971a; Muir 1981: 109).

The last two examples represent the victory of centrifugal forces over centripetal forces in federated state structures. The latter form of state territorial organization is very common where there are potential problems of territorial integration. In many cases such an arrangement has been successful in maintaining the coherence of a state in situations of high territorial diversity. It is for this reason that the federalism is often described as the most 'geographical' of state systems and has been widely studied in political geography (Dikshit, 1971b, 1975; Paddison, 1983). It is the most practical of Hartshorne's centripetal forces in that it has to be consciously designed to fit a particular situation of diversity. A sensitive and carefully designed constitution which is perceived as fair and evenly balanced can contribute to the viability of the state and may even become part of the state-idea. This has been the case for the USA and we will briefly consider federalism as a centripetal force for this example from our world-systems perspective.

The states that emerged in the core of the world-economy were of two types – the classic centralized states such as France and England where sovereign authority in the territory was vested in a single government and looser arrangements where local units retained some autonomy from the overarching state. This 'split sovereignty' was found in the Netherlands and Switzerland. This latter idea was applied in drawing up the US Constitution and has been imitated almost as often as the classic centralized state. Geographers and political scientists have attempted to specify the conditions under which federalism is the chosen state structure – Paddison (1983: 105) lists four sets of such ideas. Obviously the reasons are many and various given the many examples of federated states. But one thing does emerge. There must be a powerful group of state-builders who are able to convince the members of the territorial sub-units of the benefits of union over separation. The basis of such arguments return to our original discussion concerning territories in the world-economy. It must be shown that security and opportunity are greater in the larger territory than for separate smaller territories. This requires an alliance between the state builders and the economic groups who will benefit from the larger territorial arrangement. This is very clearly seen in the American case as Beard (1914) has argued and Libby (1894) illustrated. Both Fifer (1976) and Archer and Taylor (1981) use the latter's maps of support for the American federal constitution in 1789 to show distinct differences between different parts of the new colonies. It is not a north–south sectionalism that emerges but a commercial versus frontier cleavage that dominates. In the urban areas and commercial farming areas which were firmly linked into the world-economy, support for federation was very strong. In the more isolated areas with their more self-sufficient economy the advantages of federation were far less obvious. Suspicion of centralization prevailed and these areas tended to reject the federal constitution. The majority of world-economy linked areas finally prevailed and the USA was formed on a constitutional basis for its economic groups to challenge the world-economy order using mercantilist policies through the federal government. Although the nature and balance of American federalism has changed over time, it has contributed to the survival and rise of the state and is now very much part of the American 'state idea'.

The American example is a relatively simple illustration of the materialist basis of federalism. In the modern world most federal constitutions are devised to counter ethnic diversity. This does not mean there is no material basis to the federalism, however. We argue in the next section that such 'cultural' features may be traced to economic causes in their emergence as modern political issues. When federal constitutions help bind territories containing different cultural groups they simultaneously help bind together territories with different links into the world-economy. In every federal arrangement there are winners and there are losers and these can be defined materially with reference to the world-economy.

Hartshorne's theory of territorial integration provides a model for analysing particular cases. It has been extended by Jones (1954) in his 'unified field theory' of political geography. Hartshorne's concept of state-idea is extended to form a chain of five related concepts: political idea – decision – movement – field – political area. In the case of modern states the political idea is the raison d'être and the decision is the specific treaty recognizing the viability of the idea. Movement is Gottmann's concept as required in operationalizing the decision to produce a field as the arena in which the movement occurs. Finally a political area is defined as the territory of the state. Jones gives the example of the establishment of Israel as follows: zionism is the idea, the Balfour Declaration of 1917 is the decision permitting movement (migration) which produces a field (the immigrant settlement pattern) generating war which defines a state of Israel out of Palestine. When the chain is completed, as in this case, then centripetal forces have triumphed, when the chain is broken centrifugal forces are deemed to be too strong. In either case we are left with what is essentially a check list for studying the establishment of states.

3. Critique: developmentalism and vertical integration

These ideas of Gottmann, Hartshorne and Jones dominated political geography for over a generation being faithfully reproduced in many text books. Hence they cannot be merely dismissed as inconsequential, they must be reviewed and evaluated to produce a critical understanding of their strengths and weaknesses.

There are two basic criticisms we can make of the integration theory. First it focuses attention on the individual state. Analysis is directed towards separate treatment of each state. We are presented with some relatively abstract concepts to be applied to case studies. Such a state-by-state process undervalues the existence of the inter-state system and concentrates explanation at the state level. Hence political geographers have been enthusiastic purveyors of the error of developmentalism. Perhaps the classic example of this error in geography is political geography's 'cycle theory' whereby states were supposed to go through stages – youth, adolescence, maturity and old age – just like river valleys! (Van Valkenburg 1939; de Blij 1967: 102–5). Obviously in this study we move away from developmentalism to our world-systems approach.

The second criticism relates to Hartshorne's assertion that integration – the organization of a territory – is the fundamental purpose of the state. It is treated as self-evident that the state operates for itself. But the balance of forces that are provided to explain the success or failure of a state in its prime purpose are abstracted out of the social formation in which the states exist. At this point of the argument it is useful to repeat Schattschneider's dictum that 'all organization is bias'. The establishment and disestablishment of states represents victories for some social groups and defeats for others. This is what we have tried to convey in our brief discussion of federalism but it is equally true of all enterprises at state building. It is for this reason that we cannot banish 'vertical' integration of social groups from our political geography as Hartshorne proposes. The state can only be understood as a response to the needs of certain groups at the expense of other groups. Integration is a process that can be looked back at with pride by the winners but we should not forget the losers in such conflict. For conflict theories of the state we need to consider the Marxist literature.

MARXIST THEORIES OF THE STATE

It is well known that Marx himself never developed a theory of the state. It was a project that he set himself but never completed. Hence Marxist theories of the state are products of his many followers and this has inevitably led to alternative interpretation of what such a theory should say: there is not *a* Marxist theory of the state but many Marxist *theories* of the state. In this discussion we will consider both the differences and similarities of a small number of these theories which have recently entered political geography. We begin by briefly describing the original orthodox Marxist position before moving on to review three debates surrounding recent attempts by Marxists to update their theory. Finally we introduce one set of ideas which are particularly related to our political geography perspective.

In Marx's voluminous political writings there is much raw material for his followers to use to construct theories of the state. Two ideas have dominated Marxist political thinking. The first, from the Communist Manifesto of 1848, dismissed the state as nothing more than 'a committee for organizing the affairs of the bourgeoisie'. The second, which can be found in several writings, consists of a 'base-superstructure model' of society where this engineering analogy is used to depict a foundation of economic relations upon which the ideological and political superstructure is constructed. These two simple ideas are difficult to accommodate to the complexities of the modern state. If they are taken at face value they lead to a reduction of all politics and the state to a mere reflection of economic forces. Such crude reductionism is termed *economism*. Hunt (1980: 10) provides a good example of this type of thinking in his criticism of Lenin's contribution to state theory. Lenin proposed a strict relationship between stages of economic development and types of state. Hence parliamentary democracy is the form of state for competitive capitalism, the bureaucratic-military state emerges with monopoly capitalism and, of course, socialism replaces these with 'the dictatorship of the proletariat'. In modern orthodox Marxist theory, economics and politics are fused in another stage known as state monopoly capitalism (Jessop 1982). By directly equating the form of the state with the economic base, Lenin provides a simple explanation which we now identify as economism. Of course, this model is every much as developmentalist as the cycle theory of states or even Rostow's stages of economic growth (Wallerstein 1974b). Most modern

Marxists distance themselves from such simplistic analyses (Hunt 1980). Nevertheless this is the heritage for modern Marxist theories of the state and in what follows we show how modern Marxist theorists have attempted to avoid such economism.

1. Miliband versus pluralist theory

In the social science of the English-speaking world modern concern for Marxist theories of the state can be said to begin with Ralph Miliband's (1969) *State in Capitalist Society* which was written to counter the prevailing *pluralist* theory of the state in political science. This theory conceptualized the state as a set of institutions which manage the public needs of society. These institutions are neutral bodies to which different groups in society can appeal and so produce policies that favour their members. The state is in effect an umpire ajudicating between competing interests. Since modern society consists of very many overlapping interests – labour, farmers, business, home owners, consumers, and so on – no one group is ever able to dominate the state. The balance of interests served will vary as governments change but the state will remain pluralist in nature and able to respond to a wide range of interests. This is quite obviously the opposite of the Marxist class theory which in these terms is strictly a non-pluralist account of the state.

There are two fundamental properties of pluralist and related non-Marxist theories of the state. The first is that the state is treated as neutral; it is a body above the day-to-day politics of its constituent institutions. This property is vital to social-democratic strategies in Western European states since it assumes that if a Labour or Social Democratic party wins control of the government in an election, it can use the state to carry out its 'socialist' reforms. The state is 'up for grabs', as it were, in electoral politics. The second property of such theories is that they treat the political sphere as separate from the economic sphere. This is the basis of the whole notion of a 'political science', of course, so that no problem is envisaged in the relations of politics and economics. They are separate, though often related, processes that can be adequately studied as autonomous systems. We met this argument in discussing inter-state politics in Chapter 2 and it is repeated at all scales of analysis. From the perspective of this study pluralist theories of the state represent an important example of the poverty of disciplines.

Economism and pluralist theory can be seen as opposite ends of a scale measuring the autonomy of the political from the economic. At the economism end there is no autonomy. At the political science end there is absolute autonomy. In between we can identify different degrees of 'relative autonomy' where politics is not determined by economic processes but is not independent of them either. Most modern Marxist analyses have located themselves in the relative autonomy sector of this scale and it is from just such a position that Miliband (1969) launched his attack on the pluralist theory.

The bulwark of the pluralist theory is the existence of elections. In 1848 the state may have looked very much like a one-class institution but with franchise reforms the modern liberal-democratic state looks very much like the pluralist model. We deal with liberal democracy in some detail in the next chapter and here we will only show how Miliband attempts to uncover the class nature of the apparently pluralist state. Miliband's method is to marshall data on the social, political and economic elites of the modern state and to show that they all come from the same class background. By showing the many inter-linkages in terms of family, education and general economic interests, Miliband is able to paint a picture of a single dominant class in which pluralist competition is a myth. This dominant class is able to manipulate the state apparatus irrespective of which party is in government. This has come to be known as the *instrumentalist* theory of the state. It restates the class basis of the state and completely undermines the neutral pluralist view.

2. Poulantzas versus instrumentalism

Miliband's thesis stimulated a debate with Poulantzas (1969) upon how to construct a Marxist theory of the state. Poulantzas argued that Miliband's empirical approach, while useful and interesting, was seriously flawed because it involved analysing the state on terms laid down by non-Marxist theory. It is not that empirical analysis is wrong in itself but the way in which it is integrated with theory is important. Miliband's study reduces to a description of particular roles within the state apparatus and investigation of links between people carrying out these different roles. The inevitable result is an emphasis on inter-personal relations which is reminiscent of the original pluralist thinking. For Poulantzas the class nature of the state is not a matter of empirical verification or falsification. A state is not capitalist in nature because a dominant class with capitalist links manipulates the state for capitalist ends. The state is capitalist because it operates within a capitalist mode of production. This sets constraints on the range of action that is possible so that the state has no option but to conform to the needs of capital. The introduction of liberal democracy does not change this fundamental property. This is a *logical* argument for which empirical proof is unnecessary. Such a *structuralist* position need not reduce to economism, Poulantzas shares Miliband's relative autonomy assumption with the state dependent on the economic only 'in the last instance'.

3. Derivationists versus relative autonomy

The Miliband–Poulantzas debate was introduced into geography by Dear and Clark (1978). At about the same time, however, the work of West German Marxists was just becoming available (Holloway and Picciotto

1978) and this completely cut across the arguments that separated Miliband and Poulantzas. This *derivation* school rejected the notion of relative autonomy and so undermined the arguments of both protagonists. By assuming relative autonomy any theory implicitly accepts the separation of the economic from the political. By doing this the proponents of such theories cut politics off from the main motor of change in capitalist society, the accumulation process. For the derivationists, therefore, the key question is not about the *degree* of separation between the political and economic but why does it *appear* this way in capitalist society. The Marxist political analyses, developed by Miliband and Poulantzas in their different ways, cannot adequately answer this question because they have forsaken the holism of political economy.

For these West German theorists the solution was simple: a Marxist theory of the state must be derived from the mechanisms and concepts described by Marx in his basic theoretical work, *Capital*. To the need for competition in the economic sphere they add the need for co-operation in the political sphere. The state becomes necessary to counter the self-destructive processes of unbridled economic competition. This may even involve political processes that appear to be anti-capitalist. The evolution of the welfare state, for instance, involves ensuring the reproduction of a skilled and healthy labour force for the long-term interests of capital. In this role of co-ordinating capital and reproducing labour the state may appear neutral and above the political conflict between capital and labour. This is why non-Marxist theories of the state appear so reasonable and are so widely and easily accepted.

4. Hegemony and ideological state apparatus

Following Gold *et al* (1975), Dear and Clark (1978) introduced a further Marxist approach to the state which they term 'ideological'. All Marxist theories incorporate some notion of ideology in their formulation but Gold *et al* (1975) refer in this context to theories that specifically emphasize the state as a form of mystification whereby class conflicts are hidden behind a national consensus. This is very close to the conception of the state as the scale of ideology that we introduced in the first chapter. In the Marxist literature it is most closely associated with the work of Gramsci and his followers (Jessop 1982). Gramsci is most well-known today for his concept of hegemony. This derives from Marx's original argument that the ruling ideas in a society are the ideas of the ruling class. In Gramsci's work hegemony is the political, intellectual and moral leadership of the dominant class which results in the dominated class actively consenting to their own domination (Jessop 1982: 17). Hence alongside the coercive state apparatus (police, army, judiciary, and so on) there is the ideological state apparatus (education, mass media, popular entertainment, and so on) through which consent is generated. Notice that these ideological functions need not be carried out by public agencies – in this theory the state is much more than just the public sector. Historically the vital battle for state sovereignty involved subjugation of other authority within the state's territory, both local magnates and the universal ideas of the church. In the latter case the issue centred on education and the state's attempts to 'nationalize' its population by converting religious education into a state ideological apparatus. The successful combination of coercion and hegemony will produce an 'integral state'. Here we have a parallel with our territorial integration theory and the concept of state-idea and iconography. The notion of hegemony, however, is much more pervasive and directly derives from the class-basis of the state. In this argument Marx's original 'committee' assertion of 1848 remains broadly true: the difference between then and now merely relates to the changing relative balance between coercive and ideological means of control.

It is, of course, very difficult to summarize such a vigorous and expanding field of enquiry as Marxist theories of the state in just a few pages (Short 1982: 109). We are not able to do justice to the ideas of even the few theorists we have mentioned. Miliband's (1969) original study includes an interesting discussion of dominant class ideology, for instance and we have only dealt with Poulantzas in his response to Miliband whereas Jessop (1982) considers his work to be the most impressive of the recent spate of new theory. For a comprehensive discussion of this field the reader is referred to Jessop (1982).

We started this discussion with a description of Lenin's economism. The modern theorists have countered this problem in different ways but they have not tackled the problem of Lenin's developmentalism. Although we have brought the argument a long way forward from simple economism all the analyses described above remain rooted at the state level. For our assessment of their utility within the framework of this book it is necessary to review them in the context of the world-economy.

THE STATE IN THE WORLD-ECONOMY

The political sphere that we deal with in this study is not the single state but the whole inter-state system. Hence we need a theory of *states* where the multiplicity of states is a fundamental property of the theory. Clearly none of the above offer this type of theory. Nevertheless the various themes highlighted above do provide pointers towards provision of our need and our approach does clarify some of the contentious issues. In this discussion we begin, in a preliminary way, the bringing together of theories of the state and the world-systems approach.

1. Relative autonomy and multiplicity of states

The basic empirical problem confronting the Marxists was that the same economic system – capitalism – was producing different state forms. Although the USA and Italy were both capitalist states, for instance, they exhibited very different politics. It is this variety of politics which was to be the subject matter of Marxist political analysis (Miliband 1977, Scase 1980). The break with economism was obviously necessary and relative autonomy was a very attractive concept upon which to base these new analyses. As we have seen the derivationists have cast severe doubt on the validity of this position but they have not replaced it with another means for accounting for the variety of politics under capitalism. The world-economy approach does provide a simple explanation of this variety which makes the concept of relative autonomy unnecessary.

The notion of relative autonomy is implicitly based upon the idea that both state and economy cover the same territory. In Scase (1980), for instance, the issue of the relation between economics and politics is treated on a state-by-state basis for Western Europe. When viewed in this manner it is easy to see how the problem of relating one national economy to one state polity emerges. But this whole issue disappears with the world-economy perspective and its multi-state system. Instead of a one-to-one problem there is a one-to-many situation – one world market and many states. Hence we do not have to appeal to a relative autonomy argument to explain the variety of political forms that states take under capitalism. Instead there are numerous fragments of the world-economy each with their particular sovereign states. Since these 'fragments of capitalism' differ from one another then there is no reason to suppose that the forms that the states take should not differ from one another. Quite simply, different fragmants of capitalism are associated with different state forms. The variety of politics remains to be understood but there is no need to resort to relative autonomy for explanation.

2. Derivation of world government

Dismissal of relative autonomy brings us into line with the state derivation position. But we soon find that there are problems in applying this theory to our framework. In its initial form we have seen that the state is derived to overcome the anarchic consequences of a 'free' capitalism. If we translate this to a world-economy then this theory predicts a world government to compensate for global anarchy. This is, of course, quite the opposite to the capitalist world-economy as conceived by Wallerstein. As we have seen multiple states are necessary for manoeuvre by economic actors on the world stage. Production of a world government would therefore signal the end of capitalism as mode of production. In our framework the state does operate to maintain reproduction of labour and facilitate accumulation but not at the system level where states provide platforms for their capitals to operate in the world market.

Within the state derivation school there have been debates that have raised the issue of the world market. In particular Braunmuhl (1978) and Barker (1978) have insisted that state derivation must start from the existence of capital at the world level and not at the state level. We draw on some of their ideas and those of Chase-Dunn (1982) in our discussion below. As will be apparent by now the world-systems approach to the state is closest to the derivationist school due to its insistence on analysing the economic and political as complementary aspects of one overall process. This was expressed in Chapter 1 with inter-state system and world market as two sets of relations underlying the same process of appropriation and accumulation. We did not so much 'derive' the inter-state system from the world-economy as define it as an integral part of the overall system – it is after all one of the three fundamental characteristics of the world-economy identified by Wallerstein (1979). But we need to go further and attempt to understand the variety of states within the inter-state system. No rigorous theory for this exists but enough material is available for us to draw the outline of such a theory.

3. The variety of state forms: a space–time introduction

The form that states take depends upon the particular conjuncture of economic, social and political forces in its territory in the past and at the present time. Hence strictly speaking every state form will be unique. But we can generalize in terms of the space–time structures previously discussed. Particular conjunctures can be aggregated into a simple 3 × 2 matrix with time represented by A- and B-phases of growth and stagnation and space apportioned between core, semi-periphery and periphery. We should then be able to discuss the form that states take within each of these six positions allowing for further variation due to different histories or past positions. In all cases the states will have to carry out two basic tasks: (i) provide the conditions for accumulation of capital and (ii) maintain legitimation of the system. O'Connor (1973) identifies these two basic functions of the state in his study of the fiscal crisis with specific reference to USA. Here we will extend his ideas, based as they are on German derivationists, to states generally within our space–time categories of the world-economy. In particular we will consider the legitimation function as a varying balance between forces of coercion and consensus.

Core states are the most stable and consensus has been far more important than coercion in maintaining control. This is because the capitals of core states are strongly placed in the world market and can pass on some of their surplus to core labour. This is the process of social imperialism described in the previous chapter. It is much more than simple bribery, however, and involves the incorporation of labour into the system. These are the truly 'hegemonized' states. But the strength of this hegemony varies between A- and B-phases. In periods of growth more resources are available to keep the system stable. These are periods of building hegemony in the wake of union successes, social-security advances and finally the welfare state. With the onset of stagnation pressures to maintain conditions for accumulation lead to cut-backs in public expenditure with resulting dangers in the loss of legitimacy. In core states, however, the hegemony has coped remarkably well with the current B-phase.

The opposite situation obtains in peripheral states where instability dominates. Here there is no surplus to buy off labour which is largely left to fend for itself while being coerced into submission. The result is an 'over-developed superstructure' relative to the economic base according to Alavi (1979). But this does not represent strength, it reflects the weakness of peripheral states in the world-economy. As before in our arguments, overtly 'strong' states deceive by their appearance. Alavi (1979) argues that in post-colonial societies a military-bureaucratic group emerges to oversee the interests of three exploiting classes: (i) the metropolitan core interest, (ii) the local urban-industrial interest, and (iii) the landowning interest. These three 'capitals' have a common interest in maintaining order as the basic condition for accumulation. But they compete in terms of relation of the state to the world-economy. Generally speaking metropolitan core interests and local landowners favour an open economy whereas local industrial interests favour protection. This is the peripheral/semi-peripheral strategy dichotomy discussed in the previous chapter and illustrated using Frank's discussion of 'American' and 'European' parties in nineteenth-century Latin America. To the extent that urban industrial groups are able to have their interests promoted by the military-bureaucratic regime the state becomes more like a semi-periphery state. But such promotion can fail, of course, and the state will sink even lower into the periphery. The case of Ghana and the failure of Nkrumah's 'African socialism' is an example of this (Osei-Kwame and Taylor 1984). It is a matter of the pattern of opportunity existing for advance in the world-economy which varies with A- and B-phases, of course.

Finally we come to the most interesting examples – the semi-periphery states. As we argued in Chapter 1 this is the dynamic sector of the world-economy where political actions by states can affect the future structure of the system. According to Chase-Dunn (1982) this is where class struggle is greatest, where the balance between coercion and consensus is most critical. State governments in this zone specialize in strategies which emphasize accumulation as we have previously indicated. Semi-peripheral economic policy is all about 'catching up', it is the zone of protection in particular and mercantilism in general. This will make legitimation difficult so that much of the semi-periphery is associated with dictatorial regimes. But coercion itself is a very expensive form of control and will stretch resources to the extent of hindering the 'catching up'. Hence the semi-periphery is also associated with powerful consensus forces, specifically fascism and communism and generally nationalism. These are strategies for mobilizing the state's population behind the dominant classes without the greater material expenses of the social imperialism of the core. Putting nation before self has become the most important form of consensus, the basis of state hegemony, and the major centripetal force in the twentieth century.

NATION AND NATIONALISM

Of all the various 'isms' of modern politics nationalism is the one generally considered most geographical. Hence whereas other 'isms' are conspicuous by their absence from political geography textbooks, nationalism has, until recently, commanded the centre of the stage. This is not surprising since nationalism brings together our basic trilogy of territory-state-nation: territory becomes national 'homeland' imbued with the symbolic significance of nationalism and state becomes nation-state as the ideal expression of the political will of nationalism. It is the purpose of this final section of the chapter to explore this integration of concepts.

The words 'nation' and 'nationalism' come from the Latin word *nasci* meaning 'to be born' and imply 'common ancestry' and 'place of origin' (Tivey 1981: 4–5). 'Nation' is intended to describe an historic entity whereas nationalism is the ideology associated with this concept. Surprisingly it is the former which is more difficult to pin down (Navari 1981). If we define it simply as a historic community sharing a common culture then such entities can be identified throughout history. The people of Ancient Egypt would constitute a nation on this criterion, for example. Amin (1980) proposes just such an approach to the concept of the nation as part of his wider attempt to rid our theories of their Euro-centric bias. However much we might sympathize with Amin's motives, most studies now agree that the concept is much more useful if its use is restricted to the modern world-economy. The best way of satisfying these differences is to adopt Smith's (1982) approach where the nation is interpreted as the modern version of the older category 'ethnic community'. Hence world-empires of the past may have incorporated ethnic communities but only in the modern world-system have such communities striven for recognition as 'nations'.

As an ideology the origins of nationalism are much easier to trace. Nationalism is a doctrine based on the idea that every nation should have its own state. This idea emerges in the eighteenth century, becomes a major force in world politics in the nineteenth century and has come to dominate the politics of the twentieth century. It was originally associated with the rationalism of the eighteenth century, especially the rejection of the personal authority of the monarch as the source of a state's sovereignty. Instead sovereignty lay with the 'people'. This notion is given political expression in the famous opening sentence of the American Constitution of 1887: 'We the people . . .' The specific idea that 'the people' constitute a 'nation' appears in the French Revolution with the setting up of a *national* assembly in 1789 and the French proclaiming themselves 'le grande nation' in 1790 (Rustow 1967: 21, 27). By 1815 at the Congress of Vienna the novel idea that state should coincide with 'nation' was first expressed and Greek independence in 1821 represents the first direct result of this idea. Revolutions between 1830 and 1848 became 'national' revolutions and the concept finally triumphed at the Peace Conference in Versailles in 1919 when national self-determination was recognized as the prime criterion of the new European political order. Whatever the doubts about 'nation', 'nationalism' is most clearly an ideology of our modern world.

In our discussion we treat three aspects of nation and nationalism. We extend the brief definitions above by considering the doctrine of nationalism in more detail. This is an attempt to describe the essential character of the concepts. The variety of nationalisms is our next topic as we consider how these ideas have been applied in practice. This involves developing a typology of nationalisms. Finally we consider the problem of developing a general theory of nationalism. We present a materialist theory within our overall world-systems framework.

THE DOCTRINE OF NATIONALISM

We should never underestimate the ideology of nationalism. As Smith (1979: 1) so rightly says: 'No other vision has set its stamp so thoroughly on the map of the world, and on our sense of identity.' We all 'belong' to a particular nation, usually that based upon the territorial location of our birth. In fact the idea of nation is so embedded in our consciousness that it is even reflected in the use of terms that describe counter-national arrangements: 'Supranational' 'multi-national' and 'trans-national' all assume the prior reality of nations (Tivey 1981: 6). Similarly the two great liberal organizations of states in the twentieth century have found it unnecessary to mention the states themselves – we have had successively the League of Nations and the United Nations. Of course 'nations' that do not possess states, such as Kurds or Armenians, cannot join these organizations but states without nations such as most newly independent African states do join immediately to reinforce their sovereign status. Both the League and the UN are or were special clubs for states not nations. Their ambiguous titles merely reflect the strength of the doctrine of nationalism in the twentieth century.

1. The core doctrine

But what is this 'doctrine', this ideal that nationalists strive for? We can describe it in terms of the following propositions drawn from Tivey (1981: 5–6) and Smith (1982: 150) and related successively to our three scales of analysis.

A1: The world consists of a mosaic of nations.

A2: World order and harmony depends upon expressing this mosaic in a system of free nation-states.

B1: Nations are the natural units of society.

B2: Nations have a cultural homogeneity based upon common ancestry and/or history.

B3: Every nation requires its own sovereign state for the true expression of its culture.

B4: All nations (rather than states) have an inalienable right to a territory or homeland.

C1: Every individual must belong to a nation.

C2: A person's primary loyalty is to the nation.

C3: Only through the nation can a person find true freedom.

We can term this list the core doctrine of nationalism. It has justified the following scale effects. The world is politically divided rather than unified. The state as nation-state is the basic arena of politics. The local scale is by-passed as experiences are transcended by a 'higher' and more remote ideal.

The effects on social relations are no less profound. Other political ideologies have had to adapt or be crushed by nationalism. According to Smith (1979: 8) nationalism split with liberalism at the time of the 1848 revolutions. The simple individualism of classical liberalism had to give way to a 'national' liberalism in order to survive. At the other end of the scale the internationalism of socialism was fundamentally defeated at the outbreak of the First World War in 1914. Worker fought worker under their different national banners. Like liberalism the various brands of socialism have had to adapt to the political reality of nationalism in order to survive. Liberal individualism and socialist internationalism counted for little against the doctrine of nationalism. The result is our three-tier scale structure of the world-economy pivoting around the nation-state. We develop our ideas on the geography of these political ideologies and their nationalization in the next chapter.

2. The special secondary theories

This core doctrine is general to all nationalisms. But every nationalism is based on particularism. Each has its own character. These are what Smith (1982: 150) terms special secondary theories. Since every one is different a brief description of just a single example will have to suffice.

Watson (1970) quotes approvingly from a letter written in 1782 which lists eight features of American society which were to become American 'national characteristics'. These are: 'a love of newness', 'nearness to nature', 'freedom to move', 'the mixing of peoples', 'individualism', 'a sense of destiny', 'violence' and 'man as a whole'. The first four reflect American history, especially frontier history. The next two features are key ideological props of 'the American way of life'. Individual competition to achieve personal success – log cabin to White House – is the basis of American liberal ideology. Manifest destiny has set national goals originally continental in scope and latterly global. The final two features are contradictory as they contrast conflict in US society with the idealism of belief in rational accommodation. Together these eight features add up to what Watson calls 'the myth of America'; in our terms they are the special secondary theory of American nationalism.

Clearly it is at this level of theory that we can identify the various elements that political geographers have studied in the past – raison d'être, iconography, state idea, and so on. It has been the concentration of effort at this level of symbolism that has prevented political geographers breaking through to the general doctrine and fully understanding nation and nationalism. This is because nationalism is based upon a series of myths embodied in the secondary theories. These myths consist of distorted histories concerning society/ethnic origins, past heroic ages and betrayals and the 'special' place of the nation in world history. There may well be only one diety but he or she has certainly been generous in designating 'chosen people'! The geographical equivalents of these distorted histories are the geopolitics, the ideological heritage of political geography described in Chapter 2.

NATIONALISM IN PRACTICE

If nationalism is the dominant ideology of the world-economy we must always remember that this has not always been the case. We have already indicated that this political use of the idea of nation really dates from the French Revolution and no earlier. In the two or three centuries before 1800 the world-economy evolved without a politics based on nationalism. There were states to be sure but, as Wallerstein (1974a: 102) points out, these were anti-national where regional ethnic powers stood in the way of the absolute state's centralization. There was 'statism' or mercantilism as we have seen, but until the nineteenth century no nationalism. Since that time however, we have experienced a wide variety of different nationalisms. The first task of our discussion below is to put some order into this diversity by presenting a typology of nationalism. We then consider contrasting interpretations of these particular political practices.

1. A typology of nationalisms

The most recent description of the variety of nationalism is by Orridge (1981a). Our typology below is largely drawn from his discussion of the sequence of various nationalisms. We identify five basic types – state nationalism, unification nationalism, separation nationalism, liberation nationalism and renewal nationalism – and we consider each in turn.

State nationalism. This is the nationalism of the original core states, the medium-sized states of Rokkan's seaward Europe. This nationalism is the source of much dispute over the timing of the emergence of nation and nationalism. Gottmann (1973: 33–6), for instance, is able to trace back the idea of *pro patria mori* – dying for one's country – to about 1300 so that by 1430 Joan of Arc could freely employ such sentiments to mobilize the French knights against English encroachment on French soil. The statements of English nationalism to be found in Shakespeare's plays of the late sixteenth and early seventeenth century are even more familiar examples of this early 'patriotism'. But these are both examples of loyalty to monarch or state or even country but not to the collective idea of a people as a nation incorporating all sections and classes. Nevertheless the centralizing tendencies of these states within relatively stable boundaries did lead to a degree of cultural homogeneity by 1800 which was not found in other areas of comparable size. England and France are the key examples here but similar nation-states were emerging in Portugal, Sweden, the Netherlands and, to a lesser extent, Spain. In all of these cases state preceded nation and it can even be said that state produced nation. The result was what Orridge (1981a) terms proto-nation-states. The 'people' were entering politics but nationalism as an ideology was not fully developed until later in the nineteenth century. Hence we can say nation preceded nationalism.

Unification nationalism. For the full development of the ideology of nationalism we have to look elsewhere. In central Europe such medium-sized states had been prevented from evolving under the contradictory pressures of small (city-scale) states and large multi-ethnic empires. In particular Germany and Italy were a mosaic of small independent states mixed with provinces of larger empires. After 1800 the Napoleonic wars disrupted this pattern which had been imposed a century and a half earlier at the Treaty of Westphalia (1649).Although the Congress of Vienna in 1815 attempted to reconstitute the old Europe new forces had been unleashed which were to dominate the rest of the century. Nationalism was the justification for uniting most of the German culture area under Prussian leadership into a new German nation-state and transforming Italy from a mere 'geographical expression' to an Italian nation-state. These are the prime examples of unification nationalism and are generally considered to be the hearthlands of the ideology.

Separation nationalism. Most successful nationalisms have involved the disintegration of existing sovereigning states. In the nineteenth and early twentieth century this nationalism lay behind the creations of a large number of new states out of the Austro-Hungarian, Ottoman and Russian Empires. Starting with Greece in 1821 a whole tier of new states were created in eastern

Europe from Bulgaria, through the Balkans to Scandinavia. Surviving examples are Norway, Finland, Poland, Czechoslovakia, Hungary, Roumania, Bulgaria, Yugoslavia, Albania and Greece. Ireland also comes into this category. This type of nationalism was, until recently, considered to be a phenomena of the past at least in core countries. However in the last two decades there have been further 'autonomous' nationalisms appearing in many states. Some of the most well-known are found in Scotland, Wales, Basque country, Corsica, Quebec and Wallonia. None of these has at the present time been successful in establishing their own nation-state but each has been granted political concessions within the framework of their existing states.

This form of nationalism is currently a major topic in political geography research. The particular cases of most concern are the Canada/Quebec and Britain/Scotland/Wales national conflicts (Burghardt 1980; Williams 1981; Agnew 1981a and b; Knight 1982a). In addition Williams (1980) provides an overview of separation nationalism in Europe and Orridge and Williams (1982) attempt to set the problem in the broader context of the world-economy. Finally Knight (1982b) develops a particularly interesting argument focusing on the issue of geographical scale in defining nations and providing the basis for national separation.

Liberation nationalism.   The break-up of European overseas empires was described in the last chapter but is of interest here as representing probably the most common form of nationalism. Nearly all such movements for independence have been 'national liberation movements'. The earliest was the American colonists in 1776 whose War of Independence finally led to a constitution giving sovereignty to the 'people'. The Latin American revolutions after the Napoleonic wars were more explicitly 'nationalist' in character. These can be considered liberal nationalist movements. In the twentieth century such movements have invariably been socialist nationalist movements varying in their socialism from India's mild version to Vietnam's revolutionary version. Another way of dividing up liberation nationalism is between those based upon European settler groups and those based upon indigenous peoples. In the former case we have the USA and Latin American plus the original 'white' Commonwealth states of South Africa, Canada, Australia and New Zealand who negotiated independence without liberation movements. In the latter case there are the states of Africa and Asia which have become independent since 1945.

Renewal nationalism.   In some parts of the periphery 'ancient' cultures withstood European political capture for a variety of reasons and were able to emulate the state nationalism of the core often using a politics similar to unification nationalism. These countries had a long history as ethnic communities upon which they could easily build their new nationalism. National renewal to former greatness became the basic cry.

Hence Iran could rediscover its Persian heritage. Turkey after losing its Ottoman empire could concentrate on its Turkish ethnicity. The classic cases of this type of nationalism are to be found in Japan and China.

This form of nationalism can also occur as part of a process of creating a new state identity which attempts to redefine the relations of the state to the world-economy. As such this renewal is associated with modern revolutions. Stalin's 'socialism in one country' had many of the trappings of a renewal of the Russian nation for instance. Other renewals have occurred in Mexico, Egypt, China and most recently in Iran.

These five types and their various sub-types seem to provide a reasonable cover of the variety of nationalisms that have existed. The sequence from the early types to their emulation in the later ones illustrates, according to Orridge (1981a), the basic process of copying and adaption which has lain behind the strength of the ideology. Political leaders in a wide range of contexts have been able to appeal to the nationalist doctrine to justify their actions. This has led to a curious ambivalence in how nationalism is perceived. On the one hand it is a good thing, a positive force in world history as when it is associated with weak states freeing themselves from foreign oppression. But is also has a dark side, the negative force associated with nazism and fascism in Europe, and militarism throughout the semi-periphery and periphery. It is, as it were, both good and bad. This is most clearly seen in attitudes to nationalism after the two world wars in the twentieth century. In 1919 the First World War was blamed on the suppression of nationalism; in 1945 the Second World War was blamed on the expression of nationalism (Rustow 1967: 21). Nairn (1977), in a particularly apt analogy, calls nationalism 'the modern Janus' after the famous Greek statue which looked in two directions at once, both backwards and forwards. For Nairn this is the essence of the ideology, a simultaneous appeal to both progress and tradition.

We have packaged nationalism into five neat bundles in our typology and this is a necessary step towards explanation. But, by definition, any parsimonious description misses out most of the detail. The problem in the case of nationalism is that it is this very detail – the difference in language, folklore and other traditions – which is the essence of the ideology in practice. There is no room here to present a catalogue of such materials but what we can do is consider related case studies to illustrate difficulties of applying the doctrine in practice. The examples we take are from the political negotiations of the Peace at Paris in 1919. This is chosen for two reasons. First, it represents the apogee of the recognition of nationalism as a legitimate force in world politics. The League of Nations was largely based upon the doctrine of nationalism presented above. Second, nationalism is easier to define as a doctrine than it is to define on the ground. The negotiators at Paris had the task of redrawing the map of central and eastern Europe. The difficulties of their task and different means used to achieve their ends illustrate the two sides of nationalism in a very concrete manner. In short we present some aspects of the geography of nationalism at the peak of its influence.

During the First World War national self-determination gradually came to be regarded, especially after the entry of USA, as the principle war aim of the allied forces. By the time the Paris Peace Conference was convened new states had already been created out of the territories of the defeated states of Germany and Austro-Hungary (Cobban, 1969: 556). Hence the peace negotiators spent most of their time putting boundaries around existing political creations. National self-determination provided a simple guide to this process – states should be formed around nations as determined by the people. In strict terms the people decide which nation-state they belong to. Such choice was rare in practice and was replaced by the very negation of choice – people were allocated to states on the basis of some cultural characteristic, usually the language, of the area they lived in. We may term this process *national determinism*. Let us consider each process in turn.

2. National self-determination: plebiscites

It follows logically from one nationalist tradition that if sovereignty does indeed lie with the 'people', then the people should be consulted in any proposed changes in sovereignty. This is the principle of national self-determination which requires the use of plebiscites for changing state boundaries. Wambaugh (1936) defines three periods when plebiscites were used to decide such matters: (i) in the aftermath of the French Revolution in Savoy, Nice, Geneva and Belgium to legitimize the extension of the French state; (ii) between 1848 and 1870 notably as a tool in the unification of Italy which involved a total of nine plebiscites in the conversion of the Kingdom of Sardinia into the Kingdom of Italy and (iii) resulting from the Paris Peace conference of 1919. However use of this method was surprisingly infrequent given the allies' war aims: only six plebiscites were carried out, four to define parts of the new Germany's border and two to define parts of the new Austria's border.

One of the reasons for the infrequent use of plebiscites in 1919 was the difficulty in agreeing the ground rules. Which areas are polled and how the vote is aggregated and interpreted will affect the result. In the event four different ways of organizing the plebiscites were employed, each implying a rather different result. The simplest method is the majority method whereby a province is polled and the whole area is allocated on the basis of which rival state obtains most votes. On this basis in 1921 Sopron was allocated to Hungary despite many localities voting to join Austria. The creation of such 'national minorities' can be lessened by defining different zones in a province and allowing majorities in the different zones to opt for different state membership. This was applied in Schleswig where one zone voted to join Germany and the other to join

Denmark. Also in the Klagenfurt Basin this method was adopted but here both zones opted for Austria in preference to Yugoslavia. A more sensitive method is to allow minor border adjustments on the basis of the polling returns. This was done in Allenstein and Marienwerder in locating the boundary between Germany and Poland. Finally an attempt was made to draw the German–Polish boundary through industrial Upper Silesia on a commune-by-commune basis. Such a partition involving by far the largest poll led to many problems. Simple voting returns indicated numerous enclaves, for instance. In the end the boundary was drawn by a special commission using the plebiscite results only as a guide.

Clearly nationalism in practice was not as simple as the theory of nation self-determination implies. If the rules for Sopron had been applied to Upper Silesia, for instance, the whole province would have gone to Germany. But there were many more problems which we can only begin to appreciate this far away in time and space. Perhaps the most basic question is who is entitled to vote in such plebiscites? Wartime and its aftermath lead to much migration, some of it forced – should former residents have the vote? In Upper Silesia there were 150, 000 such 'out-voters'. In contrast in the Schlegwig plebiscites voters had to be domiciled in the province since 1900. In any case can a plebiscite ever be entirely fair when one of the two competing states has recently had sovereignty over the province being polled? In Schleswig, for instance, there had been a vigorous programme of Germanization in schools, courts and other state institutions. Similarly in the Klagenfurt Basin Yugoslavia complained about fifty years of Austrian propaganda deceiving the Slavonic voters. In fact one of the most interesting features of these minor boundary exercises was the lack of correspondance between poll results and language patterns. In the Klagenfurt Basin, with its large majority of Slovene-speakers, the people voted to join German-speaking Austria. Similarly in Allenstein, Marienwerder and Upper Siberia voting to join Germany was higher than would be expected from the language distribution. Clearly past political mobilization was cutting across current language status but this was not allowed to happen elsewhere.

3. National determinism: Jovan Cvijic's language maps of Macedonia

According to Cobban (1969) there was a change of emphasis in the practice of nationalism in the second half of the nineteenth century. Annexations occur on nationalist grounds but without asking the 'people'. The expansion of Germany is the prime example with the incorporation of Schleswig and Lorraine by conquest. Here we have a different conception of the politics of nationalism whereby people are designated members of a nation usually on the basis of the language they speak. It is this concept of national determinism which dominated the boundary drawing at Paris in 1919. But even if the language criterion is accepted as a legitimate indication of national preference, and as we have seen plebiscites do not support this assumption, there remains the problems of defining national languages and mapping their distribution. Without the prior existence of nation-states there are no 'standard' languages (except German) but rather various mixtures of dialects. This situation led to a plethora of alternative interpretations of languages and their distribution mostly based upon the nationality of the 'language-expert'. Here we will concentrate on one such author to show how his language maps change over time to reflect the increasing ambition of his own state. Our source for this discussion is H. R. Wilkinson's (1951) *Maps and Politics* possibly the most under-estimated book ever written in political geography. In this study he looks at seventy-three ethnographic maps of Macedonia from 1730 to 1946. This area is interesting because it lies between Yugoslavia/Serbia, Bulgaria, Greece and Albania. Numerous counter-claims as to its national affiliation occurred until it was finally allocated to Yugoslavia in 1919. The geographer Jovan Cvijic played an important part in legitimizing Serbian, and subsequently Yugoslavian claims, on Macedonia. We consider four of his maps here (Figure 14).

Jovan Cvijic was a distinguished physical geographer who had made his name studying the karst scenery of the Balkans. As head of the Department of Geography at the University of Belgrade his reputation was world-wide. At this time geographers were generalists rather than specialists so that it was normal for individuals to study all sections of the discipline. Cvijic, therefore, wrote books on the human geography of the Balkans and it is his ethnographic maps in these studies that concern us here. His first ethnographic map appeared in 1906 and did not attempt to distinguish between Serbians and Bulgarians, classifying both as simply Slavs. However he did tentatively introduce the term 'Macedo-Slav' at this time to indicate that the Slavs of this region were neither Serbians nor Bulgarians. This was counter to most current thinking which extended the Bulgarian nation across Macedonia. Cvijic's new concept was widely criticized and not generally accepted. Cvijic first depicted Macedo-Slavs on his 1909 map which Wilkinson (1951: 163) terms 'revolutionary'. The distribution of Serbs is extended to south of Skoplje and south of them a broad band of Macedo-Slavs are identified. In contrast the Bulgarian distribution is very limited and they are all but excluded from Macedonia. The political significance of identifying these areas as Macedo-Slav rather than Bulgarian is that it gave them *no* national affiliation so that the area was open to future Serbian claims.

This future was not far away. In the Balkan wars (1912–13) Serbia extended its territory southwards and Cvijic's cartography responded accordingly. His 1913 map shows further extensions of Serbs southwards. This does not represent migration but simply Serbian political interests. On this map Serbia gain at the expense of Albanians rather than Bulgarians to reflect the outcome of the wars – Bulgarians now occupied some territory depicted Macedo-Slav in 1909. The latter group remained,

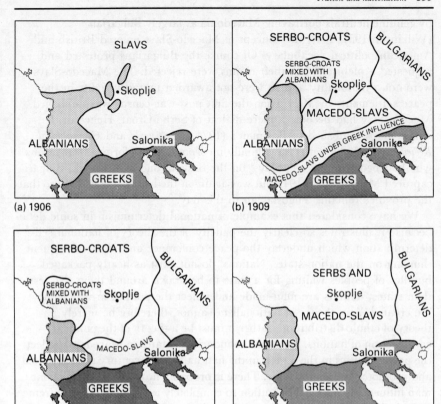

14. Cvijic's language maps of Macedonia (a) 1906 (b) 1909 (c) 1913 (d) 1918

however, as a neutral ethnic mixture transitional between the Serbs and Bulgarians. But for Cvijic they were always what Wilkinson terms 'incipient Serbs'.

In 1918 Cvijic produced his most influential map in his book on the human geography of the Balkans. The book was hailed a masterpiece and his ethnographic map was reproduced in the prestigious French *Annales de Géographie* and *American Geographical Review*. In Britain Cvijic was awarded the Patron's Gold Medal of the *Royal Geographical Society* in part for his work on the Balkans. Hence he was able to influence the Peace Conference as a most distinguished geographer and expert on ethnic distributions in the Balkans. In the 1918 map this 'expertise' now extended Serbian ethnicity into areas formerly depicted as Bulgarian. Although in hindsight Wilkinson (1951) has been able to show the continual biases of Cvijic's work, he was accepted at the Peace Conference as impartial. Whereas in 1913 Serbian annexation of parts of Macedonia was widely interpreted as usurping Bulgarian rights, by 1919 Cvijic had succeeded in justifying Serbia's right to retain Macedonia on nationalist grounds. Despite maps by genuine neutrals portraying Macedonia as largely Bulgarian (Wilkinson 1951: 204), the concept of Macedo-Slavs entered British and American political vocabulary. Of course the Bulgarians protested and requested a plebiscite but their claims were rejected. The Macedo-Slavs were not a nationality and so were not awarded minority rights in the peace settlement. By 1924 when the first post-war census was published, Macedo-Slav had become a mere dialect of Serbo-Croat. Hence in the ethnic maps published in Bowman's (1924) *New World* and *Geographical Review* in 1925 the Serbs have finally incorporated the former 'Bulgarians' who had become 'Macedo-Slavs' on the basis of one man's work. Bulgaria captured Macedonia in 1942 but was again on the losing side in 1945 so that the province remains Yugoslavian to this day.

We have considered this example of national determinism in some detail because it illustrates so clearly the paucity of the theory of national self-determination which underlay the peace conference and most subsequent thinking on the nation-state. 'Nations' do not exist as neatly packaged bundles of peoples waiting for a state to be drawn around them. No less than states, nations are man-made and reflect the politics in which they are created. Any theory of nationalism cannot, therefore be merely a theory of ethnic distribution, rather it must be a theory of the political construction of nations. The final boundaries of states in Macedonia reflect the power politics in the region in the first half of this century as interpreted and promoted by Johan Cvijic. There is probably no other example of one man influencing national definition so completely as Cvijic but this extreme case clarifies the general process. It is to the latter that we now turn.

NAIRN'S THEORY OF NATIONALISM

Although the concepts of iconography, state or nation-idea and raison d'être could have provided the raw material of a political geography theory of nationalism, in fact the theory used by most geographers is that developed by political scientist Karl Deutsch (1953, Jackson 1964: 110–18, Kasperson and Minghi 1969: 211–20). His 'communication' theory of nation and nationalism builds upon Whittlesey's nuclear area and extends it to consideration of the 'communication grid' of a country. A community based upon common language and/or memories is termed a 'people' which is separated from other peoples by a communication gap. When such a people seek power to control their own destinies through the process of nationalism a nationality results. When power is achieved a nationality becomes a nation which on acquiring its own sovereign state becomes a *nation*-state. For Deutsch this communication involves two procedures: assimilation, by which he means additions to the community, and mobilization, by which he means the rise of a political public within the community. The latter is defined by such indices as newspaper readers, literacy, school attendance and so on. Finally Deutsch combines these various concepts into a model of the growth of nations. Here we find the all-too-familiar stages of development, this time 'national development'. Six stages are envisaged as people progress from initial economic exchange processes to the final national stage.

This is a beautiful example of the error of developmentalism. As we have seen in our discussion on nationalism in practice, nations do not simply evolve in a linear sequence. They are made and in their making they encompass contradictory expressions. The rationalism of modernity is combined with the irrationality of ethnic traditionalism. No simple developmental model can cope with both sides of the Janus-like concept simultaneously. We need to move beyond considering nation and nationalism case-by-case as separate processes and see all nationalism as part of a larger unfolding process which started in the nineteenth century and is with us still. This grander perspective is what the world-systems approach offers political geography and we will now apply it to nation and nationalism.

1. Nationalism and uneven development

Nationalism did not occur in isolation. As well as this new political phenomenon, the nineteenth century witnessed many other economic and social changes often summarized by the terms industrialization and urbanization. Of course this parallel is not a coincidence but adequate linkages between the various strands have been difficult to find. Nairn (1977) has provided the basic model to integrate these great processes of change and what follows draws upon his work. Nationalism is the result of the 'tidal wave of modernization' that swept Europe in the nineteenth century. This 'modernization', or more precisely economic development, was not evenly spread, as we know, so that western Europe was more advanced than central and eastern Europe. Nationalism is then a compensatory reaction to this uneven development. Beginning in the area bordering the advanced zone the new rising urban-industrial interests were unable to compete with the more efficient core producers. They have to evolve strategies to survive, to prevent their peripheralization. We have already discussed one part of their reaction, List's new economic theories which led to the Zollverein customs union in 1843. But economic policy alone is not enough. How can workers be persuaded that dearer food caused by tariffs is in their interests? The answer is to appeal to 'higher' values than mere material needs. The *only* resource available to these local capitalist interests not available to the metropolitan interests was their cultural affinity to their 'people'. By emphasizing differences between ethnic communities, local interests could form broad national alliances with which to challenge the core. Hence the regions where nationalism blossomed as a major new force on the European stage were central Europe and the unification nationalisms of Germany and Italy. From this beginning nationalism spread like a wave following the uneven development unleashed on the world by 'modernization'. Next came the separation nationalisms of eastern Europe to be followed by the nationalisms outside Europe in the twentieth century. But nationalism became more than a reaction of semi-periphery and periphery. With the demise of British hegemony, the new vigorous nationalism spread to the core as a major force in the subsequent political competition resulting, as we have seen, in the second phase of formal imperialism. By the twentieth century nationalism was to become the dominant ideology throughout all zones of the world-economy. Quite simply it was too good a territorial strategy to pass over. After all the initial upheavals it settled down to become what we previously identified as the seventh of the territorial strategies in Table 6 – the obscuring of social conflict.

Where do the two sides of nationalism fit into this theory? So far the use of 'tradition' has been made clear but what of the 'progress' side of the ideology? Although the urban-industrial interests of the semi-periphery and periphery used images of an idyllic past to mobilize the people, they could not be true conservatives and prevent progress. The whole purpose of the strategy was to close ranks with a view to catching up the core. This could only be done by borrowing the salient features of the modernization against which the movement was reacting. A 'mediaeval' Germany or Italy would be no match for a modern Britain or France. Hence the rhetoric of nationalism with its glorification of the past was ultimately only a cover for rapid modernization. The classic case is, of course, late-nineteenth-century Germany where massive industrial growth went hand in hand with a popular German cultural 'revival'.

2. Nationalism and 'mass society'

This model describes, in Nairn's (1977) term, the 'contours' of nationalism as a diffusion process out from its central European heartland. But there is something missing. Both Gellner (1964) and Nairn (1977) point out that there is an important psychological aspect to nationalism. As Giddens (1981) observes the dominant elites did not have to force-feed the masses their nationalism, there was a receptive public out there waiting to be mobilized. The primordial sentiments that were aroused indicate a particular need for identity. As well as threatening the dominant interests outside the core, the tidal wave of modernization was undermining the everyday life of ordinary people. Many were migrating to industrial zones where their existence was routinized in ways never previously experienced. Here we have the alienation of mass society based upon the breakdown of tradition. Nationalism gave the people back their tradition and provided an identity in an alien-world. It is for this reason that nationalism is particularly associated with periods of radical disruption such as wars and as, Giddens (1981) emphasizes, strong charismatic leadership. In short nationalism acts as compensation for the alienation of mass society.

3. Nationalism and intellectuals

Finally what of figures such as Cvijic in Serbia? The intelligentsia have played an important role in the rise of nationalist movements everywhere (Smith 1981: 81), not least by giving them a respectability they hardly deserved. The new class of intellectuals of nineteenth-century Europe, often from lower-middle-class backgrounds, were able to provide the historical, philosophical, ethnographic and even geographical basis of the new nationalisms. As Nairn (1977: 100) puts it, the dilemma of underdevelopment only becomes nationalism when it is 'refracted' into a society in a certain way. The intellegentsia were the agents of refraction, the most 'advanced' part of the new national middle class. Nairn (1977: 117) postulates a social diffusion process starting with a small intelligentsia, initially reacting to the French Revolution, which he terms phase A. This is followed by phase B, from 1815 to 1848 in Europe where the ideology spreads through the middle classes. But it is still a minority movement and this accounts for its ultimate failure in the 1848 revolutions. Phase C occurs in the second half of the nineteenth century in Europe when it diffuses to the lower classes and modern popular nationalism is born. The intelligentsia were therefore the initial purveyors of ideas to be used for the general interests of their class. But they continued to be of use in sustaining and developing the special theories underlying each nationalism. Jovan Cvijic fits in to our story as a dominant intellectual justifying and charting an expansionary minor nationalism of the early twentieth century.

Partly because of this intellectual input, nation and nationalism will remain a controversial topic both within and beyond political geography. Like all general social theories which cover complex topics, Nairn's arguments are open to many criticisms from political enemies. In his case we can identify both Marxist and non-Marxist criticisms. The latter have been presented by Orridge (1981b), and Gellner (1983) has developed some of the ideas presented above while being careful to distance himself from Nairn's neo-Marxism: the spread of capitalism/industrialization is replaced by the spread of education. Marxist criticism is best represented by Blaut (1980) who objects to Nairn's 'relegation' of class struggle to below nationalism, the association of nationalism to fascism in the Janus. model and more generally to the Euro-centric 'diffusionalism' of Nairn's model which under-rates the contribution of the non-European periphery to nationalism and 'national liberation' in particular. Blaut provides an alternative space – time identification of nationalism with the source in USA (1776) and Haiti (1804). Blaut's critique raises several important questions involving definitions and whether identification of nationalism as a false consciousness relegates or enhances the fundamental theoretical importance of class struggle. These other writings should be consulted for further debate on this subject. We are arguing here that we have the outline of a materialist theory of nationalism to counteract the production of ideology by nationalist intellectuals. Whatever the criticisms, for the most part misplaced, the fact remains that Nairn's theory provides a major attempt at explaining nationalism which transcends the ideology itself. In Nairn's (1977: 332) own words:

> My belief is that the only frame of reference which is of any utility here is world history as a whole . . . Most approaches to the question are vitiated from the start by a country-by-country attitude. Of course it is the ideology of world nationalism itself which induces also this road by suggesting that human society consists essentially of several hundred different and discrete 'nations', each of which does (or ought to) have its own postage stamps and national soul. The secret of the forest is the trees, so to speak.

By interpreting the world-economy as the 'forest' we are able to provide a far better understanding of the individual 'trees' or nations. Nation and nationalism is a topic which clearly illustrates the advantages of a world-systems approach and as such can be integrated into the political geography being developed in this book.

Chapter 5

RETHINKING ELECTORAL GEOGRAPHY

THE LIBERAL HERITAGE

Quantitative electoral geography

1. Geography of voting
2. Geographical influences in voting
3. Geography of representation

A systems model of electoral geography

1. Input, throughput, output
2. Critique: liberal assumptions

Coulter's global model of liberal democracy

1. Liberal democracy and social mobilization
2. Two interpretations of a relationship

THE GEOGRAPHY OF POLITICAL IDEOLOGIES

International political groupings

1. Socialist 'internationals'
2. International groupings on the 'right'

The geography of liberalism

1. Discontinuity or continuity?
2. Conflicts and ideologies
3. Aggressive and defensive liberalisms

PARTIES AND POWER

Party and government: the 'great act of organization'

1. Alternative organizations of control
2. Section and party in USA, 1828–1920

Party and state: the dialectics of electoral geography

1. The two geographies of elections
2. Contrasting geographies of power and support

Parties and world-economy: the reality of power

1. 'New politics' and the world-economy
2. Changing agendas in British politics

Chapter 5

RETHINKING ELECTORAL GEOGRAPHY

If success can be measured by quantity of production then electoral geography is the success story of modern political geography. In the last two decades there have been hundreds of studies on the geography of elections, so much so that some have argued that the growth has been 'disproportionate' in relation to the general needs of political geography (Muir, 1981, 204). In fact, as Muir (1981: 203) points out, ideas on the role of electoral geography in political geography range from those who imply that it is 'the very core and substance of political geography' to those who feel that it does not belong in political geography at all! Obviously the position taken in such a debate depends ultimately on the definition of political geography being employed. In our political geography elections play a key role at the scale of ideology in channelling conflicts safely into constitutional arenas. Hence we need to consider electoral geography but not necessarily in its usual form.

There is a second debate on the nature of electoral geography which is much more important. Given the rapid increase in these studies, what is it they are adding to our knowledge of political geography? It is not at all clear where electoral geography is leading. The goal of most studies seems to be nothing more than understanding the particular situation under consideration. The result has been a general failure to link geographies of elections together into a coherent body of knowledge. In short we have a 'bitty' and unco-ordinated pattern of researches which have produced a large number of isolated findings but few generalizations. There are some exceptions, and these are described below, but on the whole quality has lagged behind quantity of production and few would now claim electoral geography as a 'success story' Hence the need for some rethinking.

Although electoral geography has not been explicit in its theorizing its implicit theory is easy to identify. In effect electoral geography has simply accepted the political assumptions of the core countries in which it has developed. These assumptions can be summarized by the term 'liberal democracy' and in the first section of this chapter we review electoral studies in geography as a 'liberal heritage'. Unfortunately the narrowness of these past studies has led to major omissions in coverage. In particular comparison between elections in different countries is only conspicuous by its absence in electoral geography. Hence we have to 'bolster' this liberal heritage by drawing on some work in comparative politics which enables us to appreciate more fully the implications of the liberal assumptions.

Problems of omission of important topics is the reason why the title of this chapter has had to be prefixed by the phrase 'rethinking'. In the second section we deal with the geography of political ideologies which is, apart from the major exception of nationalism, a completely new subject for political geography. In our discussion we relate liberalism and socialism to our previous discussion of nationalism and set them both within a world-systems framework. In the final section of this chapter we come to consideration of what elections are all about – the allocation of political power. To understand this fully we need to give much more attention to the role of political parties than is usual in electoral geography. In this section we come across our old friend Schattschneider again and develop his ideas in conjunction with the theories of the state discussed in the previous chapter.

THE LIBERAL HERITAGE

In some ways electoral geography is like geopolitics in being represented in the work of some of the founding fathers of modern geography. In the case of electoral geography we can cite Andre Siegfried of the French regional school whose 1913 study of western France under the Third Republic has long been regarded as a classic of its genre. Siegfried is usually considered the 'father' of electoral geography because of his method of mapping election results and comparing them with maps of possible explanatory factors. At about the same time Carl Sauer (1918) was contributing to the perennial American debate on how to define congressional districts. As the founder of America's cultural-regional school of geography it is perhaps not surprising that his solution involved representation by geographical region. Other studies could be cited but until the 1960s electoral studies in geography were sporadic with no sustained effort except perhaps in France.

All this changed with the so-called quantitative revolution in geography. This affected human geography in particular and resulted in the decline of qualitative regional studies and the rise of quantitative systematic studies, especially in economic and urban geography. As we noted in Chapter 1, most of political geography was passed by in these intellectual upheavals but this is not so for electoral geography. The regular publication of volumes of electoral data neatly organized by electoral areas provided a wealth of material for the new quantitatively orientated geographers (Taylor 1978). Hence the massive rise of electoral studies in geography and the 'disproportionate' effort that electoral geography attracted within political geography. The first part of this section describes this quantitative electoral geography, the second part describes an attempt to co-ordinate this effort in a systems framework and the final part looks beyond these electoral studies to a critique of a global model of liberal democracy that geographers never achieved.

QUANTITATIVE ELECTORAL GEOGRAPHY

There were three aspects of the new quantitative approach which were applied to electoral geography. The most common we can term 'standard statistical analysis' which was widely used to study the *geography of voting*. Within geography there was a growing interest in the role of spatial factors and this is reflected in the theme *geographical influences in elections*. Finally probability modelling of spatial distributions was employed in studies of the *geography of representation*. This triology of electoral geography studies was first identified by McPhail (1971) and subsequently used by Busteed (1975) and Taylor and Johnston (1979). This latter source provides a comprehensive 'state of the art' review for the 1970s and in this discussion we summarize the salient features of that study.

1. Geography of voting

This follows in the Siegfried tradition in that its purpose is the explanation of particular voting maps. In modern geography of voting studies, however, cartographic comparisons have given way to statistical analysis. It is these studies which have born the brunt of the criticism of electoral geography. Generally speaking the explanation of a particular voting pattern has become an end in itself with the result that many sound quantitative analyses added up to very little in terms of understanding elections. Taylor and Johnston (1979) attempted to overcome this fundamental deficiency by introducing the work of Stein Rokkan (1970) into electoral geography to provide a framework in which geographies of voting could be interpreted.

We have already come across part of Rokkan's modelling in Chapter 2 where we introduced his geopolitical model of Europe. Associated with that model is a second model that concentrates upon the conflicts *within* each state. Rokkan (1970) argued that there have been four major conflicts in modern Europe which result from the two fundamental processes of modernization, the national revolution emanating from France and the industrial revolution emanating from Britain. Each of these processes produces two potential conflicts. These are subject versus dominant culture and church versus state from the national revolution and agriculture versus industry and capital versus labour for the industrial revolution. Each conflict may produce a social cleavage within any one country. But each country has a unique history in which these conflicts are played out. Rokkan argues that the particular mixtures of cleavages that occur among European states deriving from these conflicts are reflected today in the variety of political party systems in Europe.

Rokkan (1970) terms this a model of alternative alliances and oppositions. For each European state the nation-building group made alliances with one side or other in these various conflicts forcing the opposition to forge a counter-alliance. Before the full effects of franchise extensions were felt (*c.* 1900) nation-builders in the dominant culture had a choice of secular or religious alliances and agricultural or industrial alliances. According to Rokkan (1970) the choices made in these conflicts has largely determined the great variety of political parties on the centre and right of European politics. After 1900, as franchise reforms became effective, the final capital–labour cleavage came into operation to produce much more uniformity on the left in European politics.

Let us consider some examples of the process Rokkan describes. In Britain the nation-building group allied with a national church and landed interests (the Tories and later Conservatives) against an alliance of dissenters, industrial interests and minority cultures (the Whigs, Radicals and later Liberals). After 1900 the rise of the Labour Party has produced a particular right–centre–left cleavage represented by three political parties whose pattern of support in terms of votes still reflects these historical cleavages. Although the Conservatives have eclipsed the Liberals and taken their 'industrial interest' vote, the latter party has remained strong in non-conformist and particularly peripheral zones of Britain. Throughout their decline Liberals maintained MPs from celtic Britain (Cornwall, central Wales and northern Scotland) when everywhere else rejected their candidates.

A different set of alliances developed in Scandinavian countries. Here the nation-builders allied with national church and urban interests leaving an opposition alliance of periphery, dissenters and landed interests. In Norway the latter formed the 'Old Left' which defeated the King's government alliance in 1882 to usher in liberal democracy. After 1900 and the gradual rise of the Labour Party, the Old Left alliance disintegrated so that Norway has inherited a five-party system of Conservatives on the right, Liberal, Agrarian and Christian Peoples Parties from the 'Old Left' and Labour on the left. The cleavages are reflected in this party system as follows:

- Northern periphery (Labour) versus South-east Core (Conservative)

- South-west periphery (Liberal, Christian) versus South-east Core (Conservative)

- Bokmal language (Liberal) versus Nynorsk (Conservative)

- Teetotal (Christian) versus Non-Teetotal (Conservative)

- Dissenters (Christian) versus National Church (Conservative)

- Rural (Agrarian) versus Urban (Conservative)

- Rural workers (Labour) versus Landowners (Agrarian)
- Urban workers (Labour) versus Industrialists (Conservative)

Not all of these cleavages are equally important so that Labour has been the largest single party since it formed its first government in 1936. The major difference with Britain is the separation of the dissenter vote from the Liberals through the Christian People's party and the separation of rural and urban conservative interests in the Agrarian and Conservative parties. Rokkan has illustrated how these cleavages continue to be reflected in the geographical pattern of votes for these five parties (Taylor and Johnston 1979: 172–7).

Rokkan identifies eight different patterns of nation-building alliances and opposition counter-alliances all of which are reflected in at least one Western European state today. This particular model summarizes European history and is not, therefore, generally applicable outside Europe. Nevertheless the process of modernization that Rokkan describes has spread beyond Europe and similar cleavages can be identified in non-European countries. This is further explored in Taylor and Johnston (1979: 196–206).

It is the core–periphery cleavage which has attracted most geographical research attention as might be expected. Even in the longest established nation-states political mobilization may not be complete as we have seen in the brief discussion of resurgence of national separatism in the last chapter. Models incorporating a core–periphery dimension such as those of Deutch and Rokkan imply a lessening of the relevance of location as socio-economic criteria come to dominate modern politics. Hence to many social scientists recent expressions of separation nationalism were unexpected. But they did not appear out of nothing. In Britain, for instance, Scottish and Welsh nationalism may have only become a significant political force in the late 1960s and 1970s but that does not mean that before then Scottish and Welsh voters all behaved as typical British citizens. Hechter (1975) has shown that sectionalism persisted in British politics throughout both of the two party systems of Conservative–Liberal and Conservative–Labour. Figure 15 shows a small part of his results. Eight elections from 1885 to 1966 were analysed by counties in terms of predicting the Conservative vote from seven socio-economic variables. The residuals from each analysis indicate how the vote percentage in a particular county deviates from that expected due to its socio-economic structure. Positive residuals indicate a pro-Conservative bias and negative residuals an anti-Conservative bias. The average residuals over all eight elections are distributed in Figure 15(a) where two distinctive 'tails' are prominent. On the pro-Conservative side there are three overwhelmingly strong counties – the three most protestant Ulster counties which consistently voted Unionist and hence Conservative in this period. The anti-Conservative tail is larger and includes fourteen counties, all in celtic Wales and Scotland. The geography of these extreme residuals is shown in Figure 15(b) which defines three contiguous sections which have not conformed to normal British voting behaviour. Quite simply British elections were never completely nationalized and sectionalism persisted to be reactivated in part as 'nationalism' after 1966.

2. Geographical influences in voting

For some geographers analysis of voting data by areal units is not considered sufficiently 'spatial' to form a distinctive electoral geography (Reynolds and Archer 1969). Standard statistical techniques, such as the regression analysis used by Hechter above, ignore the spatial context of the areal units which are each treated as separate and independent observations. For this group of researchers such simple geography of voting analyses were throwing away the geography! Hence standard statistical analyses of voting returns were replaced by location models which emphasized the local context within which voting occurred. In this way simple descriptive geography *of* voting would be replaced by a more sophisticated geographical influence *in* voting. This argument fitted in well with the behavioural school of geography which was emerging in the late 1960s. The basic position is summarized by the title of Cox's (1969) seminal paper: 'The voting decision in a spatial context'.

There are four basic processes that may lead to local influences on voting decisions. (i) *Candidate voting*, more commonly termed 'friends and neighbours effect', has been shown to occur in American, Japanese, Irish and New Zealand elections (Taylor and Johnston 1979: 274–94). It merely consists of a candidate receiving additional votes from his or her home area. The most obvious example of this is in American presidential elections where candidates usually do better in their home state. (ii) *Issue voting* occurs where a particular topic in an election is of more importance to some areas than others. (iii) *Campaign effects* reflect differential influences of the campaign. This may involve particular targeting as in presidential elections when additional effort is put into key states or more simply local campaigning differences in terms of resources used (Johnston 1977). (iv) The *neighbourhood effect* is the most studied geographical influence in voting. It attempts to explain why it is that parties do better than expected in their strongest areas.

The neighbourhood effect postulates the following process. For any individual in an election campaign there are two sources of information. The general information from the mass media available to everybody and the particular information derived from local contacts. The latter will be biased to the extent that the individual lives in a partisan area. Hence general information will go through a partisan filter in the voting decision-making process. The result will be that *all* classes living in working-class areas will be more likely to vote for the 'natural' party of the area and *all*

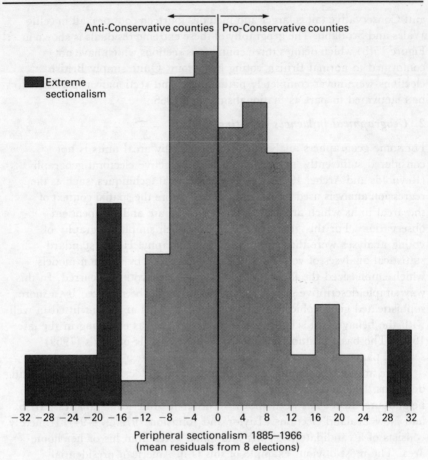

Anti-Conservative counties | Pro-Conservative counties

■ Extreme
  sectionalism

Peripheral sectionalism 1885–1966
(mean residuals from 8 elections)

15.   Sectionalism in British elections, 1855–1966 (a) Distribution of residuals
(b) Geography of extreme residuals (on page **149**)

classes living in middle-class areas will be more likely to vote for the
'natural' party of that area. It has been shown from survey data, for
instance, that working-class voters living in working-class districts are
more likely to vote Communist in France, Labour in Britain and
Democrat in USA than working-class voters living in middle-class areas. A
simple example will illustrate this effect. In Britain the two extreme
locations in political terms are mining constituencies and resort
constituencies. In their 1960s survey, Butler and Stokes (1969: 183) showed
that whereas 91 per cent of working-class residents voted Labour in
mining constituencies, only 48 per cent of working-class residents voted
Labour in resort constituencies. This large difference can be explained, in
part at least, by the neighbourhood effect.

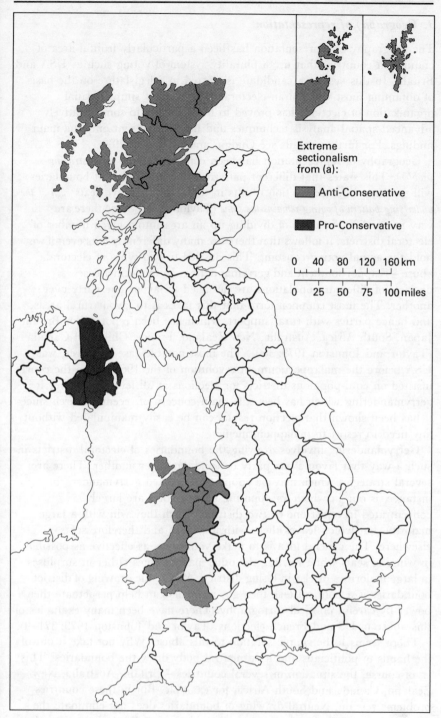

15. (b)

3. Geography of representation

The geography of representation has been a particularly fruitful area of enquiry in countries that use a plurality system of voting such as USA and Britain. In this system a candidate is elected to a legislature on the basis of obtaining most votes in an electoral district. This simple spatial organization of elections has proved to be amenable to some relatively advanced spatial analysis techniques and here we present only the main findings. For further details see Gudgin and Taylor (1979).

Geography of representation has been concerned with the *districting problem*. This states that different patterns of electoral district boundaries will produce different election results in terms of legislative seats *even if the underlying pattern of voting remains the same* (Taylor 1973). Since there are very many different ways of dividing up an area into a given number of electoral districts, it follows that there are many different results even if we hold the actual voting constant. This has led to two types of electoral abuse – reapportionment and gerrymandering. In the former case districts of different populations are designed to favour one party over another. The most common form that this takes is to favour rural areas, and hence parties with rural support, which has been reported for Britain, Japan, South Africa, Australia, New Zealand, France, Chile and Canada (Taylor and Johnston 1979: 360). The most notable case, however, was USA before the malapportionment revolution of the 1960s when the courts insisted on equi-populous districts for elections at all levels. However it is gerrymandering which has been the main concern of recent research since it has been shown that election results can be easily manipulated without any need to resort to malappointment.

Gerrymandering involves drawing the boundaries of electoral districts in such a way that favours one party or candidate over another. There are several strategies which may be adopted. A stacked gerrymander, for instance, is one in which an opposing party's votes are largely concentrated into just one or two districts which they win with a large majority, but which leaves them with few votes and therefore seats elsewhere. The general idea is to make your votes as effective as possible in winning seats while wasting the other party's votes either in surpluses in large majorities or else in losing districts. Where the drawing of district boundaries is a political task then governments can help perpetuate their power by careful political cartography. There have been many examples of this abuse in US and French elections (Taylor and Johnston 1979: 371–9).

There seems to be simple solution to this abuse. Why not take it out of the hands of politicians and let a neutral body draw the boundaries? This is, of course, the situation in several countries – Britain, Australia, New Zealand, Canada and South Africa, for example. But in these countries problems remain. Neutral drawing of boundaries does not eliminate the districting problem: it merely removes the intent to discriminate against an opponent. A neutrally drawn districting plan will not necessarily be neutral in effect. To think otherwise is to subscribe to what Dixon (1968; Taylor and Gudgin 1976a) terms the 'myth of non-partisan cartography' Such districting is merely 'innocently partisan' and employs 'the three monkey's policy – speak no politics, see no politics, hear no politics' (Dixon 1971). This is the most concrete example in political geography of Schattschneider's dictum that 'all organization is bias'.

But what is the nature of the bias instilled in election results even by neutral commissioners? This depends upon the spatial pattern of voters as reflected in the level of segregation of voters supporting different parties. Since party systems are based upon social class, religious and/or ethnic criterion which are also important in defining residential segregation, it follows that we can usually identify areas of support for different parties. In short the spatial distribution of support for particular parties is relatively uneven. When district boundaries are added to this map they produce districts with different mixes of each party's supporters. This process can be modelled to show the possible effects of the procedure. The basic result is that arbitrary (or neutral) drawing of boundaries will inevitably tend to favour the majority party in the area being districted. In Britain, for instance this means that Labour gets a higher proportion of seats than votes in urban and industrial counties whereas Conservatives obtain a higher proportion of seats than votes in suburban and rural counties. Overall the two biases tend to cancel themselves out although the majority party in the country as a whole (either Labour or Conservative depending on the election) will have a disproportionate majority in Parliament. This is sometimes known as the cube-law and results from the particular mix of social segregation and scale of constituency underlying the spatial organization of elections in Britain (Taylor and Johnston 1979: 392–6).

If partisan districting (gerrymandering) and non-partisan districting (innocent gerrymandering) are unsatisfactory why not employ bi-partisan districting where parties agree between them on the district boundaries? This solution has become quite popular in USA where both informal and formal bi-partisan commissions have been created so that bi-partisan districting has been widespread since the reapportionment revolution (Tufte 1973). The problem is that such districting omits one important interest from the negotiations, namely that of the voter. Bi-partisan districting tends to produce sets of safe districts for each party. This means that there are few marginal seats where voters may effectively cause a seat to change hands. Bi-partisan districting takes the uncertainty out of elections! The classic case of this occurred in the 1974 congressional election in the immediate aftermath of the Watergate scandal. This hurt the Republican party in the polling booths but not so much in Congress since the existence of a relatively large number of safe Republican seats insulated the party from the worst effects of its unpopularity (Taylor and Johnston 1979: 406–7).

Since bi-partisan districting lessens the influence of voters on election results it is sometimes referred to as bi-partisan gerrymandering (Mayhew 1971). This is a final confirmation that in the geography of representation all organization is bias.

A SYSTEMS MODEL OF ELECTORAL GEOGRAPHY

The organization of quantitative electoral geography is in many ways unsatisfactory. Two problems stand out. First the subject matter consists of three distinct areas of interest with little cross-reference. Second the subject matter is not integrated into the mainstream of political geography. To be sure examples of both linkages can be found – the relation between geography of representation and the segregation in geographies of voting and the relation between geography of voting in peripheries and more general core–periphery models in political geography, for example – but such links have been no more than perfunctory and undeveloped. For all the research effort of the 1970s electoral geography had become an unco-ordinated and isolated sub-discipline.

The way out of this impasse was not for more empirical research but for a new synthetic framework to integrate these various themes. Such an approach was readily available in systems analysis which had been around in political geography for more than a decade without making any important impact. Although text books (for example, Bergman 1975, Muir 1981) paid lip service to systems thinking, this did not go as far as actually influencing the presentation of most of their political geography (Burnett and Taylor 1981). The simplest model employed was Easton's (1965) political system which could be reduced to just four elements – input, throughput, output plus feed back. Such a framework seems to fit electoral geography – which is, after all, commonly thought of as dealing with electoral *systems*. Johnston (1979) attempted to use this approach to integrate studies of elections with administrative *systems* but no satisfactory overall framework was produced.

1. Input, throughput and output

The most explicit use of systems thinking in electoral geography is Taylor's (1978) use of systems concepts to order his discussion in a review of electoral geography (Figure 16). Geography of voting and geographical influences in voting become the input to the system. Geography of representation becomes the throughput leaving the geographical effects of the resulting legislature/executive as the output of the system. Three implications of this reordering of the literature were identified. First, electoral geography was given a purpose and focus beyond the elections themselves. Second, the current emphasis on one part of the system – the input – seemed excessive in comparison with the other parts. Third, in contrast, the massive neglect of the output was highlighted. This was the reason electoral geography seemed to have no clear direction. By treating

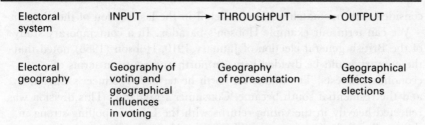

Electoral system	INPUT ⟶	THROUGHPUT ⟶	OUTPUT
Electoral geography	Geography of voting and geographical influences in voting	Geography of representation	Geographical effects of elections

16. A systems model applied to electoral geography

elections as an end in themselves, the actual purpose of election – the producing of legislatures and governments – had been largely forgotten. Hence the systems approach pointed towards a redirection of electoral geography beyond input and throughput.

Johnston (1980b) has taken the argument one stage further and located electoral geography as part of a systems-orientated political geography. Feedback loops between input and output round off the system and integrate electoral and political processes. This is clearly illustrated by American pork-barrel politics whereby politicians ensure the area they represent is well treated by government and they expect, in return, the gratitude of citizens to be expressed in their votes. In the US Congress, for instance, representatives and senators try to obtain places on spending committees that affect policies most relevant to their own constituents interests. If they can achieve such committee positions, especially chairmanships, then they can usually benefit the district or state they represent. Although this process is difficult to substantiate statistically (Johnston 1982) there is no doubt that it is an important element of American politics. Although less recognized, the same process will occur in other countries such as Britain, where there are other explicitly geographical government effects such as in regional and inner city policy.

2. Critique: liberal assumptions

While providing a solution to the problems of electoral geography enumerated at the beginning of this discussion, the systems approach has proved to be more important for what it reveals rather than what it solves. Quite simply the systems approach has opened up a real pandora's box. The assumptions upon which electoral geography has been built are laid bare. They turn out to be the classic liberal assumptions of the twentieth-century core states: a receptive government responds to an electorate that articulates its demands through its representatives. All of a sudden, conflicts have disappeared, history is forgotten and political parties are nothing more than vehicles for transmitting candidate and voter preferences. But things are never as simple as they seem. Sometimes there is a complete mismatch between input and output. When this occurs it is difficult to see how the simple liberal model can cope with the evidence. I will give just one example here to illustrate the argument and we will consider such mismatches in more detail in the last section of the chapter.

We can term our example Hobson's paradox. In a contemporary study of the British general election of January 1910, Hobson (1968) noted that the country could be divided between north and south in terms of economic interests. The industrial north he termed 'Producer's England' and the residential south became 'Consumer's England'. This division was reflected heavily in the voting returns with the Liberals polling strong in the north and the Conservatives likewise in the south. The interesting point, however, is that this voting pattern is inconsistent with each region's economic interests. Both parties inherited nineteenth-century traditions based upon the old urban–rural cleavage so that Liberals maintained their free-trade stance and Conservatives campaigned on a policy of tariff reform (protectionism). The paradox is that Consumer's England voted for protection and hence increased prices whereas Producer's England voted for free trade exposing its industries to American and German competition. We will not resolve this paradox here – it is difficult to see how the systems approach can cope with it beyond designating it as an historical anomoly. We will provide other paradoxes below to show that such 'anomolies' are indeed quite common.

The reason why electoral geography can get into such a muddle is that its liberal assumptions are interpreted as self-evident and innately proper. The liberal democracy model upon which it is based is a normative argument which regards itself as the rational and correct culmination of the western political tradition. But if it is so good why has the 'West' had so much trouble transplanting its parliamentary ideals to the periphery? The popular will as expressed in elections may produce changes in government in core countries but elsewhere several other procedures can be found. For example, on Figure 17 all 'irregular executive transfers' as identified by Taylor and Hudson (1971: 150–3) for the period 1948–67 are

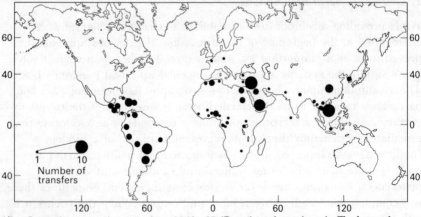

17. Irregular executive transfers, 1948–67 (Based on data given in Taylor and Hudson 1971)

plotted. They define these as a change of government accomplished outside the conventional legal procedures in effect at the time of the change and with actual or threatened violence. Their period of study covers the post-Second World War economic boom in the world-economy but this did not prevent 147 of these irregular transfers occurring. Only one occurred in the core – de Gaulle's return to power in France in 1958 – and there are only two other cases in Europe, in Czechoslovakia in 1948 and Greece in 1967. The remaining 144 cases are in Latin America, Africa and Asia. This is a classic case of a periphery political process which is almost entirely missing in the core. Electoral geography should no longer treat elections as an ideal for they should be seen realistically as just one of several means of choosing governments, and one with an extreme geographical bias.

The only political geographer to comment on the relative lack of liberal democracy in the periphery is Prescott (1969: 378) but he treats it merely as a data problem which prevents 'profitable geographical analysis'. Clearly the *geography* of elections as the global pattern of a particular government-creating institution is a topic sorely missing from quantitative electoral geography. Fortunately it is not a theme neglected by political scientists. Given our world-systems approach it is important that we consider global scale analyses of liberal democracy as a prelude to our own interpretation. We present one such study whose methodology is entirely consistent with quantitative approaches in modern geography.

COULTER'S GLOBAL MODEL OF LIBERAL DEMOCRACY

A major contribution of political science to the rise of modern quantitative social science was the production of large scale data sets covering almost all countries in the world (for example, Banks and Textor 1963; Russett *et al*. 1963). This allowed researchers to carry out comparative political studies on a scale never previously achieved. The comparative politics study most well-known to political geographers is Russett (1967) and Berry's (1969) 'moribund backwater' review briefly alluded to in Chapter 2. Russett's work has subsequently been introduced into political geography (for example, Muir 1981: 198–203) but in many ways Coulter's (1975) study of liberal democracy is much more relevant to political geography. Russett's (1967) study appeals to geographers because of its use of the regional concept and its relation to political integration. But such integration between states is not a major issue in most parts of the world. Coulter (1975), on the other hand, attempts to test Deutch's (1961) model of social mobilization at a global scale. Since Deutch's work is widely used in political geography it follows that Coulter's study is of particular interest in linking Deutch's model to the global scale.

1. Liberal democracy and social mobilization

Coulter uses a classic quantitative geography research design. The first step is to define the 'problem map' to be explained. This involves measuring degrees of liberal democracy across eighty-five different states. He identifies three aspects of liberal democracy – political competitiveness, political participation and public liberties – and combines them into a single index (Coulter 1975: 1–3). Multi-party elections, voter participation and freedom of group oppositions are all elements of this index so that it effectively measures the variations in the degree of importance of elections in determining governments. Variations in liberal democracy for the period 1946–66 are shown in Figure 18 which can be interpreted as the obverse of Figure 17.

In defining the variables to explain this map he keeps very close to Deutch's ideas on social mobilization and democracy. This is another aspect of Deutch's communication model of political development which we have previously discussed in its application to nation and nationalism. In the case of liberal democracy Deutch (1961) postulates the mobilization of people out of traditional patterns of life and into new values and behaviours. This occurs to the extent that a population is urbanized, is literate, is exposed to mass media, is employed in non-primary occupations and is relatively affluent. Coulter (1975), therefore, defines five sets of variables to produce indices of urbanization, education, communication, industrialization and economic development. These are measured both as levels for 1960 and as rates of change for 1946–66.

The global model of liberal democracy is a multiple regression analysis with liberal democracy as dependent and the five aspects of social mobilization as independent variables. The results are reasonably good with economic development being the best explanation of liberal democracy followed by the communication index. However, these are not really separate explanations since they are very highly correlated (r = +0.94). Nevertheless Coulter (1975) has shown that liberal democracy can

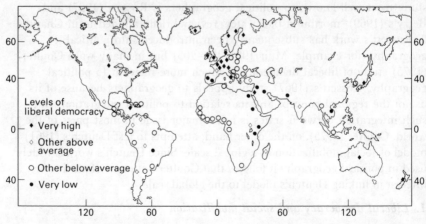

18. World map of liberal democracy (Based on data given in Coulter 1975)

be statistically accounted for, in large measure, by the indices of social mobilization.

2. Two interpretations of a relationship

Coulter's results are summarized in Figure 19(a) which shows the basic trend line whereby an increase in social mobilization is associated with an increase in liberal democracy. Also shown on this diagram is Coulter's interpretation of his results. All countries which lie within one standard error of the trend line are termed optimally democratized. By this he means that the level of liberal democracy in these countries is about as high as would be expected on the basis of their social mobilization. By using the term optimal he implies that politics in these countries is correctly adjusted to their social situation. Among this group we find all the Western European states as we might expect but Haiti and South Africa are also designated optimally democratized. Countries which lie below the optimally democratized band in Figure 19(a) are designated under-democratized indicating a lower level of liberal democracy than expected on the basis of social mobilization. Such countries include Spain and Portugal and so we might be tempted to argue that the democratic revolutions in these two countries after 1966 represent a move to conform with Deutch's model of political development. Countries lying above the middle band are designated over-democratized since they have 'more' liberal democracy than their social mobilization would warrant. These include Greece, Uganda and Chile and we may interpret moves against liberal democracy after 1966 by the Greek colonels, Idi Amin and General Pinochet as similarly contributing to their country's conforming to Deutch's model.

Perhaps the most surprising result of this analysis is that Coulter (1975) finds USSR to be optimally democratized and the USA to be under-

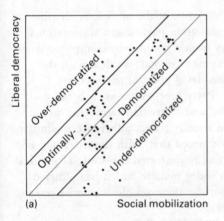
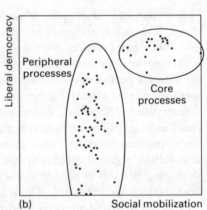

19. Liberal democracy and social mobilization (a) As a trend line (b) As two clusters

democratized! This is counter to our expectations although it does not mean that the USSR is more liberal than the USA but simply that, relative to their respective levels of social mobilization, the USSR scores higher on liberal democracy. This result must make us wonder about the model, however. Either the measurements are unsatisfactory or else the structure of the model is incorrect. We will argue here that both are at fault. In Figure 19(b) the same scatter of points is presented in a completely different way. Instead of concentrating on a trend line we identify two clusters of points one defined by a vertical oval and the other by a horizontal oval. They represent separate, non-overlapping levels of social mobilization. But as we have seen the most important component of social mobilization is economic development. We shall, therefore, interpret these two distinct levels of 'social mobilization' as representing economic core and periphery processes. Now the scatter of points begins to make some sense. *All* core countries experience liberal democracy. In peripheral countries there are a wide range of political systems showing many different levels of liberal democracy. This will depend upon the nature of the peripheral state discussed in the previous chapter.

This interpretation makes much more sense than Coulter's global model. It is entirely consistent with our world-systems framework in its emphasis upon two different sets of processes operating in the world-economy. Once again a world-systems interpretation has been found to be superior to a developmental one, in this case one that sees countries on an 'optimal' ladder of political development. Quite simply politics do not develop separately country-by-country but are all part of a larger unfolding system of political-economy.

THE GEOGRAPHY OF POLITICAL IDEOLOGIES

This section has the purpose of rectifying two of the omissions identified above. First, we concentrate our discussion on parties at a transnational level. Our initial step in moving away from a country-by-country analysis is to describe international party groupings. Second, we deal with the ideologies of parties to counteract the model of political parties that operates in most electoral geography. Party labels such as 'Liberal', 'Conservative', 'Socialist', 'Communist' and 'Christian Democrat' are found in many different countries and usually reflect adherence to similar sets of political ideas. We have already noted that, with the exception of nationalism, political geography has totally neglected the study of political ideologies. But this is part of a much wider malaise which has afflicted most modern social science. The reason for these problems can be traced back to alternative definitions of ideology.

'Ideology' literally means the 'logic' of 'ideas'. But right from its beginning it has been associated with the idea of bias. The first use of the word is usually traced back to Napoleon who used it as a derogatory term to describe some liberal academics who opposed his authoritarian rule. Seliger (1976) argues that from this time onwards ideology has had two distinctive meanings which he calls the *restrictive conception* and the *inclusive conception*. The former relates to the derogatory sense of the word and is used to label opponents' political views. The assumption is that there is a set of correct political values which are opposed by incorrect 'ideologies'. This was most fully developed by Marx in his development of 'scientific' (that is, non-ideological) socialism which opposed the mystification of ruling-class ideas which were therefore ideological. Seliger (1976: 19) points out the irony in the parallelism between Marx's use of the derogatory restrictive meaning of ideology and post-1945 social science use of the same restrictive meaning to label modern Marxism. Whereas Marx defined pro-status-quo ideas as ideological, modern social science has designated anti-status-quo ideas as ideological! At the height of the cold war between the USA and the USSR social science played its part in justifying the American position. The 'end of ideology' was proclaimed (Bell 1960) on the assumption that practical and rational politics dominated core countries with ideologies only represented by minority extremists such as communists and fascists. Two convergences were identified – between liberalism and democratic socialism in the West to produce the welfare state and between communism and fascism in the East to produce the totalitarian state. In this context the study of ideology became the study of extreme political sects.

Seliger's (1976) inclusive conception of ideology covers all sets of political ideas. Hence it does not presuppose that any one set of ideas is superior to any other. This position is now generally accepted in social science, because the 'end of ideology debate' is regarded as an 'ideological aberration' of the first order. The inclusive conception is consistent with our use of the term ideology to the degree that all major politics are distorted by their channelling into national arenas. Hence in what follows we treat all sets of political ideas as they currently operate as ideologies. The ideology of liberalism will come under particular scrutiny but before we deal with it we consider liberal and other parties in their international context.

INTERNATIONAL PARTY GROUPINGS

The simplest way of ordering political parties is on a left–right spectrum. This distinction between parties has an interesting relation to the international dimension of party organization. Quite simply parties of the right tend to have few international links whereas on the left 'Internationals' are an important part of the history and tradition of parties. The reasons for this contrast are many. In part it is to do with the variety of party labels used on the right. There are not, to my knowledge, any parties calling themselves the 'Capitalist Party'. Rather parties of the right emphasize their non-economic values as a means of attracting support. This will normally entail more use of their country's special secondary theory of nationalism than other parties. Hence despite the cultural similarities of English-speaking liberal democracies, their right-wing parties all have different names – USA: Republican; Britain: Conservative; Canada: Progressive Conservative; Australia: Liberal; and New Zealand: National. There are no international organizations of Republican, Conservative (Progressive or otherwise) or National Parties. There is a 'Liberal International', as we shall see, but the Australian party is not a member. In fact, as Goldman (1980) laments, neither major American party, Republican or Democrat, has any transnational party links, leaving the CIA as the major American tool for influencing parties in other countries.

1. Socialist 'internationals'

On the left of the political spectrum there has been over a century of international organization. In 1864 Karl Marx and Frederick Engels added substance to their 1848 call 'Workers of the World, Unite' by forming the International Working Men's Association subsequently known as the First International. This was mainly a joint effort of just a small number of British and French trade unions but it began a tradition that lasts till this day. The First International was disbanded in 1877 but was re-activated as the much more substantial Second International in 1889. This had affiliates from socialist parties throughout Europe ranging from moderate reformist parties such as in Britain to revolutionary socialists such as the Russian Bolsheviks. Although merely an association of nationally based parties, it did profess genuine international ideals (Liebman 1964). It proclaimed its opposition to war which was condemned as an innate property of capitalism. In 1907 a resolution was passed committing all member parties to intervene in the event of war being declared to prevent worker fighting worker. For some war meant revolution. The Socialist International was in session when war broke out in 1914. Delegates hurried home to their respective countries and most supported their own government's war efforts. The greatest shock was in Germany where the most influential and radical socialist party supported the war. In the German Diet only one socialist member voted against credits for the government to pursue the war. Worker did fight worker as nationalism triumphed and international socialism disintegrated. 1914 confirmed the world-economy's political structure: the inter-state system, buttressed by the most powerful of modern ideologies, nationalism.

The First World War produced the 'great schism' of socialism (Liebman 1964). The moderate reformist parties were integrated into their national societies via war service and the revolutionaries continued their policy of class warfare. With the Bolshevik success in Russia in 1917 the

split became permanent, leaving two heirs to the Second International.
The Third International was convened in Moscow in 1919 and continued
as a grouping of Communist Parties until 1943. There have been two
successor organizations to the Third International but currently no
international grouping of Communist Parties exists. Nevertheless Day and
Degenhardt (1980) have compiled a list of Soviet-recognized Communist
Parties which are shown in Figure 20(a). Many of these are illegal or in
exile but the global spread is impressive. The other heir to the Second
International, the reformist socialists, formed a Labour and Socialist
International in 1923 and this was reformed in 1951 as the Socialist
International which is still active. Member Parties in 1980 (Day and
Degenhardt 1980) are shown in Figure 20(b). Although not common in
Asia and Africa, this international grouping does have a global
distribution.

2. International groups on the 'right'

The only right-wing parties with major trans-national organization are the
Christian Democrats. These parties formed throughout Catholic Europe in
the second half of the nineteenth century in response to the rise of secular
parties. Their first international congress was held in 1925 but the
Christian Democratic World Union was not formed until 1961. The
distribution of member parties (Figure 20(c)) clearly reflects the
distribution of Roman Catholic populations in southern and central
Europe and Latin America. In effect this pattern is an expression of the
first imperialism of the world-economy, that of Spain and Portugal, even to
the extent of including parties in the East Indies. In complete contrast
membership of the Liberal International is much less global (Figure
20(d)). This organization was formed in 1947 but remains a grouping of
parties in core countries only. Also shown in Figure 20(d) are parties that
label themselves 'liberal' but which are not affiliated to the international.
In two cases, Australia and Japan, the ruling right-wing party has a
liberal label but are generally considered 'conservative' rather than 'liberal'
parties. The Latin American examples are much more interesting since
they represent the political heirs of Frank's nineteenth-century 'European'
parties. But these labels have long since ceased to have ideological
meaning. One of the liberal parties shown in Figure 20(d), for instance, is
the dictator Somoza's National Liberal Party which ruled Nicaragua in a
very illiberal manner before being overthrown by the Sandinistas in 1979.
What this example does show is that international groupings are useful for
defining 'orthodox' representatives of political ideologies irrespective of
labels.

The distribution of members of the Liberal International (Figure 20(d))
is both instructive and misleading. It is instructive in its limitation to core
countries hence confirming the failure of liberalism in poorer countries.
But it is misleading if we conclude that liberalism has only influenced the

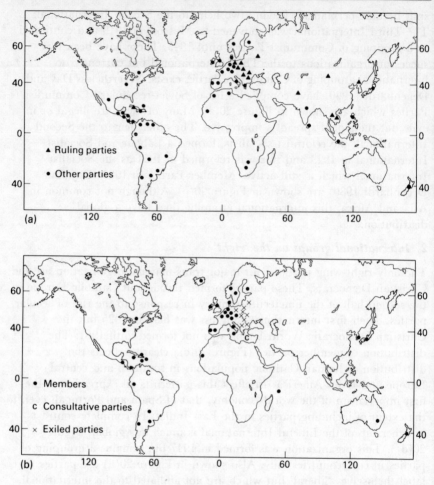

20.   International groupings of political parties (Based on listings given in Day and Degenhardt 1980) (a) Soviet-recognized Communist parties (b) Socialist International (c) Christian Democrat World Union (d) Liberal International and other 'Liberal parties'

core of the world-economy. The current pattern of orthodox liberal parties does not adequately express the role that liberalism has had in the evolution of the modern world-economy. In the remainder of this section we concentrate on liberalism and set the ideology within our world-systems framework. The stimulus for this 'geography' of an ideology comes from de Crespigny and Cronin's (1975: 13) assertion that 'The same or apparently equivalent words vary in their meanings both within and between countries and from time to time.' We will show that this variety of 'meanings' is very clearly illustrated by the ideology of liberalism in the world-economy.

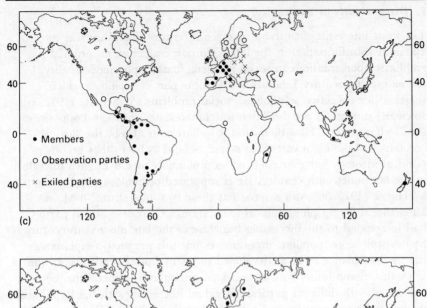

(c)

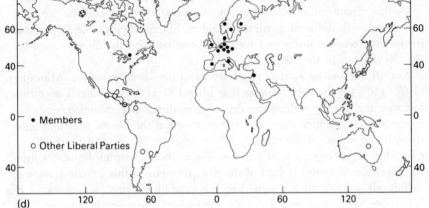

(d)

THE GEOGRAPHY OF LIBERALISM

The term 'liberal' meaning a political opinion was new to the nineteenth century and was originally coined in 1820 to describe the Spanish rebels fighting against the Bourbon monarchy (Collins 1957). As the term came to be accepted as a label for 'progressive' politics, it was soon applied in retrospect to earlier thinkers and movements. Hence Adam Smith, whose *Wealth of Nature* was written in 1776, becomes a major liberal thinker and the American War of Independence becomes a liberal revolution. And this is right because it is the ideas rather than labels which are important. Hence Laski (1936: 9) is able to assert that liberalism has been 'the outstanding doctrine of Western civilization' for four centuries.

Nevertheless we will begin by considering liberalism as a nineteenth-century ideology directly linked to party politics before we consider it in the context of the world-economy as a whole.

1. Discontinuity or continuity?

The most interesting feature of nineteenth-century liberalism was its apparent transformation in the late Victorian era. From an original emphasis upon solutions to social problems based upon individuality, by the end of the century Liberals had become part of a politics which searched for collective solutions to social problems. As Schultz (1972: xi) so clearly puts it: 'Is not the "nightwatchman state" the logical opposite of the "welfare state"? How then can the welfare state also be the "logical corollary" of the nightwatchman state?' Schultz believes that no other political ideology has ever changed so profoundly as did English liberalism in the late nineteenth century. He is supported on philosophical grounds by Hayek (1975: 56) who asserts that these two 'liberalisms' 'rest on altogether different philosophical foundations'. Of course liberal parties had to respond to the increasing franchise of the late nineteenth century by devising more 'popular' programmes but this pragmatic explanation hardly does justice to ideas developed to justify both liberalisms. In the USA this discontinuity was less obvious since the two liberalisms became associated with different parties: individual liberalism with the Republicans in the nineteenth century and welfare liberalism with the Democrats after the 'New Deal' in the 1930s.

Not all authors agree that there are two liberalisms, however. Manning (1976: 140), for instance, admits that liberal ideas have changed over time but that this merely reflects 'an on-going evaluation of changing circumstances'. Hence there are 'variants within the liberal tradition' and there is 'no universal liberalism' (Manning 1976: 58, 60) but there is, nevertheless, an overall continuity in liberal thought which he traces from the seventeenth century. Part of the disagreement in this debate relates to definitions – when do 'variants' become 'new liberalisms', for instance? But it is more basic than that. Liberals, themselves, have a vested interest in showing a continuity since it provides a very prestigous pedigree of thinkers. In this discussion we will follow the discontinuity argument.

2. Conflicts and ideologies

In any materialist explanation ideologies do not exist in a vacuum but are developed to justify positions taken by different sides in social conflicts. In the geography of voting we identified four such conflicts which Rokkan (1970) has used to explain the internal development of European states. These conflicts can be loosely related to liberalism and competing ideologies. In Figure 21 we list the four conflicts in order of their approximate time of emergence and identify each side as either a 'new' or 'old' group interest. Ideologies cut across these conflicts in such a way that their initial stimulus as a 'progressive' force supporting a new group interest becomes converted into a defence of the status quo. It is this conversion in liberalism which underlies the unity/disunity debate.

In each conflict in Figure 21 the new interest group combines elements of the old ideology with the new one. This is, in effect, the battleground for the emergence and establishment of new ideologies. Once the progressive ideology becomes established it is used to support the system it has helped create. Hence traditional feudal ideas are used to bolster peripheral and church interests in the first two conflicts and they are opposed by a combination of core traditionalists and new mercantilist ideas and old mercantilist and new liberal ideas respectively. In fact Laski (1936: 59–66) sees mercantilism as the first step in creating a secular state but argues that it was soon realized that the wider principles of liberalism offered more opportunities than narrow mercantilism. Mercantilism is thus both a precondition for liberalism and an opponent when it becomes reduced to serving the reactionary landed interest. But just as 'old' mercantilism is defeated, liberalism is challenged in its urban centres by the new ideology of socialism. Liberalism now adopts a status-quo position of defending middle-class and employer property rights against the working class. In the final stage of this model we have added the basic

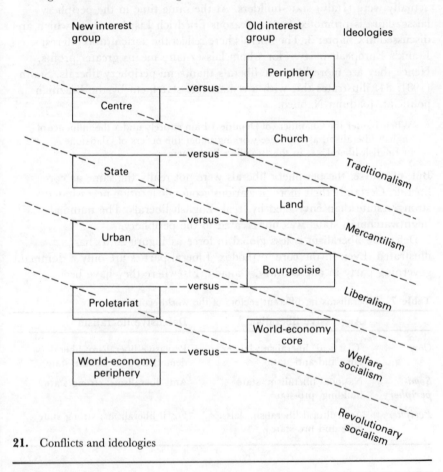

21. Conflicts and ideologies

cleavage of the current world-economy, core versus periphery on a global scale. This enables us to identify welfare socialism as a new status quo ideology in the core reflecting the social imperialism described earlier, with revolutionary socialism as the ideology of the periphery.

3. Aggressive and defensive liberalisms

The two liberalisms identified earlier can now be interpreted as *aggressive liberalism* fighting old social forces emanating from above in church and state, and *defensive liberalism* fighting new social forces emanating from below. Aggressive liberalism emphasizes individualism against the restrictions of traditional and mercantilist policies whereas defensive liberalism had to develop new corporate ideas to combat socialism. But this is only the story in the core. In Table 7 these two liberalisms are extended to their other expressions outside the core. Hence whereas 'classical' liberals of the core emphasized laissez-faire and were broadly anti-state in their ideas, in the semi-periphery 'national' liberals dominated who were pro-state to the extent that they attempted to be (Germany) or actually were (Italy) state-builders. At the same time in the periphery laissez-faire is promoted for the reasons Friedrich List has given which are discussed in Chapter 3. The liberals here reflect the agricultural interest – Frank's European party – for whom laissez-faire means greater profits. Hence they are more like core liberals than semi-periphery liberals. Smith (1981: 34) illustrates this with a remarkable statement by the Brazilian politician Joaquim Nabuco:

> 'When I enter the Chamber (of Deputies) I am entirely under the influence of English liberalism, as if I were working under the orders of Gladstone . . . I am an English liberal . . . in the Brazilian Parliament.

But, of course, the periphery liberals were not really the same as core liberals. Certainly their more precarious economic location necessitated a stronger state than envisaged by 'real' English liberals. The minimal 'nightwatchman state' was not created in the periphery.

Defensive liberalism is less global in force as Figure 20(d) has illustrated. Even in the core 'orthodox' Liberal parties are only a dominant governing party in one country, Canada. Elsewhere they have been

Table 7   Liberalisms in different sectors of the world-economy

	Aggressive liberalism	Defensive liberalism
Core	'Classical' liberalism: laissez faire and anti-state	Pervasive liberalism: liberal democracy and welfare state
Semi-periphery	National liberalism: state building, pro-state	Anti-liberalisms: strong state
Periphery	Agricultural liberalism: laissez faire and pro-state	Fossil liberalisms: strong state

squeezed into the 'centre' between Socialist parties and various right-wing parties who have adapted better to the nationalism of the twentieth century. In the semi-periphery the emphasis upon strong states has largely eliminated liberalism and in the periphery the liberal parties that still exist in Latin America are not, as we have seen, 'recognized' by the Liberal International. Clearly defensive liberalism has not been nearly as successful on the world stage as aggressive liberalism was before it. But we should not under-estimate it. Liberal parties may have been eclipsed as major forces in most core countries but in many ways the things that they stand for have been achieved by welfare socialism. As Salvadori (1977: 93) so neatly puts it – 'liberalism with a small "l" survives Liberalism with a capital "L"'. Part of the argument of the 'end of ideology' proposers was that liberalism and socialism had come together. This is true if we accept that liberalism is the pervasive ideology in the core. This is implicitly assumed when we use the term 'liberal democracy'. In the core Liberal Parties are a victim of the success of liberalism. But only in the core.

PARTIES AND POWER

The first two sections of this chapter have presented political parties either as reflections of public opinion or as purveyors of political ideologies. Parties may carry out either or both of these roles but they are much more than this. The concept conspicuous by its absence from our discussion so far is power. The major purpose of political parties is to obtain power. This may be achieved constitutionally as in liberal democracies or by overthrowing the state by revolutionary parties. In this discussion we will continue with our concern for liberal democratic politics.

The argument of this section proceeds through three levels of analysis. First, we consider the way parties dominate the formation of governments. Second, we look at how party government satisfies the basic functions of the state. Finally we take a realistic look at the power of political parties within the overall context of a dynamic world-economy.

PARTY AND GOVERNMENT: THE 'GREAT ACT OF ORGANIZATION'

A competitive party system depends upon opposition groups being perceived as alternative governments rather than as threats to the state. From the nineteenth century onwards state-building groups in core countries and some peripheral countries have come to accept this position so that elections become the means of selecting governments. In the USA this fundamental position was reached in the second party system of Democrats versus Whigs which developed in the 1830s. In the first party system a generation earlier each party fought elections with the view of eliminating their rivals from the political scene – eventually the Democrat-

Republicans succeeded in reducing the Federalists to political impotence. In contrast the Democrats and Whigs fought elections merely with a view to securing the presidency for their candidate (Archer and Taylor 1981: 54–61). The defeat of President Carter in 1980 was the nineteenth transfer of executive power in USA by election.

This transfer of government office is not as open as the above discussion implies. Government formation is not a free-for-all but is a carefully controlled process. And this is where parties come in. In many countries there is a duopoly of power to form governments. In the USA, for instance, *all* presidents since the Civil War have been the nominees of the Republican or Democratic Parties. In Britain Conservative and Liberal Parties until the 1920s and then Conservative and Labour parties have had a similar duopoly of power. Even in multi-party systems there remain severe constraints on voter choice with relatively few effective votes available. But this is the whole point of a party system. From the vast range of positions on a large number of topics, voters are asked to support just one of a limited number of 'manifestoes' or 'platforms'. This is what Schattschneider (1960: 59) terms 'the great act of organization' with political alternatives reduced 'to the extreme limit of simplification'. The power of parties is simply that electors can vote for or against particular party candidates but they cannot vote for or against a party system (Jahnige 1971: 473).

For Schattschneider (1960) this power over choice enables parties to define the politics of a country. There are an infinite number of potential conflicts in any complex modern society. By controlling alternatives offered to voters parties decide which conflicts are organized into a country's politics and which conflicts are organized out. Hence electoral politics is defined by the party system producing massive constraints on the nature of the political agenda.

1. Alternative organizations of control

Electoral politics as constrained by political parties is, therefore, an important control mechanism in liberal democracies. The actual organization operating at any particular election, however, is not normally designed for that election. As we have seen, parties and party systems are the product of the specific histories of their countries. The manipulation of the political agenda is not a conspiracy of ruling elites but rather reflects the relative power of different interests in the evolution of a party system. The ultimate constraint on this process is the nature of the state which the government runs. For the state to continue as a capitalist institution in the world-economy it is necessary for anti-capitalist politics to be organized off the agenda. This has been achieved in four major ways:

(i) The hegemonic solution. Initially in Britain and later in USA socialist parties were unable to become effective parts of the party system. In the

nineteenth century Britain had the weakest socialist tradition of the western and central European states and the Labour Party only adopted a socialist constitution in 1918 long after Britain's fall from hegemony. At about this time the Socialist Party in USA was failing in its push to become a major party. Hence in both hegemonic states oppositional politics was relegated to the harmless fringe: Socialism was organized off the political agenda. This is partly related to the social imperialism process which can be much more effective in affluent hegemonic states but the process includes more specific mechanisms such as ethnic rivalries in USA.

(ii) The accommodation solution. Where a socialist party becomes an alternative government then the political agenda is potentially dangerous. This danger can be lessened if the party emphasizes reform policies rather than revolutionary ones. Reformist socialism does not attempt to change the nature of the state but merely tries to redistribute resources within the state. Such redistribution policies can be accommodated without major problems for the dominant class. It is in this situation that the most explicit examples of social imperialism occur where governments combine 'progressive' home policies with 'conservative', usually bipartisan, foreign policies. Accommodation is possible because of the state's role in the world-economy. The classic case of this is Britain and the Labour Party whose reformist policies have been labelled 'Labourism' to distinguish them from socialism (Miliband 1961). With the decline of Britain in the world-economy Labourism and the accommodation solution have become harder to sustain.

(iii) The coalition solution. In most of Central and Western Europe the multiple cleavages described by Rokkan are reflected in a multi-party system. The voting system sustains this arrangement by using proportional representational schemes in place of plurality voting. This prevents the geography of representation operating to produce a majority party and hence one-party government. Instead attention is directed away from government and towards the composition of the legislature. A classic developmental argument is employed to show that PR represents the culmination of a democratic reform movement. The four stages of electoral reform usually identified (for example, Gudgin and Taylor 1979: 2–3) are reform of the franchise, to extend the vote to all classes and sexes, reform of electioneering to outlaw corruption and malpractices, reform of distribution to reduce malapportionment and finally reform of representation to generate proportionality between a party's vote proportion and its seat proportion in the legislature. Only the latter relates directly to parties and was to become popular in the first half of the century at the same time that socialist parties were becoming a threat. Its effect is to insulate government from voters by ensuring that it is party managers who negotiate to produce coalition governments *after* an election.

It raises the threshold to 50 per cent for election of a socialist government. In practice socialist parties have had to trim their policies to satisfy coalition partners. We return to this theme below.

(iv) The coercion solution.   If the above strategies fail and an uncompromising radical government is produced by an election then dominant classes will revert to coercion to prevent its policies operating. The classic case remains the coalition of Chilian middle classes and the CIA to undermine and finally overthrow the democratically elected Marxist president of Chile, Salvadore Allende, in 1973. Similar de-stabilization accompanied the electoral defeat of Michael Manley in Jamaica in 1980. This has been the solution of the semi-periphery and periphery. Of course where this solution has failed, for example the White Russian counter-revolutionaries before 1921, the threat of the anti-capitalist state has been contained by the structural logic of the world-economy as described in Chapter 2.

The end-result of these solutions is to produce 'safe' governments which do not challenge the dominant economic interests within the state. The country with the longest continuous democratic tradition is USA and this country also has the longest history of party control of the political agenda. We conclude this discussion, therefore, with a brief look at this process in operation.

2. Section and party in USA, 1828–1920

Here we briefly report on a part of Archer and Taylor's (1981) analysis of American presidential elections from 1828 to 1980. Using the percentage vote for all Democratic candidates, Archer and Taylor derive different patterns of party support across states. When several elections show the same pattern these are defined as 'normal votes' in the sense that a tradition of voting has been established. For the analysis of eastern states from 1828 to 1920 two such patterns dominate the analysis and we report on this finding and its relation to our previous discussion.

In Figure 22 we show the strength of these two patterns over time. They clearly represent pre-civil war and post-civil war normal vote patterns with the first being important from 1836 to 1852 and the second from 1876 onwards. In Figure 23 their respective distributions across states are shown and from this we have derived their respective names – the non-sectional normal vote and the sectional normal vote. The latter represents what was the usual pattern of voting in USA for much of the twentieth century: solid Democratic south, less solid Democratic 'border states' and a slightly pro-Republican north with Vermont and Michigan particularly so. This is the sectional voting for which America was famous. It contrasts strikingly with what went before. In the non-sectional normal vote pattern strong Democrat states are found both north and south. The distribution seems haphazard, even random. Northerners and southerners supported

(a) Non-sectional normal vote

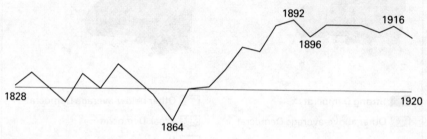

(b) Sectional normal vote

22. Normal vote profiles: USA, 1828–1920 (a) Non-sectional normal vote
(b) Sectional normal vote

both Whigs and Democrats with relatively little sectional favour. This is best illustrated by identifying the most pro-Whig and pro-Democrat states of this era. Interestingly enough they turn out to be contiguous – Vermont and New Hampshire which are as similar a pair of states in social, economic and ethnic terms, as you could expect to find in pre-civil-war USA. This is non-sectional voting par excellence.

There are several important aspects of this finding. First political developmental models which assume a decline in the territorial basis of voting over time are exposed here. In the USA the extreme sectional voting *follows* non-sectional voting. It seems that the USA was highly 'integrated' before the civil war. This interpretation is consistent with an emphasis on the voting pattern but must be laid aside as soon as we consider the party system. What the non-sectional voting pattern represents is merely a conglomeration of local alliances which come together on the national stage to support a selected presidential candidate. The forums for this national activity are the two political parties, Democrats and Whigs. This local agglomeration produced 'national' parties for the only time in American history (McCormick 1967: 109).

There is a paradox here. Just as the country was undergoing the strains of sectional competition which was to erupt in the civil war, elections show no sectional bias. This means that the north versus south cleavage was

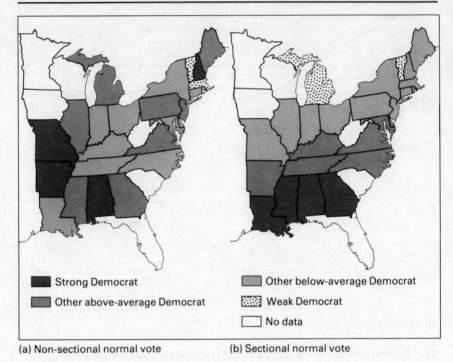

Strong Democrat

Other above-average Democrat

Other below-average Democrat

Weak Democrat

No data

(a) Non-sectional normal vote   (b) Sectional normal vote

23. Normal vote patterns: USA, 1828–1920 (a) Non-sectional normal vote
(b) Sectional normal vote

being kept off the political agenda. Quite simply there was no 'north'
party or 'south' party to vote for until the 1850s. Hence the tensions
developing in the country were organized off the political agenda by a
non-sectional party system. The parties acted as an integrating force in a
politics of sectional compromise. Van Bureen, President from 1836 to 1840,
is usually credited as the architect of this highly successful control of a
political agenda (Archer and Taylor 1981: 81–4). This was party versus
section and, for a generation, party won. It was in Ceasar's (1979: 138)
words 'a complete antidote for sectional prejudices'. This remains a classic
example of mass politics being diverted from a major issue by political
parties.

The system did not survive and in 1856 the Republicans replaced the
Whigs and the Democrats split into northern and southern factions. The
upheavals of the civil war and subsequent reconstruction produced no
normal vote pattern for nearly two decades. By the late 1870s however a
new politics was arising based upon the sectional normal vote. This
politics of sectional dominance coincides with the establishment of the
northern section as the economic core of the state. The state's territory
becomes integrated as one large functional region serving the
manufacturing belt. And here we have a second paradox, economic

integration is accompanied by political separation. In effect north and south become two separate political systems, the former dominated by the Republicans the latter even more so by the Democrats. This arrangement suited the industrial leaders of the country since northern states are able to outvote southern states. The presidency, therefore, becomes virtually a Republican fiefdom with only two Democratic presidents between the civil war and 1932. Hence one party was able to control the political agenda by relegating its opponents to a peripheral region.

What about the electors? What were they voting for while this control was going on? Fortunately historians have attempted to answer this question by using correlation and regression methods on voting and census data. Their findings are fascinating. The major determinants of voting in this period are always cultural variables (McCormick 1974; Kleppner 1979). Hence voters were expressing religious and ethnic identification in elections. And yet in this whole period there are only two 'cultural' policies which reach the political agenda – slavery as a moral issue at the beginning of the period and prohibition at the·end. Through the whole of this period the major dividing line between the parties was protection (Republicans) versus free trade (Democrats). Hence while voters were expressing their culture in elections, party elites were competing for economic stakes in terms of US relations to the world-economy. There can be no clearer example of the separation of voters from government by parties.

PARTY AND STATE: THE DIALECTICS OF ELECTORAL GEOGRAPHY

The success of a party system in organizing the political agenda depends upon the parties being able to mobilize an effective proportion of the electorate in their support. The free trade versus protectionism agenda in US politics above relied upon ethnic and religious mobilization by the parties. More generally the fact that millions of electors regularly go through the procedure of voting in their respective countries for a small number of major parties legitimizes the state and in particular the nature of the state reflected in the party system. This represents the single most important achievement of liberal democracy and we may term it 'the great act of mobilization'.

Mobilization is a major concern of Rokkan's (1970) electoral studies. With the gradual extension of the franchise in all core countries parties were set the task of mobilizing these new voters into the political system. Hence parties have been a major integrating force in the modern state. In fact the power of the state is very much dependent upon parties converting inert subjects into participating citizens. The geographical dimension of this process is the mobilization of the periphery, one of Rokkan's favourite themes (Taylor and Johnston 1979: 129–47).

In some ways this integrating role of parties is paradoxical. 'Party' comes from the same root as 'part' and indicates a division within a political system. Political parties, therefore, have the second role of accommodating differences within a state. Hence the social conflicts and resulting cleavages that Rokkan identifies do not ultimately pull the state apart but rather become part of the state. Parties can therefore convert even potentially rebellious subjects into mere voters. The rise of Christian Democratic parties throughout Europe, but especially in Italy, represents a victory of the state over the transnational pretentions of the Catholic Church. Devout Catholics became mobilized into state politics via their church parties.

1. The two geographies of elections

The two 'great acts' that parties achieve, organizing the agenda and mobilizing the voters, can be brought together into a single argument by relating them both to the theory of the state developed in the last chapter. In particular O'Connor's (1973) classification of the necessary functions of every modern state, promotion of capital accumulation and legitimation of the system, are pertinent here. Parties are agents which contribute to both functions with mobilization contributing to legitimation and agenda organization contributing to accumulation. We are now in a position to develop our theory of the state to incorporate political parties.

Every election incorporates two distinct processes. First there is intra-class competition within the dominant class over state tactics for promoting accumulation. Second there is interclass conflict over distribution issues. The former will include state relations with the rest of the world-economy, the latter will concentrate on domestic issues. Gamble (1974) terms these two processes the *politics of power* and the *politics of support* respectively. Political parties operate in both these politics by promoting special interests in their policies and mobilizing voters in their campaigns. The activities of the parties in this regard produces *two* electoral geographies, a geography of power and a geography of support. This revised model is shown in Figure 24. This should be compared to the simple systems model of electoral geography (Figure 16). The single linear sequence is replaced by two loops representing the two politics involved in every election.

The most important feature of this model is that the two processes occur as separate geographies. There is no general relationship between them; there are only particular relations for every state depending upon the class relations within the state, the relation of the state to the world-economy and the history of these two relations. Nevertheless there are structural tendencies which we can identify (Taylor 1984). The following five statements provide the basic propositions of the model:

1. There is no structural need for the two processes to provide a single

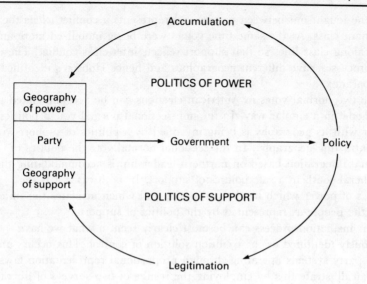

24. A revised model of electoral geography

consistent basis for a party's actions. In fact the contradictions in the state's function will normally translate into tensions within parties.

2. There is a structural need to mystify the dual role of parties. Without this mystification the power function of the party becomes impossible. This is one of the purposes of liberal theories of the state.

3. The balance between action based on one or other of the two processes will vary in terms of whether a party is in office or opposition. Opposition parties operate more in the politics of support, for instance 'social democratic' parties become notoriously 'socialist' in periods of opposition.

4. The prime basis of action in the politics of power is class whereas there will be a variety of bases for the politics of support. In fact the mystification function is facilitated if the politics of support is *not* based upon class (that is, the hegemonic solution, above).

5. Parties may operate involuntarily to deflect attention on contradictions away from the state by taking the blame for the situation: a potential crisis of the state becomes a crisis of the party, for example, Republicans in the USA in the 1930s and Labour in Britain in the 1980s.

This new model of the electoral process enables us to make better interpretation of some of our previous examples. Hobson's paradox of voting in the British 1910 election now reduces to a simple contrast between a geography of support and a geography of power. The tariff issue was one fought out between parties and represents a conflict *within* the dominant class. At the same time voters were being mobilized more and more along class lines so that support reflects inter-class conflict. These two processes have different geographies and hence Hobson's identification of a paradox.

The two normal votes in American elections can be accommodated to our model in a similar way. In the non-sectional normal vote a politics of power with its geography is being mystified by a politics of support with its contrasting geography. In the sectional normal vote the politics of national integration based on northern leadership is accommodating the peripheral south in a safe politics of support. In both cases it is the politics of power which lies behind policy and which insulates the state from the people as represented by the politics of support.

This insulation process can be most clearly seen in what we have previously identified as the coalition solution of control. This occurs under multi-party systems operating through proportional representation laws. We can illustrate this by employing the results of two surveys of liberal democracies carried out by Arend Lijphart. In the first study (Lijphart 1971) the electoral cleavage is investigated by finding the percentage bias of different groups towards their 'natural' party. In the first two columns of results in Table 8 we report on just the religious and economic cleavages for seven European countries that have employed a PR system. The figures represent the percentage bias of church attenders towards Christian Democrat parties and the percentage bias of manual workers towards socialist/communist parties. For the European liberal democracies reported here the most outstanding feature of these results is the predominance of the religious cleavage. In the final two columns of Table 8 Lijphart's (1982) results for a study of coalition formation for these same countries are shown. Using information on all governments for the period 1919–79, Lijphart defines each coalition as either religious or economic on the basis of party membership. Table 8 shows the total years of government for each category as a percentage of all years of coalition government. The most notable feature of these results is their contrast with the electoral cleavage findings. Roughly speaking religion is three times as important as the economic cleavage in voting patterns whereas economic criteria are eight times as important as religion in the process of forming governments. This is the classic case of mobilizing voters on cultural grounds while forming governments around economic coalitions.

2. Contrasting geographies of power and support

Most of electoral geography has been concerned with the geography of support. This is partly a result of data-availability. Elections must be very public exercises to function as legitimizing forces so that voting returns are easily available to produce geographies of support. As we pointed out at the beginning of the chapter this has been the basis of the spectacular

Table 8 Contrasting politics of support and power in seven western European countries

	Politics of support		Politics of power	
	Electoral cleavages*		Coalition formation†	
	Religious	*Economic*	*Religious*	*Economic*
France	59	15	25	75
Italy	51	19	0	75
Germany	40	27	12	70
Netherlands	73	26	0	100
Belgium	72	25	17	70
Austria	54	31	5	95
Switzerland	59	26	0	49

* Percentage bias towards religious and socialist parties by church attenders and manual workers respectively.
† Percentage of 'coalition years' for the period 1919–79.

rise in electoral geography in recent years. But data availability for the politics of power is much less likely to be available. Where the politics is based upon covert actions we may never know about it. CIA funding of 'friendly' foreign parties or destabilization of 'unfriendly' foreign governments are part of the geography of power in some states which are only sporadically reported. Certainly we cannot expect simple official tabulations to produce geographies of power in the way that we can produce geographies of support. And yet both are equally essential to the smooth operation of liberal democracy. We should not neglect one merely because it is more difficult to investigate. The major lesson of our reformed model is to redirect electoral geography towards its neglected half, the geography of power. Fortunately we can begin to learn this lesson through recent research in South Africa which provides a glimpse of a geography of power to contrast with a more familiar geography of support.

The National Party has been in power in South Africa since 1948. With the collapse of the opposition Union Party it is now firmly entrenched with no rival alternative government on the horizon. The National Party came to power with a geography of support showing a strong rural bias. As the party has come to increase its popularity the relative strength of its urban support has increased but the rural bias remains (Peele and Morse 1974). And yet under National Party control South Africa has developed from a peripheral state based upon primary exports into a strong semi-peripheral state based upon massive industrial-urban growth. Hence there seems to be a paradox that a rural-based party has promoted urban expansion. The answer to the paradox is now becoming familiar – the party's power base is distinct from its support base.

Although the National Party is the dominant political expression of
Afrikaner nationalism the vanguard of this movement is a covert
organization, the Broederbond. This was founded in 1918 as a self-help
ethnic society for newly urbanized Afrikaners. It has grown into a country-
wide organization of over eight hundred cells with some twelve thousand
members (Pirie *et al.* 1980: 99). Membership is strong in all the key
professions – education, law, clergy, journalism – in business and
commerce and in political positions at all levels. In 1977 the latter
included the state president, prime minister, 19 cabinet and deputy
ministers and 79 members of parliament (Pirie *et al.* 1980: 100). Although
by definition, the exact influence of a secret society can never be fully
explored, the web of contacts represented by the Broederbond clearly
represents the power behind the South African government. And the
geography of this power is urban, reflecting the society's origins. The three
major centres of Broederbond members are Pretoria, Johannesburg and
Cape Town respectively whereas in electoral terms the latter two are
important centres of anti-National voting. There is, of course, no reason
for the geography of support and the geography of power to coincide, as
we have previously argued, but the differences are not usually as extreme
as in this urban – rural cleavage in South Africa. Clearly to concentrate
only on the geography of support would be to fundamentally
misunderstand the nature of the National party and the way in which it is
steering the South African state. This represents a straightforward
vindication of our reformed model of electoral geography.

PARTIES AND THE WORLD-ECONOMY: THE REALITY OF POWER

Our revised electoral geography has directed attention away from the voter
to the party. The main effect has been to introduce the concept of power
into our analysis of elections. But we must not go too far along this path.
For all parties' dominance of government in liberal democracies, they are
still constrained by state functions as we have seen. And beyond that there
is the world-economy. Although parties may be powerful within their
state's territory this is no guarantee of power beyond the borders. This
'external' power of parties depends upon the position of the state in the
world-economy. There may be opportunities for parties to pursue policies
which act to enhance the state's power and hence the position of the party
within the country. The best example of this is the Republican Party
which, having consolidated northern dominance of US economy, embarked
upon an imperialism, both formal and informal, at the end of the
nineteenth century which was to be a springboard for twentieth-century
US hegemony in the world-economy (Archer and Taylor 1981: 113–16,
130–4). But such success is the exception rather than the rule in the
world-economy. In the case of Britain, for instance, the twentieth century
has been a period of economic decline irrespective of the party in power.

These failures have only been hidden by military successes in 1914–18, 1939–45 (Nairn 1977) and most recently 1982 in the South Atlantic War. In this final section we investigate the relation between parties and the world-economy in which they have to steer their states.

1. 'New politics' and the world-economy

The problem for all political parties is that whereas the politics of support is an internal matter within their country, the politics of power inevitably extends beyond the boundary of the state. As we have seen the world-economy does not develop in a smooth linear fashion but is typified by major booms and recessions. Every time the world-economy moves from an A-phase to a B-phase, or vice versa the constraints and opportunities facing every individual state fundamentally changes. Political parties operating within these states have to tailor their policies accordingly. The result is a series of 'new politics' within each state corresponding to the particular reactions of the political parties to the new world circumstances. The recent demise of Keynesian economic management and the return of monetarism as a guide to government policy throughout the world is an important aspect of the new politics of the current recession in all countries.

The most interesting feature of these 'new politics' is that they do not necessarily arise out of elections. Usually there is not an election whereby voters are asked to choose between 'old' and 'new' politics: this is not a matter of the politics of support, it is largely an issue of the politics of power. For each new politics old assumptions are swept away and new items appear on the political agenda but all major parties accept the new politics. A new party competition arises but takes place *within* the new politics being limited to matters of emphasis and degree. Hence the mobilizing powers of the parties are usually able to bring the voters into line with new economic circumstances. It is for this reason that the stability of voting patterns commonly found in electoral geography is not a good index of the changing politics of a state.

The idea of linking changes in party systems to economic changes is not a new one, of course. In the USA changes in party systems are clearly linked to economic depressions. The two key 'critical' elections commonly identified as changing the post-civil war party system are 1896 and 1932. Although the Republican and Democratic party labels continued to be used these elections are part of a process ushering in the fourth and fifth party systems respectively (Burnham 1970). These changes involved new alliances of party support first confirming Republican dominance in 1896/1900 and then asserting Democratic dominance in 1932/36. It should be noted that mobilization around new issues – American imperialism and the New Deal respectively – each occurred *after* the so-called critical elections (Archer and Taylor 1981) which is entirely consistent with our argument above.

2. Changing agendas in British politics

Perhaps the best country in which to study this process, however, is
Britain. Its long-term economic decline has elicited a variety of political
responses. If we consider the period from the First World War we can
identify six phases of 'new politics' each developing as consecutive pairs of
responses to the A- and B-phases of the world-economy. These are shown
in Table 9 and we will consider each new politics in turn.

We begin this sequence of politics with the depression following the
First World War. The initial reaction is a *politics of crisis*. The old party
system of Liberal versus Conservatives crumbles and the new Labour
versus Conservative system emerges. But two-party politics does not arrive
straight away. Since no party has the 'answer' to the economic problems
every election leads to the defeat of the governing party, often to be
replaced by a weak minority government. This process ceases in 1931. The
culmination of the political crisis is the fall of the Labour government and
its replacement by a coalition 'National' government confirmed by general
election. Labour retreats to the political wilderness as the National
government maintains support through the 1935 election. This replaces
two-party competition as the electors are mobilized to reduce their
economic expectations.

The Second World War sweeps away the assumptions of the 1930s. A
new *social democratic consensus* emerges and with the return of a Labour
government in 1945 a 'welfare state' is created. The revision of the
domestic agenda does not extend to foreign affairs. The combination of
funding the welfare state and maintaining a global military presence leads
to severe economic cycles – the famous 'stop-go' sequence of British
economic performance. The problem becomes acute when the relative
performance of Britain becomes a political issue. The 'reappraisal of 1960'
and the return of a Labour government in 1964 promising 'a white hot
technological revolution' usher in a new *technocratic politics*. This involves
widespread reform of state institutions to make Britain as competitive as

Table 9 'New Politics' in Britain since 1918

Period	World-economy	'New' politics	Major events
1918–31	Stagnation B(i)	Politics of crisis I	Rise of Labour Party, National Strike
1931–40	Stagnation B(ii)	Politics of national interest I	Dominance of National Coalition
1940–60	Growth A(i)	Social Democratic Consensus	Establishment of Welfare State
1960–72	Growth A(ii)	Technocratic politics	Application to join EEC
1972–82	Stagnation B(i)	Politics of crisis II	Conflict/accommodation with Unions
1982–	Stagnation B(ii)	Politics of national interest II	South Atlantic War

its rivals. Reorganization becomes the key word as local government, the welfare state and other central state departments are 'streamlined' for 'efficiency'. In foreign affairs the retreat from global power to European power is sealed by membership of the European Economic Community – the ultimate technocratic solution to Britain's problems.

With the onset of the current recession it soon became clear that tinkering with the administration of the state was not working. Once again we enter a politics of crisis. Haseler (1976) actually identifies thirty-five events between 1966 and 1975 which he interprets as signifying the breakdown of the political system. Once again no party is seen as having the answer and we return to electoral defeats for governing parties and even a period of minority government. The party system is under stress with the rise of nationalist parties in Scotland and Wales, increased support for the Liberal Party and finally a split in the Labour Party. All this changes with the rise of a new *politics of national interest* in the 1980s. The Conservative government is returned to power with a large increased majority as voters have learnt to mellow their demands and expectations.

Further details of these new politics can be found in Taylor (1982b). For our purposes here there are just two main points requiring further emphasis. First the various 'new politics' have not emerged at elections. In 1931 the new political battle lines were drawn before the election. The key example, however, is probably the practice of identifying the new politics of the social democratic consensus with the 1945 Labour victory. This is incorrect. Although the Labour government was responsible for setting up the welfare state, the major policy decisions had been agreed by the Conservative-led wartime coalition government. Hence we can date the emergence of this new politics to 1940 with the creation of the new coalition government. Similarly technocratic politics were not the result of any one election – the appraisal of 1960 came just *after* a massive government election victory which presumably endorsed past policies! I have dated the emergence of the new politics of crisis in 1972 when the Conservative government gave in to Miners' Union demands and became tarnished by their 'U-turn' image. Finally the South Atlantic War of 1982 produced a nationalistic reaction among voters represented by a turn-around in Conservative government popularity which they consolidated in the 1983 election. This obviously marks the beginning of the current politics of national interest. Hence in all cases 'new politics' have emerged independently of elections. The politics of power precedes the politics of support.

The second main point is that throughout this period of six new politics there was only one major geography of support. Generally speaking the areas voting Labour and Conservative in the first politics of crisis have continued their political biases right through to the present day: Labour maintains a northern, urban pattern of support with strongholds on the coalfields while Conservatives are the rural and suburban party. Despite electoral swings back and forth between the parties this electoral geography has remained remarkably stable. Even the rise of a centre political alliance in 1983 could not break this geographical mould. The two major political parties may not have been able to counteract Britain's steady decline in the world-economy but they have continued successfully to mobilize the voters through thick and thin. This fascinating mixture of impotence and strength is the hallmark of political parties of all countries.

Chapter 6

POLITICAL GEOGRAPHY OF LOCALITIES

THE ECOLOGICAL HERITAGE

The rise and fall of urban ecology

1. Ecological theory: the hidden political dimension
2. Ecology as spatial structure: apolitical urban studies

Recent debates in urban studies

1. Reaffirming space: Pahl's managerialism
2. Disposing of space: Castell's collective consumption
3. Disposing of 'urban': Abrams's phenomenon
4. Return of locality: Urry's special spatial effects

SOCIALIZATION IN PLACE

Neighbourhood effect revisited

1. 'The neighbourhood effect won't go away'
2. 'A process of massive indoctrination'
3. Breakdowns in socialization

Ideology and locality

1. Dominant ideology for all
2. Milieux

3. Dominant ideology and Conservative success in British elections

Place and protest

1. Protest and size of place
2. A political location theory
3. Planning for harmony

LOCATION OF LOCAL POLITICS

Geography of locational conflicts: politics of change

1. From ecology to pluralism
2. From locality to political economy

Geography of physical access: politics of mobility

1. Aggregate patterns of access
2. Reconstructing patterns of access

The geography of local government: politics of boundaries

1. Removing boundaries: the reform of US city government
2. Maintaining boundaries: the fragmented US metropolitan region
3. Redrawing boundaries: delocalization in Britain

Chapter 6

POLITICAL GEOGRAPHY OF LOCALITIES

We have reached the scale of experience in our framework for political geography. The range of this scale is defined by the day-to-day activities of people in the ordinary business of their lives. We may start with Hagerstrand's time geography concept which treats the strict space–time constraints on an individual's behaviour. Starting from his or her 'home-base' every person's day-to-day life consists of a series of regular paths that must be organized to enable return to the home-base every night. The range of these paths depends upon the transport available to the individual. This 'physicalist' view of geography places a 'space–time' prism of constraint around every individual which is unique to that individual. Hence everybody's direct experience of the world is distinctive to that person.

Being distinct does not mean being unrelated, of course. Society does not consist of an aggregation of random 'prisms' but is a highly organized and structured phenomenon. Space–time prisms are clustered as anybody who has spent time in a city's rush hour knows only too well. In much of the modern world these clusters are the 'daily urban systems' of activities around our major cities. Although usually defined just in terms of commuting, these urban systems incorporate a wide range of people's needs in modern society including shopping, education, recreation as well as employment. In core countries and many other parts of the world daily urban systems are the limit of routine behaviour and therefore represent in concrete terms the scale of experience.

Before we consider the nature of this scale we must emphasize once again that our identification of scales is a pedagogic devise and does not indicate any separateness of different systems at different scales. Every individual in his or her prism which is part of a daily urban system are no less members of a nation-state as citizens and participate in the world-economy as producers and consumers. Although the dependency heritage of the world-systems approach emphasizes the global scale, the second heritage we identified in Chapter 1, the French *Annales* school of history equally emphasizes day-to-day activities of ordinary people. For Braudel (1973) it is these routine behaviour patterns which provide the long-term structures in which 'world-events' occur. The scale of experience is just as integral to the world-economy as the scale of reality.

As we have already indicated contemporary studies of the scale of experience will normally be urban in nature. Urban studies in social science have been the largest growth area in the twentieth century. Cities have been a major concern of sociologists, political scientists and geographers for several generations. Political geography, however, apart from its treatment of capital cities, has been largely immune to this academic endeavour and urban political geography can only be said to start from about 1970. Since then studies at the urban scale have been a major growth point in political geography rivaling electoral geography as the spearhead of the sub-discipline's resurgence. Why therefore has this chapter not been entitled 'Urban political geography' or, in the style of past chapters, 'Rethinking urban political geography'? The reason is simply that we will argue in this chapter that attempts to produce 'urban theory' prefixed by any adjective is bound to fail. The richness of the empirical heritage of urban studies must not blind us to the poverty of the theory that has been produced to order that information.

This is the subject matter of our first section in which the 'ecological heritage' of urban studies is criticized and we conclude that there can be no urban theory. The importance of local studies is not thereby diminished however. We replace the distinctively 'urban' by the more general idea of locality and search for the nature of the relationship between experience defined by locality and the nation-state and world-economy that encompasses it. This relationship is the subject matter of the second section of the chapter when neighbourhood effects reappear as socialization in place. This represents a quiet on-going process of politics which goes unreported in public political debate. In contrast the final section looks at the variable content of localities which is the very stuff of what is normally recognized as 'local politics'. Locational conflicts, questions of access and the jurisdiction structure of localities have been the subject matter of the new 'urban political geography' and we treat these topics in this concluding discussion.

THE ECOLOGICAL HERITAGE

Every geography student and every researcher in urban studies is familiar with Burgess's zonal model of the city. As a spatial structure it is probably even more well-known than Christaller's central place hexagons and von Thunen's agricultural zones. But Burgess's model comes from a very different tradition than the economics of Christaller and von Thunen. It is part of the Chicago school of human ecology whose studies employed biological concepts to understand the city. The term 'ecology' now appears in geographical literature to mean analysis of areal data as in 'ecological correlation' or 'factorial ecology' so that the biological origins have all but been forgotten. In this discussion we return to this biological heritage and consider the political implications of this approach. These political implications remained when the biology was erased to leave behind confusion as to the nature of modern urban studies. We will use this debate to derive our political geography of localities.

THE RISE AND FALL OF URBAN ECOLOGY

Although E. W. Burgess's zonal model is the most well-known product of this school, the leader of the school is Robert Park. The school can be said to start from 1916 with Park's appointment to the University of Chicago's Sociology Department and the publication of his 'The City' Suggestions for the Investigation of Human Behaviour in the Urban Environment' (Park 1916). In this paper Park put forward the idea of using the city as a laboratory for investigating human behaviour and in subsequent years, with the help of of Burgess and others, this suggestion developed into the first major school of thought in urban studies. This empirical basis is nicely captured in the following quotation attributed to Park (Reissman 1964: 95):

> I expect that I have actually covered more ground tramping around cities in different parts of the world, than any other living man. Out of all this I gained, among other things, a conception of the city, the community and the region not as a geographical phenomenon merely, but as a kind of social organism.

Park's vast experience was supplemented by the work of countless students in their Chicago fieldwork for Park and Burgess to produce the most sustained research effort on one city ever mounted. It is not too far off the mark to suggest that many recent geography students have known more about Chicago in the 1920s than about their own city today!

1. Ecological theory: the hidden political dimension

The interesting feature of this work, however, was that it attempted to go beyond description. The flavour of the theoretical project is glimpsed in Park's use of the term 'social organism' to describe the city. Park evolved his ideas in a period when crude social applications of Darwin's theory of evolution were still popular. This social Darwinism used biological concepts to justify social inequalities in terms of such notions as 'survival of the fittest'. In such arguments the poorest areas of the city, the slums, could be explained by the genetic inferiority of their inhabitants. One of the results of the Chicago empirical studies, however, was to show that the same areas remained slums, in Burgess's zone of transition, as different ethnic and racial immigrant groups passed through them (Faris 1967: 57). Hence slums were problems of the area and not the individuals that lived there at any one point in time. This change in focus from individual to area led to a changing biological brief, from genetics to ecology.

Ecology evolved out of Darwinian biology as the study of the relationship between an organism and its environment. These relationships

defined a 'web of life' in which inter-relationship between different
organisms – plant and animal – and the environment produced an
'ecology'. Distinctive patterns of equilibrium were produced in a
'purposeless' manner by the laws of nature. These laws or processes were
not 'directed' or 'planned' but nevertheless resulted in stable and clear-cut
patterns of organisms. What Park did was to transfer these ideas to the
organization of the city where human patterns could be similarly
interpreted.

In Table 10 I have listed some ecological concepts and provided
examples for animal/plant ecology and for human ecology. Every
'environment' must be bounded to define an ecological unit in which
equilibrium can be reached. A salt marsh is a good example of such a
distinctive environment. In human ecology nation-state, region or city
provide such units although in practice it was the city that was the prime
ecological unit. Hence human ecology was in reality only urban ecology.
Within the city 'natural' processes occurred as competition for scarce
resources in the same way as they occurred in other ecology. The process
of adaption and specialization were thought of as general means by which
resources were used and allocated, in biology among species, in human
ecology among occupation groups and land-use classes. All are not equal
in these processes and dominant species/groups will control the community
as trees do in woodlands through their control on light and business does
in the city through its central location. Hence the city is ordered around
the central business district in Burgess's model just as shrubs, grasses and
mosses are ordered with respect to trees.

Of course Park did not believe that this ecological approach could fully
describe the city. The cultural components of the city had no equivalent in
animal or plant ecology. Park, therefore, divided the study of society into

Table 10 The 'Nature' and Politics of Human Ecology

Ecological concept	Animal/plant ecology example	Human ecology example	Political implications
An 'environment' as an ecological unit	e.g. salt marsh	e.g. city	Analysis is restricted to locality
Natural processes	Biological competition for scarce resources	Economic competition for scarce resources	Market processes are universal and inevitable
Adaption and specialization	Different species in different ecological niches	Occupation groups/land use classes in 'natural areas'	Class system is merely specialization which benefits all
Dominance and control of community	e.g. trees in a woodland community	e.g. Commerce and industry in the city	Dominant classes are as benign as trees

two levels – the biotic substructure which could be described as ecology and the cultural superstructure which incorporated a moral order beyond ecology. The biotic order was based solely on the prime need for survival as expressed through competition. It is Park's version of the survival of the fittest and must not be confused with the classical Marxist base and superstructure model. Whereas the economic base in Marxism defines the structure governing society specific to a mode of production, Park's ecological processes are eternal and natural. As such they provided a new justification for the inequalities of the city to supersede the increasingly discredited genetic explanations. As Castells (1977) points out the competition Park describes is not ecological: it is merely a particular expression of laissez-faire capitalism. In the final column of Table 10 some of the political implications of the use of ecological concepts are shown. As illustrated throughout this book, the proposition that some human behaviour is 'natural' is usually a justification for a particular status quo. Quite simply, dominant classes are not like trees, and the processes of their control are anything but natural and 'purposeless'.

2. Ecology as spatial structure: apolitical urban studies

This type of political argument did not enter urban geography until the 1970s. Urban ecology was originally criticized on empirical grounds – 'are the zones really circular?' – and then in terms of the impossibility of separating 'biotic' and 'cultural' levels. This disposed of the ecological theory but many of the ideas, especially concerning spatial structure, remained. These were incorporated into two forms of developmentalism in sociology. First, the folk–urban continuum of Robert Redfield (1941), Park's son-in-law, used human-ecology ideas to define the 'modern' end of a sequence of communities which subsequently fed into the modernization theory discussed in Chapter 1. Second, the new emphasis upon social as opposed to ecological processes generated a social-area analysis (Shevky and Bell 1955). This latter is interesting for two reasons. It represents an explicit break with human ecology's treatment of the city as separate from society. In social-area analysis modernization trends for society as a whole are extrapolated down to the city scale. General processes of urbanization and industrialization lead to specific processes such as skill differentiation and new family functions which are reflected in urban social patterns as social areas. It is these ideas which were enthusiastically taken up by urban geographers who eventually were able to show an equivalence between social-area analysis and 'ecological' structure (Murdie 1969) using the techniques of factor analysis in 'factorial ecology'. In this way urban geography was placed within the overall developmentalism of modernization theory.

Ecological theory was dead but ecological structures survived. Natural areas were replaced by social areas and purposeless processes gave way to household decision-making on where to live. The best example was

Alonso's (1964) trade-off model whereby rich people chose to spend money on commuting and suburban living while poor people chose to live in overcrowded inner-city conditions, hence saving on commuting costs. Kirby (1976) has shown how this trade-off between housing costs and commuting in reality does not exist: it merely models what are structural constraints as individual choices. This point has been made more generally by Gray (1975) who argues that urban geography was both mythical and mystical in its emphasis upon choice in explaining urban spatial structures. Burgess's zones may not be due to natural ecological processes but neither are they the result of households simply choosing to live where they wished. A conservative naturalism had given way to a conservative liberalism but both had similar political implications: justification of the status quo. The inequality reflected in slums is neither an inevitable effect of natural processes nor the result of such areas being attractive to the people who live there. The idea that people might not want to live in such poor conditions but had no choice because they could afford no other locations was missing from apolitical urban geography (Gray 1975). In short, power – and hence politics – is ignored in an ideal world where the dominant classes dominate and nobody notices.

RECENT DEBATES IN URBAN STUDIES

The debates in urban studies since the fall of urban ecology have had a strange twist to them. It all revolves around what is and what is not 'urban'. First, urban is represented by spatial structure as 'politics' are added to traditional ecological themes. Second, the spatial basis of urban is dismissed and it becomes equated with particular activities of the modern state. Third, this is taken a step further when urban is dismissed as a meaningful category for study. Finally, space, and with it urban space, is rediscovered as a neglected theme in social science.

At first glance it would seem that this debate has gone round in circles. In fact the debate is vital for understanding how the concept of locality used in this study relates to urban political geography. We do not arrive back at urban ecology, instead we find a new basis for analysis. Hence we deal with each step of the argument in turn in order finally to reach a justification for the study of locality.

1. Reaffirming space: Pahl's managerialism

The redefinition of urban sociology that came in the late 1960s did more than add politics to the processes of residential differentiation. Park had separated out the city as an 'ecological unit' and social-area analysts had treated the city as reflecting societal trends but neither had doubted the existence of a distinct phenomena – the city. This urban entity was usually defined in opposition to rural areas but, as the latter declined, society as a whole began to resemble an 'urban society'. In such highly urbanized societies as Britain the notion of an urban sociology separate from general sociology seemed increasingly archaic. R. E. Pahl (1970) set about the task of redefining urban sociology and in the process emphasized constraints on behaviour rather than choice and so introduced power into his project.

In order to find a new urban sociology Pahl (1970) drew a parallel with industrial sociology. Although we live in an 'industrial society' the social relations of authority in the industrial system constitute a viable industrial sociology. Similarly an urban sociology should study the social relations of authority in the urban system. Pahl's (1970) schema is famous for introducing the notion of social gatekeepers – planners, social workers, estate agents, developers, and so on – who organize and control the scarce urban resources. Hence industrial managers have their counterpart in urban managers. The result is a socio-spatial system which reflects power in society as mediated by these managers. Pahl, therefore, proposes a *spatial* sociology where the organization and control of facilities, access to such resources and their effects on the life-chances of individuals replaces traditional urban sociology's emphasis on the study of a particular type of place identified as 'urban'.

Pahl's approach has come to be known as the managerial thesis and has initiated a large debate. While generally praised for emphasizing the constraints that exist in the urban system over individual choices, the nature of the constraints identified by Pahl are controversial. In short he is criticized for dealing with the 'middle dogs' at the expense of the top dogs of the system. By this it is meant that by concentrating on the immediate managers of urban resources, such as public housing managers, the ultimate constraints on their actions are neglected. Middle managers may control 'who gets what' to some degree but they have little or no say in how much there is to distribute in the first place. Unlike the industrial system where a hierarchy of managers can easily be identified pursuing a definite goal in terms of company profit, in the urban system there seems to be no equivalent pursuit. It remains an amorphous mixture of different managers controlling a wide range of resources with no overall coherent purpose in Pahl's scheme of things. But of course there are processes operating in the urban system no less than in the industrial system which define the nature of the system and the overall constraints in which it operates.

Pahl's programme of 'spatial sociology' in Britain was paralleled by a similar argument for a spatial urban political science in USA by Williams (1971). While being more explicit in his ecological heritage, Williams attempted to move modern urban ecology away from individual choice emphasis to one in which space is socially controlled to manipulate accessibility to resources. Spatially defined interest groups rather than managers are the focus of attention but the result is similar to that of Pahl. Analysis of the urban field consists of studying the spatial organization of urban resources and facilities and the conflicts this generated. Not surprisingly these ideas appealed to geographers and it is at this time that urban political geography can be said to begin, the first substantial works being David Harvey's (1973) *Social Justice and the City* and Kevin Cox's (1973) *Conflict, Power and Politics in the City: A Geographical View*. But no sooner had geography found a spatial framework to borrow, this framework came under severe attack. With its spatial emphasis it is arguable whether these new studies represented the final death throes of the urban ecology tradition or the birth of a genuinely new urban political geography. Whichever interpretation is preferred matters little since this interpretation of urban as spatial has been largely replaced by more holistic political economy analysis. We will return to some of the themes of this work in our final section below.

2. Disposing of space: Castell's collective consumption

Although urban studies have been largely neglected in Marxist thought (Tabb and Sawers 1978), the most influential urban study of the 1970s was undoubtedly Manuel Castells's (1977) *The Urban Question* which derived directly from the French school of structuralist Marxism. The popularity of Castells's work was not so much due to its Marxist credentials, indeed as we shall see his most enthusiastic followers have been non-Marxists, but because it directly confronted the whole gamut of problems in urban analysis from the ecologists onwards and it offered a new exciting programme of research. In short it represents an abrupt break in a tradition that was being seen increasingly as an albatross. With the publication of Castells's work urban ecology could be well and truly buried, for the very last time.

Castells (1977) approaches the concept of the urban as an 'everyday notion'. It is, in his words, the 'domain of experience' where people live their day-to-day lives. Thus the urban unit is 'the everyday space of a delimited fraction of the labour force' (Castells 1977: 445). Hence the 'domain' corresponds to the daily urban systems we identified in the introduction to this chapter. So far, therefore, Castells's schema is entirely consistent with our scale of experience. But Castells narrows his concern to only certain activities within daily urban systems. In advanced capitalist societies he argues that the processes of production and reproduction can be interpreted as relating to essentially different scales of operation. Whereas production is organized at a national and international scale, the reproduction of labour remains an urban phenomenon. This reproduction involves consumption processes in which the state has become increasingly involved. This is termed *collective consumption* and includes urban planning, public transport, public housing, education, public health care, and so on. Hence the city becomes a 'unit of collective consumption' (Castells 1978: 148) which explains why 'urban problems' usually reduce to local conflicts over public management of consumption in transport, planning, housing, and so on. The result of this argument is what Dunleavy

(1980: 50) terms a 'content' definition of the urban field. This replaces the 'urban ideology' of the ecological heritage with the equation 'urban = collective consumption'. On this basis Dunleavy has defined an urban political analysis in which the spatial basis of 'urban' or 'city' is entirely banished. All we are left with is a set of processes concerning the reproduction of labour which are deemed to be 'urban' in nature.

3. Disposing of 'urban': Abrams's phenomenon

The final demise of the urban as a distinct object for study can be found in the work of Philip Abrams (1978). He castigates the whole ecological heritage as reifying the city as if it were a social object whereas in reality it is 'nothing more than a phenomenon' (Abrams 1978: 10). Hence the reason why we have no adequate theory of the city is because it is impossible. The city is not an entity that we can develop theory around because it is not an operating system. Here we return to Pahl's problem of the lack of a goal for his urban system. Whereas the factories, firms or companies operating in industrial systems are units that contribute to the operation of the system, there is no parallel way in which towns and cities operate in the urban system. Hence attempts to ascertain the role of cities in the rise of capitalism in the core, or in modern peripheral under-development, are misplaced. City and towns are merely arenas for the unfolding of social relations, they do not themselves represent social relations. In Abrams's (1978: 31) words towns should be seen 'as battles rather than monuments'.

4. Return of locality: Urry's specific spatial effects

A major advantage of the idea of collective consumption is that it links 'urban problems' directly to increased state activities as described by, among many others, O'Connor's (1973) work on the functions of the capitalist state. It is, of course, true that the fiscal crisis of state expenditure is acutely seen in our inner city areas due to the disproportionate dependence of their populations on the state: cuts in state expenditure have been most severely felt in our cities. Dunleavy's urban political analysis is able, therefore, to harness many 'non-local' processes as necessary components in the study of urban policy. But somewhere along the way the 'urban' concept as it relates to places we know as towns and cities seems to be lost. We need to return to consideration of towns and cities as places as 'the context in which people live out their daily routine' (Mellor 1975: 277).

In the work of John Urry (1981) the argument has come full circle. He bemoans the *neglect* of the 'spatial' element in social science. In particular he criticizes Castell's (1977) argument that space has no meaning outside the social relations that define it. Although space *per se* can have no independent effect, Urry argues that the spatial arrangement of social objects *can* effect their social relations. Hence he dismisses the idea that there can be a *general* spatial social science as attempted by Chicago human ecologists in the 1920s and quantitative geographers in the 1960s but there are specific spatial effects which are local in scope. Hence we return to the notion of a locality which in most core situations, and many periphery situations, will be the daily urban system as the local labour market. Although social classes are mobilized politically at the national scale their distribution among localities will be uneven. Different mixes of social groups or classes will lead to different patterns of social relations. These differences in experiences will not automatically be evened out by nationalizing processes. In fact, according to Urry (1981) with increasing economic control at the national and international scales we can expect more politicization of localities as particular labour markets suffer the recession. And this is not just important for reproduction of labour, it can have local effects on production processes.

We accept Urry's argument in this chapter. This is not a new position of course but a restatement of the contextual effect of localities (Filkin and Weir 1972). From our perspective localities are important since they provide different experiences for their populations and these will have political implications. But we are not trying to contribute to or develop any new 'urban' theory. The localities we deal with below are largely daily urban systems but the emphasis is upon the variety of contexts they provide in terms of class balances and resources rather than as some general notion of 'the city'. In short, we have moved on from city as ecological unit to locality as social context.

SOCIALIZATION IN PLACE

Political socialization theory has been one of the major growth areas in political science (Renshon 1977). It has come to be seen as a key process for the stability of a political system. Quite simply political control can be by coercion or by consensus. The former is extremely dangerous and expensive and the latter is the preferred option where possible. In every society there will be a balance between coercion and consensus and this will vary throughout the world-economy. The contrast between the distribution of irregular executive transfers (Figure 17) and liberal democracy (Figure 18) has already illustrated the geography of the coercion/consensus balance. The consensus in the core is reproduced and sustained by political socialization processes. This involves the learning of the necessary political values through family, school, mass media and other communication. It is these processes as they operate within liberal democracies which are the concern of this section.

NEIGHBOURHOOD EFFECT REVISITED

Massive growth in a field of study does not necessarily mean any major extension of our knowledge. In the case of political socialization attempts to develop universal theory have been unsuccessful (Renshon 1977). Political socialization does not consist of universal processes but involves particular processes operating in *concrete* social situations. It is the experiences of individuals within their specific localities which provide the context and raw material for socialization. And this process is normally termed the 'neighbourhood effect' which we described briefly in the last chapter. In electoral geography neighbourhood effects are generally considered to be relatively unimportant. Although Cox (1969) and Reynolds and Archer (1969) attempted to develop a 'spatial' electoral geography around this concept their ideas have not been generally followed up. Explanation of voting patterns has continued to be centred upon the political cleavages among the electors with the neighbourhood effect brought in to account for minor deviations. Hence Taylor and Johnston (1979: 267) conclude that its impact is 'negligible'. Here we reverse this conclusion and bring neighbourhood effects back to the centre of the stage not as an abstract location theory but as socialization in place.

1. 'The neighbourhood effect won't go away'

One of the interesting things about studies of neighbourhood effects is that evidence for this process seems very clear-cut and firm at the aggregate scale but it has been much harder to find at the individual scale. An example of the sort of impressive findings for aggregate analysis can be found in Almy's (1973) study of 55 referenda voting patterns in 18 different American cities between 1955 and 1972. These referenda covered a wide range of topics including fluoridation of water supplies, education and public works. Almy compared voting returns for precincts with socio-economic data to define what he termed 'electoral cohesion' within social groups. This simply means whether similar precincts in socio-economic terms voted together on a particular referenda proposition. Almy found 19 cases of low electoral cohesion and 36 cases of high electoral cohesion. Why do these different levels of cohesion occur? Almy argued that cities with high levels of residential segregation would foster high electoral cohesion as a neighbourhood effect. Conversely in an integrated city a neighbourhood effect is cancelled out. The hypothesis is justified by his results. Sixteen of the 19 cases of low electoral cohesion occur in integrated cities and 31 of the 36 cases of high electoral cohesion occur in segregated cities. Clearly the inference that the spatial structure of these cities affects voting patterns through neighbourhood effects is a very reasonable one on this evidence.

Inferences from aggregate data may seem clear-cut but they remain only indirect 'tests' of the neighbourhood effect. Some researchers have looked at individual voters and attempted to find a neighbourhood effect in interactions among residents in local areas. Fitton (1973), for instance, surveyed 87 voters in three streets in Manchester, England during the 1970 election campaign and found some evidence for residents conforming to the pro-Labour sentiments of their neighbours but the quantity and frequency of political discussion did not suggest that the neighbourhood was a potent force in national politics. This is, of course, in line with surveys that show that most people obtain their political information from the mass media, especially TV. In fact it is becoming increasingly difficult to equate the aggregate findings for neighbourhood effects in elections with modern campaigning techniques of advertising whether 'making' presidents or prime ministers. This has led some researchers to suggest that the neighbourhood effect reflects altogether different processes. Dunleavy (1979), for instance, argues that deviations from class voting is due to consumption issues – housing and transport – and not the neighbourhood effect. However Johnston (1983) has tested Dunleavy's ideas by adding consumption variables to class variables to his analysis and still finds evidence indicating a neighbourhood effect. In Johnston's words, despite the efforts of many sceptics, 'the neighbourhood effect won't go away'.

2. 'A process of massive indoctrination'

The only way out of this dilemma is to relate neighbourhood effects back to the overall socialization process of which they are part. This means a change of emphasis from cross-sectional studies to a longer time horizon. Instead of trying to find evidence of a process in a particular campaign as Fitton (1973) does, we consider political socialization, in Miliband's (1969: 182) words, as 'a process of massive indoctrination' from birth to death. This involves neighbourhood influences but it includes much more than that. Other findings in electoral studies soon fall into place in such a socialization perspective. In their massive survey of British electoral behaviour, for instance, Butler and Stokes (1969) found that the best predictor of a person's party preference was their knowledge of their parents voting behaviour, especially their father's. This obviously reflects socialization within the family as the prime process. But there are other factors at work relating to a voter's experiences. In particular the 'political climate' during their first voting experience seems to be subsequently important. Butler and Stokes (1969) employ a 'generational model' to show how 'pro-Labour' generations (for example, from 1945) and 'pro-Conservative' generations (for example, from 1959) have moved through time as identifiable voting cohorts.

In electoral geography the most direct evidence of this overall socialization process is not the neighbourhood effect *per se* but the stability of voting patterns. With the exception of modern USA, liberal democracies have very stable voting patterns that have lasted for several generations. It has been shown that, for instance, in post-1945 elections in EEC countries, most parties have a consistent pattern of support within the country. In some cases this can be traced back further. In Britain we noted in the last chapter that the national pattern of support for the Labour Party has remained basically the same since its first major election campaign in 1918. These stable patterns are what we previously termed 'normal votes' in our discussion of past voting stability in USA in the last chapter. Normal votes represent the ability of parties to mobilize support but they do not start from scratch in every election, they build on basic socialization processes that operate either for or against them in particular localities.

3. Breakdowns in socialization

We might wish to refer to this as the 'silent campaigning' of the locality. It only really appears as an observable process when it breaks down. This occurs when a change in party system operates in such a way that the 'normal' allegiance of a locality is no longer consistent with the material interests of the locality. Obviously such a change will not happen overnight. Lewis (1965) has described just such a process in Flint, Michigan in the 1930s. The black residential districts are initially solid Republican areas, still 'voting for Abraham Lincoln', but they become equally solid Democrat areas as the New Deal policies evolved. This is not an even process. In Flint there are two black residential areas and it is the northern one that converts to Democrat first. Here we have differential local neighbourhood effects operating so that in some elections, in 1942 for example, the two black districts voted in different directions.

More insights into the processes going on in localities during periods of political realignment can be found from Gregory's (1968) study of politics in mining communities in Britain before the First World War. In the late nineteenth century mining constituencies were the safest Liberal seats in the country but by the 1918 election they had become the safest Labour seats. The process of this changeover involved the miner's union and their affiliation to the Labour Party in 1907. But it was not a simple procedure of the union directing their members to vote Labour. There were different traditions of radicalisms among the coalfields which Gregory relates to working conditions. Hence the North East coalfield was relatively 'moderate' whereas South Wales was more 'radical'. This was reflected in voting so that in 1910 the Liberals maintained MPs in the North East but not in South Wales. The way in which changes occurred can be glimpsed by a look at a by-election at Houghton-le-Spring, Durham in 1913. When the sitting Liberal MP died the Liberal Association adopted a commercial traveller to defend the seat. Labour nominated the president of the Durham Miners Association to challenge. Since over half the electors were miners it might be expected that this would be a Labour gain. In the event villages and even households throughout the constituency were divided from top to bottom. Generally speaking it was the younger miners who were changing to Labour but the older miners remained loyal to the Liberals. The result was a Liberal victory with Labour remaining in third place with 22 per cent of the vote (Gregory 1968: 80–1). This was a rare competitive election for a mining constituency. Socialization between generations was breaking down as the community was adjusting to a changing national party system. After 1918 Houghton-le-Spring took its place among the safe seats in Labour's 'traditional' heartland.

IDEOLOGY AND LOCALITY

Our conclusion from the above discussion is that the neighbourhood effect is much more than a matter of inter-personal relations. It is not just whether the quantity of political contacts a person experiences are biased for one party or another, it is the fact that localities are places in which the general process of socialization occurs which is important. And this is not just a matter of favouring one party or another; it is to do with the setting up and sustaining of ideologies within which parties have to fit. These ideologies are, as we have seen, first and foremost national ideologies as individuals are socialized into becoming citizens of a particular country. This has led to the idea of different political cultures existing in different countries. The most famous study along these lines is Almond and Verba's (1963) *Civic Culture* where they used an international social survey to show that British and American citizens held attitudes more condusive to liberal democracy that German, Italian and Mexican citizens. Britain and USA, therefore, had 'civic cultures' with the British being particularly deferential. In the discussion that follows we will develop this finding of Almond and Verba's by relating it to locality.

The problem with their concept of 'national' political culture is its unitary nature. From their sample survey Almond and Verba derive one culture per country. This precludes differences in culture within countries developing in response to material inequalities experienced in different localities. In effect Almond and Verba base their concept upon an extreme consensus model of society which assumes a homogeneous pattern of values and attitudes within countries. This is no longer acceptable. In sociological studies of local communities, for instance, there is a strong tradition of describing a 'working class' culture which is not easily accommodated in the unitary concept of political culture. In this discussion we follow Jessop (1974) in equating political culture with the notion of dominant ideology and use Parkin's (1967, 1971) scheme for identifying variety within this domination.

1. Dominant ideology for all

Starting with the basic Marxist dictum that the ruling ideas in a society are the ideas of the ruling class we will define the political culture of a country as the *dominant ideology*. This is a moral framework of ideas and values that endorse the existing system. In all countries with market economies it will endorse capitalist ideas although it will vary between countries in terms of the particular values emphasized for social control in different national contexts – in Britain there is a dominant ideology supporting the capitalist ethos but with a deferential cultural addition according to Almond and Verba (1963).

If the dominant ideology is to be useful in avoiding the need for physical coercion to maintain the status quo it must be accepted, in part at least, by the vast majority of all the population, rulers and ruled. Parkin identifies two direct expressions of the dominant ideology in the dominated class: *deferential* and *aspirational*. In both examples the subject accepts the status quo but in the former he also accepts his low status, in the latter he is striving *individually* to raise his position within the system. A related value system is the subordinate one which indirectly expresses the dominant system. In this case the status quo is accepted but within a moral framework which emphasizes communal improvement within the system. This is an *accommodative* set of values which amount to a 'negotiated' version of the dominant ideology (Parkin 1971: 92). The dominant ideology is filtered to day-to-day needs so that it continues to provide the abstract moral frame of reference while the subordinate value system deals with the concrete social situation involving choice and action. Parkin (1971: 95) refers to this as two levels of normative reference – 'the abstract and the situational'. Deferential, aspirational and accommodative values all contrast with *oppositional* values based upon a radical ideology which is designed to counter and replace the dominant ideology. In a stable liberal democracy the latter needs to be relegated to the status of fringe politics.

One important corollary of this argument is that we no longer have to subscribe to Almond and Verba's rather simplistic notion of Britain's 'deferential' civic culture. Such a model of the dominant ideology is unnecessary since stability can be maintained without coercion through aspirational and accommodative value systems as well as deference. This is important because Jessop (1974) has found feelings of deference less important in Britain than Almond and Verba's study would imply. The latter survey was part of a comparative politics exercise which highlighted British deference. It may well be that the British population is less aspirational than their American counterparts and less accommodative than the Swedish population (Scase 1977) but this does not mean that these two value systems are not important in Britain. In all stable Western countries ideological dominance will be reflected in various mixes of deferential, aspirational and accommodative value systems. The particular mixture in any one country will depend on the strategies of the dominant classes in the past and the concrete experiences of dominated classes in their day-to-day activities.

2. Milieux

And so we return to localities. Lockwood (1966) has explicitly linked these alternative value systems to 'the vantage point of a person's own particular milieux' and 'their experiences of the social inequality in the smaller societies in which they live out their daily lives'. Three types of locality are identified. (i) The urban-industrial milieux with large factories and a dominance of impersonal inter-class relations enables an accommodative value system to develop. (ii) The rural-agricultural milieux with small traditional industry and personal inter-class relations is condusive to the maintenance of deferential value systems. (iii) The suburban-residential milieux with its competitive conspicuous consumption is the location of the aspirational value system.

These milieux are implicit in much discussion of British politics. In quantitative electoral geography they appear as variables in attempts to explain aggregate voting patterns (Piepe, Prior and Box 1969; Crewe 1973; Crewe and Payne 1976). In the most sophisticated model, for example, Crewe and Payne (1976) add to their basic social-class model of voting, first, specific variables identifying 'agricultural' constituencies and 'mining' constituencies and, second, measures of the previous level of party voting in constituencies to take into account other abnormally 'strong' Labour or Conservative localities. The result is a highly successful model which statistically accounts for about 90 per cent of the variation in Labour voting among constituencies in 1970. But milieux imply much more than additional variables for cross-sectional statistical analyses. Milieux are living communities which have distinctive histories. The most comprehensive investigation of such communities using a long historical perspective is Newby's (1977) study of rural communities in East Anglia. He begins by using the ideas of Parkin (1971) but finds that identifying a deferential value system is more difficult than initially supposed. How far is the imputed deference of agricultural workers merely a realistic behavioural adjustment to the powerlessness of their situation? Or is it a matter of values being formed to match the constraints on the day-to-day lives of the workers? These are not problems to unravel here but the influence of locality is not in doubt.

3. Dominant ideology and Conservative success in British elections

Many observers have commented on the seeming paradox of Conservative success in British elections. As long ago as 1867 Engels lamented the success of the Conservative Party in the wake of franchise reforms which gave many working men the vote for the first time. This most traditional of political parties has shown itself most adept at mobilizing support in over a century of elections. Despite a majority of working-class voters since 1885, there have been only three anti-Conservative governments with a clear majority in Parliament in this period (Liberal 1906–10, Labour

1945–51 and Labour 1964–70). In contrast Conservative or Conservative-dominated governments have controlled Parliament on thirteen occasions since 1885. Clearly very many working-class voters have supported the Conservative Party over these years. Such voting has been considered 'deviant' on the grounds that first Liberal and then Labour are the 'natural' party of the working class (Mackenzie and Silver 1968).

By employing a socialization and dominant ideology approach a very different picture emerges. Parkin (1967) considers *any* voting for Labour to be deviant to the extent that it is interpreted as anti-dominant class. Labour voting reflects a less than satisfactory socialization into an accommodative value system. In order for such a voting position to be maintained 'barriers' are required to insulate voters from the full weight of the dominant value system. This is where locality comes in either as a working-class community or as a large workplace. Where they are combined – dockland, mining communities – insulation is greatest and hence Labour voting highest. The least insulated members of the working class are housewives and the retired, both of whom are typically least Labour-orientated. Jessop (1974) has tested some of these ideas by devising a 'structural score' in terms of such barriers and confirms Parkin's ideas.

Clearly the neighbourhood effect when viewed as socialization in place is anything but negligible. Modern British politics can be interpreted in terms of the differential abilities of the parties to mobilize support among persons with different value systems in contrasting localities. Whereas industrial and rural milieux have consistently been Labour and Conservative orientated respectively, it is in the aspirational milieux that elections have increasingly been won and lost. In the social democratic consensus and technocratic politics phases Labour appealed to aspirational values and were relatively successful. In the two phases of national interest Conservatives have been able to push Labour back into its traditional industrial heartlands. This is, of course, the nature of the dominant ideology. In times of recession the material needs of the dominated class are accepted as being against the national interest (Miliband 1969: 207).

PLACE AND PROTEST

Ideology as it relates to voting intentions is only one part of politics. Other forms of political activity can be related to locality as many researchers have shown. Tilly (1978) has traced the changing 'reportoire' of protest from the early world-economy to the emergence of liberal democracy. Traditional parades, burning of effigies, sabotage, petitions, strikes, mass demonstrations, insurrection and revolution – all have distinctive social and ideological structures based upon experience of economic relations rooted in locality. But there is no simple relation between political activity and locality. Tilly (1978) argues that material interests alone will not produce protest but that, in addition, organization, mobilization and opportunity are required. Hence even the very plausible 'isolated mass hypothesis' of Kerr and Siegel (1954) that segregated homogenous workforces such as miners and dockers/longshoreman are prone to high strike levels is shown to be untenable as a general process (Tilly 1978: 67).

Nevertheless there are numerous studies that have related localities to political activity. Brigg's (1963) critique of Mumford's (1938) characterization of the nineteenth-century city as the appalling 'Coketown' depends upon drawing a distinction between different locales. Although Mumford's model fits Manchester with its large factories and resulting large social distance between classes it does not fit Birmingham with its small workshops and closer contact between classes. This idea that the industrial nature of a locality will be reflected in social relations and hence politics is similarly drawn by Read (1964: 35) when he describes Birmingham and Sheffield as 'cities of political union' and Manchester and Leeds as 'cities of social cleavage'. The most detailed study of the way local social structures are reflected in political activity is the comparison of Oldham, Northampton and South Shields by Foster (1974). These studies of social relations in place are interesting but too specific for our purposes and we will not describe them in detail here. Instead we concentrate on two topics – the relation of size of place to political activity and attempts to plan places to control political activity.

1. Protest and size of place

To many observers in the nineteenth century large cities were the centres of agitation and protest. This is certainly the opinion of Engels (1952) and of the pioneer town planners as we shall relate below. But recent statistical analysis of protest and organization have shown a remarkable regularity that disputes the militancy of large cities. In nineteenth-century Britain Lees (1982) has shown that strikes were more likely in medium-sized towns. Similarly in late nineteenth-century USA labour organizations and socialism were found to be stronger in medium-size towns than in large cities by Bennett and Earle (1983). Let us consider the processes involved for each case.

Lees's (1982) evidence relates to strikes in Yorkshire, Lancashire, Nottinghamshire and Leicestershire in two 'strike-waves', 1842 and 1889–91. He divides these counties into settlements of different populations and computes strike rates for each of five size categories. Strike rates in small (less than 2,000) and large (over 300,000) settlements are consistently the lowest. Highest rates are usually found in his middle category of towns from 20,000 to 100,000. Lees's explanation is that different sized towns had qualitatively different forms of relations with political authority and that this changed over the two periods. In the 1840s large towns were incorporated and had their own local political

authority including justices and police. In contrast other towns were
controlled by outside (county) authority with policing carried out by the
army. In the incorporated towns there was more likelihood of mediation
and less likelihood of provocation by the authorities. By the 1890s these
contrasts were even more marked. The various organs of mediation in
work disputes – general trade councils for labour and chambers of
commerce for capital often combined in conciliation boards – were
particularly developed in the larger towns and cities. In Tilly's terms, the
repertoire of protest could be extended towards more 'legitimate' politics
and the single weapon of the strike blunted. The strike in nineteenth-
century Britain, therefore, seems to have been a phenomenon of the social
relations and authorities of medium-sized towns more than other places.

Bennett and Earle (1983) consider the two 'surges' of socialism in the
USA in the late nineteenth and early twentieth centuries. In the 1880s the
Knights of Labour reached a membership approaching two million and in
1912 the Socialist Party presidential candidate obtained nearly one million
votes. In investigating the geography of these two movements Bennett and
Earle find that size of place is important. The Knights of Labour
'displayed surprising strength in unexpected places, notably the small
towns and cities of the Middle West' (Bennett and Earle 1983: 47). In the
regression analysis of the 1912 Socialist Party vote by counties, population
of county is found to be a significant variable. For counties with
populations under 85,000 socialist vote and population size is positively
correlated whereas for counties over 85,000 the relationship is an inverse
one. That is to say the Socialist Party obtained less votes in small *and*
large localities. American socialism was a feature of the medium-sized
settlement, localities where paternalistic social relations persisted and
interfered with the domination of capital (Gordon, 1976).

2. A political location theory

Gordon (1976) has incorporated the processes described above into a more
general location theory of labour control. He argues that there are two
forms of efficiency, quantitative efficiency related to improved technology
and qualitative efficiency related to control of workforce. The latter can be
indexed by strike activity. In the process of capital accumulation firms
which combine both efficiencies will be the successful competitors in the
market. Gordon argues that it is qualitative efficiency that has dominated
location decisions for investment. Before 1870 in the USA for instance,
industrial growth was spread among towns of all sizes. After 1870 however
there is marked concentration of growth in large cities at the expense of
medium-sized towns. This reflects the qualitative inefficiency of the latter
as described above. Gordon takes the argument further forward in time.
Concentration of workers in large cities eventually led to local commerce
losing political control of their cities. This is accompanied by the

suburbanization of industry symbolized by the development of Gary steelworks *beyond* Chicago. Gordon describes the 'sudden' emergence of the de-centralization strategy and relates it directly to the rise of corporate capitalism. The late 1890s are a period of phenomenal merger activity which produced large corporations able to take broad strategic decisions such as decentralization of plant. The qualitative efficiency explanation is far superior to quantitative efficiency explanations which emphasize changes in transport and land needs. Gordon is able to document that the decision-makers at the time were clear in their motives (Gordon 1978: 75). Cities had become 'hotbeds of trade unionism' and corporations were relocating investment to non-union plants in the suburbs. The final stage in this process is the regional shift from unionized North-East USA to the less-unionized South and West of the present day. The 'rise of the sunbelt' can thus be seen as the third location strategy in US capital's battle to keep control of US labour.

This process has not been documented in detail elsewhere but the general pattern seems to fit. In Britain for instance we have described the militancy of medium-sized towns and they certainly grew slower than large cities in late-nineteenth-century Britain. Similarly de-centralization and regional shifts in investment have also been inversely related to unionism in the twentieth century. The qualitative efficiency argument is clearly attractive here also. It is, of course, consistent with the 'runaway shop' process that has typified the world-economy from its inception. Wallerstein (1980a: 194) shows how the stagnation of the logistic B-phase was combated in part by a relocation strategy in many industries. Throughout central and western Europe the power of labour guilds was broken by moving industry to the countryside. This physical dispersion led to weaker labour organization and lower wages. And, of course, today's runaway shop to peripheral countries – Korea, Mexico and so on – is the latest example of the qualitative efficiency strategy. Here we have a political location theory rather than the economic location theory which has dominated geography.

3. Planning for harmony

The lesson of the above discussion is that ultimately capital, by investment, creates and destroys places. In core countries in the twentieth century this power of capital has been mediated by the state through the activity of 'town planning'. 'Planning' is sometimes contrasted with 'market' and is then assumed to be anti-capitalist in some way. In fact in the theory of the state we developed in Chapter 4 planning occurs as an alternative way in which the interests of dominant classes can be safeguarded or promoted. Sarkissian (1976) has described how planning has attempted to apply the neighbourhood effect to promote social harmony.

Planners have a long history of promoting the social mixture of communities. Why should social mix be preferred to segregation of classes which the housing market left to itself would produce? Early planners argued that by mixing classes the behaviour of the lower classes would be raised by emulating their more affluent neighbours. In this way social harmony could be created and social tensions reduced. In some ways this was an anti-urban 'back-to-the-village' movement but it also encompassed ideas such as equality of opportunity for all classes and provision of leadership for the urban poor. But the emphasis upon emulation meant that social problems were reduced to individual behaviour. It was just a matter of teaching the poor to behave.

The practical application of these ideas can be traced back to George Cadbury's building of Bourneville on the outskirts of Birmingham in the 1880s. This was a paternalistic project – it was a temperance settlement, for example – but social mix was an integral part of the plan to produce an ideal 'balanced community'. The idea of a balanced locality is most developed in Ebenezer Howard's Garden City Movement which is probably Britain's major contribution to town planning. Although his book is now well known as *Garden Cities of Tomorrow* it was originally published in 1898 as *To-morrow: A Peaceful Path to Real Reform* which clearly places the movement in political perspective. This planning in no way challenged the basic forces operating in British society, rather it steered them into politically safe directions. Howard's motives were explicitly anti-revolutionary as his original title suggests. In fact Garden City advocates were careful to maintain segregation at the neighbourhood level because complete integration implied 'equality and hence mediocrity' (Sarkissian 1976: 236).

These ideas became popular after the Second World War. The 'classlessness' of national sacrifice became directed towards reconstruction and in Britain, in particular, this involved town planning dominated by garden city ideas. The neighbourhood unit as a small balanced community fitted into this planning ideology and was imported from the USA. The whole process was promoted in both countries by the onset of the Cold War with the USSR. Balanced neighbourhoods where different classes had equal opportunities became an important element in the 'free' 'democratic' world's claim to continue to be the 'true' 'progressive' force in the world (Sarkissian 1976: 239). In the USA this inevitably led to the issue of racial segregation and ultimately to the Supreme Court desegregation victories in education and housing. There is a continuity of ideas from Bourneville, England to Little Rock, Arkansas centring on opportunity but ultimately based on containing social conflict. Originally benevolent capitalists with foresight and then the state have used planning in an attempt to produce places of harmony to replace places of strife. It is ironic, therefore, that planning as a reformist solution to 'urban' problems should often appear today to be part of the problem.

LOCATION OF LOCAL POLITICS

We began this chapter by pointing out that urban political geography has rivalled electoral geography in its recent growth. In this final section we describe some of the more interesting parts of this work as they relate to our previous discussions. We concentrate on three themes in the location of local politics. First we continue the place and protest theme by reviewing the findings of 'geography of conflict' studies. These are concerned with concrete examples of political conflicts over land-use issues. Generally speaking protesters are objecting to the cost of proximity they are being forced to pay for some land-use change. A major road development, for example, will lower the 'real income' or quality of life of adjacent residents. The result is a politics of urban change in which local groups attempt to preserve their localities.

The purpose of any urban change is to generate benefits for some groups in the community. The disbenefits in a few localities is an unintentional effect – an externality – to be set against the benefits of other groups in other locations. The new road development, for instance, will provide benefits of accessibility for road users well beyond the 'externality field' of disbenefits. The second theme we deal with below is the geography of accessibility. Benefits from any transport policy will depend upon where a person lives and that person's particular mobility. The resulting politics of mobility is much more subtle than that expressed in locational conflicts. This has been a classic area of political non-decision-making.

The distribution issue created by different people experiencing costs of proximity and benefits of accessibility is more generally expressed as the free-rider problem in local government. This involves a politics of boundaries so that for the residents of a favoured locality, costs of providing a service are avoided while benefits of the service are enjoyed. The classic case is the independent suburb with its low tax rate whose residents use services such as transport provided by a central city with its high tax rate. We consider this and other politics of boundaries in our final discussion of the geography of local government.

GEOGRAPHY OF LOCATIONAL CONFLICTS: POLITICS OF CHANGE

The study of locational conflicts became a major theme in urban political geography in the early 1970s with the work of Julian Wolpert and his associates (Wolpert *et al*: 1972) and Kevin Cox (1973). Initially these studies focused upon single conflicts and attempted to identify patterns of gains and losses in the local community and how these were articulated or not articulated in the conflict. This approach was subsequently extended to deal with aggregate patterns of large numbers of conflicts which could be mapped to produce a 'geography of locational conflicts'. The method was to analyse the local press over a specified period and produce a list of all 'identifiable conflicts'. In this way the geography of locational conflicts in London, Ontario for 1970–72 (Janelle and Millward 1976) and 1970–73 (Janelle 1977), Vancouver, BC for 1973–75 (Ley and Mercer 1980) and Columbus, Ohio for 1971–78 (Cox and McCarthy 1982) have been produced. The most interesting thing about this small set of studies is that whereas they all produce very similar findings on the geography, they exhibit a wide range of interpretations which encompass most of the issues we have discussed earlier in this chapter.

Between them the four studies cited above mapped nearly one thousand locational conflicts. Not surprisingly they found that the patterns of conflicts were neither evenly distributed nor merely random. A definite structure emerged with conflicts concentrated in three areas – the core of the urban region, the decaying inner city around the core and the newest developments at the edge of the city. In the 1970s these were the major areas of change in the North American city and this is reflected in these geographies of conflict. But how do we interpret this structure?

1. From ecology to pluralism

In the first study Janelle and Millward (1976) provide us with an ecological interpretation. They down-grade the influence of zoning and planning and argue that this geography represents the 'adaption of the urban environment to changing human needs and expectations' (Janelle and Millward 1976: 103). They identify different types of issues on the basis of land-use categories and summarize the patterns using a factor analysis. This produces just two general patterns of conflict – a transition zone factor relating to housing, transportation and preservation issues and a CBD redevelopment-peripheral expansion factor relating to retail, school and redevelopment conflicts. This generalized description of the geography of conflicts is therefore interpreted in terms of Burgess's concentric zone model as reflecting the 'competitive ethic operating within a free market economy' (Janelle and Millward 1976: 104).

Janelle's (1977) subsequent study moves away from identification of general aggregate processes of the ecological tradition and concentrates instead on the actors involved in each conflict. Proposers of land use change and the objectors to the change are each identified so that the nature of the conflicts can be assessed. Using this revised methodology Janelle was able to identify major conflict-participant categories which go beyond simple ecological inferences. The basic finding was that the 'economic sector' (developers, corporations) was the most common proposer of change, followed by the public sector (planners, public institutions) with the 'household sector' (residents) a very poor third. In terms of objections however the reverse was true with households being responsible for nearly two-thirds of all objections, the public sector accounting for nearly one third and the economic sector hardly ever objecting to land-use change. Unlike his previous study, Janelle (1977) now emphasizes the complexity of the inter-dependencies of conflict participants in land-use change. Simple ecological interpretation is replaced by a pluralist model of the geography of conflict.

2. From locality to political economy

Ley and Mercer's (1980) interpretation is much more political. For them locational conflict represents a challenge to market equilibrium. Their study includes two new developments. First they recognize that 'identifiable conflicts' are only a subset of all potential conflicts which appear on the political agenda. They produce, therefore, a geography of development by mapping a sample of permits awarded by the city government for land-use changes. This turns out to be a highly structured geography with a distinct concentric zonal pattern reflecting the city's zoning policy. But when this is compared to the geography of conflicts an interesting contrast emerges: the conflicts have a sectoral pattern instead of a zonal one. Whereas change permits are distributed equally between east and west sectors in Vancouver, more than eight times as much conflict is generated in the west (Ley and Mercer 1980: 100). This is explained in terms of Ley and Mercer's second new development – the linking of conflict to social cleavages and city politics. The sectoral contrast reflects a basic social cleavage in Vancouver which had become politically activated at the time of the conflict survey. In the late 1960s the ruling Non-Partisan Association, a free-enterprise business party, was challenged by a new urban reform party, The Elector's Action Movement (TEAM), offering the ideal of the 'liveable city' as an alternative to 'boosterism' and urban growth. In 1972 this new party won control of City Hall so leadership passed from business to the new professionals – university professors, teachers, lawyers, architects, and so on. The electoral base of TEAM was the affluent west sector. In fact Ley and Mercer (1980: 107) describe the party as 'a product of a distinctive urban subculture', in short a neighbourhood effect. Hence the conflict pattern is part of a larger political process that was changing the nature of Vancouver politics. A new political agenda was being devised in the west of the city which entailed resident resistance to commercial development. Ley and Mercer, therefore, provide a very political geography of conflict.

Finally Cox and McCarthy (1982) have taken the argument one step further. In their study of variations in the resistance of residents to commercial development they have been able to show that home-owners and families with children at school had higher rates of neighbourhood activism than renters and families without school children. This suggests a 'politics of turf' centred on the different stake that families have in their localities. But Cox is unwilling to leave the matter there as a purely local phenomenon. He looks at the conflicts in which neighbourhood activism plays its part and shows that over two-thirds are concerned with a particular type of antagonism – 'between those who are interested in an expanded urban infrastructure and the conversion of land parcels to higher yielding land uses, and those whose interest in the urban environment is essentially that of use value' (Cox and McCarthy 1982: 211). This is Ley and Mercer's finding interpreted in political economy terms. The 'politics of turf' becomes the link between the private and public restructuring of space to facilitate capital accumulation and the victims of that restructuring in their neighbourhoods. The geography of locational conflict reflects adverse local experiences which have been mobilized against a changing capitalist world-economy. Since the mobilization is location-based and may therefore incorporate diverse occupational groups such conflict can cut across traditional national political cleavages. Following Castells (1977) such local challenges to the system are generally referred to as *urban social movements*.

GEOGRAPHY OF PHYSICAL ACCESS: POLITICS OF MOBILITY

The question of access has long been a popular theme in geography. The resulting location theory has generally neglected access to public facilities, however. Current concern with physical access to services provided by government is usually traced back to Tietz's (1968) call for a location theory of public services. But no such theory has been produced. As Dear (1978) has pointed out it is not a location theory that is required but a theory of the state in which allocation of services form one part of state activity. We have dealt with this theme in previous chapters. Here we concentrate on the empirical work carried out on accessibility. We begin by describing some findings from a quantitative approach to this theme before unravelling the politics that lie behind the policy.

1. Aggregate patterns of access

Accessibility has been measured in different ways in different studies. The simplest measure is simply distance to the nearest facility from any particular location. More sophisticated measures take into account the quantity of service provided at a facility and replace distance by travel time. The most common method is to produce an aggregate access score to all facilities for each residential area. This is achieved as follows. The access of each residential area to each facility is computed as the access ratio. This is the quantity of service at a facility divided by the distance or travel time between the facility and residential area. For instance a residential area adjacent to a large facility would have a large access ratio (high service/low distance). Such ratios can be computed between a residential area and all facilities. The sum of these access ratios provides the aggregate access score for that residential area. Such scores can be computed for all residential areas to produce a map of accessibility to the service under consideration. Jones and Kirby (1982) provide examples of maps of access to general medical practitioners and dental practitioners in Reading, England, for example.

Once we have produced such a map the next step is to try and explain the spatial distribution displayed. If we adhere to a simple instrumentalist view of the state we expect government policy to provide facilities so that the local dominant class has better access than other groups with less power to influence decisions. Such 'who gets what?' exercises have been carried out by correlating access scores with variables describing the socio-economic characteristics of census tracts. The interesting feature of these researches is that generally speaking the simple instrumentalist model is not supported (McLafferty 1982). In most cities it seems that low-income groups have better access to public facilities than high-income groups. In fact this reflects the concentration of lower-income groups in the inner city who are therefore closer to services centralized in the core of the urban region. In short the spatial structure of the modern city counter-acts the expected bias in the political process (McLafferty 1982).

This 'surprising' finding has been challenged empirically in two different ways. First it has been argued that studies of accessibility do not take into account the quality of service provided and that inner-city residents often experience the worst public services. In Britain, for instance, it is well documented that small single-handed medical practices run by the oldest doctors are disproportionately located in the poorer central areas of cities (Knox 1982: 183). Such effects, while being very real and important, cannot be easily incorporated into accessibility analyses. This is not the case with the second reason given to challenge the spatial structure effect. This argument relates to differential mobility between social groups which has been investigated by McLafferty (1984) and we will briefly review her findings here.

McLafferty (1984) selected twelve medium-sized US cities to carry out simulation experiments. Facilities were spatially 'allocated' to these cities many times in a random fashion. In the vast majority of cases it was found that the resulting access scores were negatively correlated with income (that is, low-income groups have best access). This is the spatial structure effect operating merely because of the more central location of lower income groups. However when these simulations were repeated by incorporating differential mobility levels between income groups very different results were produced. In the case of allocating four centres to each city, for example, in all but two cases the original bias towards lower income groups was conclusively reversed. McLafferty (1984) is able to conclude that mobility differences counter-act the spatial structure effect: lower income groups are not as favoured by public facility location as had previously been assumed.

This finding does not mean we have to return to a simple instrumental model of city politics. As Kirby (1983) has pointed out, the role of the state in providing public facilities is much more complicated than mere political favouritism. But we can go further and note that state activity in urban areas is concerned with much more than providing services. The restructuring of urban areas which underlies Cox and McCarthy's (1982) interpretation of the geography of conflicts is part of a major process of reordering space in the twentieth century which is usually termed suburbanization. In Alonso's (1964) terms suburbanites have chosen to reduce their access to services (and jobs) for the benefits of the quality of life in the suburbs (including low local taxes as we shall see). This does not mean that suburbanites have been left 'stranded' on the edge of cities, of course. A major aspect of reordering space included the development of a new physical infra-structure to meet the needs of the new suburbanites. In the post Second World War period urban transport policy evolved to reconstruct patterns of access. The resulting politics of mobility was anything but neutral.

2. Reconstructing patterns of access

In the 1950s and 1960s transport planning became a major concern of urban government in many countries. For the most part it was not treated as a political issue but merely as a technical exercise necessary for making the city work. The planning was based on advanced computer modelling procedures which enhanced the scientific and objective credentials of the process. This was typified by the Land Use/Transportation Studies carried out in cities throughout the world. Starting in Chicago in the mid-1950s, this type of analysis spread to London by 1962 and by the mid-1970s Atkins (1977) could enumerate ninety-nine such studies in Britain alone. It had become in his words 'big business' with specialist consulting firms competing to carry out the studies. And yet Atkins (1977: 62) was able to conclude in the following damning manner:

> 'We have a series of excessively complicated and expensive models using unsubstantiated and biased techniques to provide information of dubious accuracy for answering the wrong questions'.

Let us pursue some aspects of this criticism.

At the very heart of these large-scale transportation studies we find a data-gathering exercise known as origin and destination surveys. This consists of sampling a large number of road users and asking them where they have come from and where they are going. Every origin and destination is then allocated to one of a pre-defined set of traffic zones. From this data 'desire lines' of movement between zones can be described at different levels of intensity. Hence an objective data base was generated to plan for the future. In every case the key problem was found to be peak-hour commuting flows in the morning and late afternoon. The only solution was to plan for massive new investments in roads to ensure the city of the future could cope with traffic of the future. Above all the traffic must be kept flowing or else the city will be 'strangled to death'.

The problem with this procedure is that it was anything but objective. By only surveying current road users existing inequalities in mobility were projected into the future (Wachs and Kumagai 1973: 441). For example a community with a large number of car-less households will be under-represented in an origin and destination survey in contrast to an affluent community with many two-car households. Hence the latter's needs are much more likely to be incorporated into the planning process. In Hillman *et al.*'s (1973: 107) words these surveys 'have led to car orientated plans . . . weighted in favour of the "mobile rich" at the expense of the "immobile poor"'. Generally speaking the modelling served the needs of white-collar middle-class male commuters at the expense of children, women and the elderly without continuous access to a car (Hillman *et al.* 1976).

The most fascinating aspect of this whole planning movement was that it went largely unchallenged for nearly two decades. Transport policy was kept off the political agenda and left to experts so that 'nowhere is the basic conflict between motorised movement and non-motorised movement admitted' (Hillman *et al.* 1973,: 107). This was political non-decision-making at its very best. It reached its apogee in Glasgow, Scotland. While other cities were abandoning their transport plans Glasgow continued with a massive road-building programme in the early 1970s. The result was the paradox that the city with the lowest proportion of car-owners in Britain had the highest rate of miles of planned motorway per head in Britain (Cable 1974). And this planning was carried out by a Labour administration whose support base lay in the relatively car-less inner-city areas. Clearly this geography of support is irrelevant to the politics of power in this situation. For the geography of power we have to look beyond Glasgow to the Scottish Office and the 'road lobby' (construction companies, road transport firms, car manufacturers, car owner organizations, and so on) using politicians and planners who wanted to make Glasgow the 'envy of Europe' (Cable 1974: 605).

By the late 1960s transport planning was beginning to creep on to the political agenda. By 1972, for instance, London's motorway plans were a major political issue resulting in the election of a Labour administration committed to stopping further motorway construction (Hall, 1982). This did not occur because of the issues raised above, however. There was no uprising of the poor car-less against the redistribution of resources to rich car-owners. It was the environmental impact of the transport plans that was their undoing, especially when they impinged on middle-class areas. Once the extent of disruption of localities became clear, pressure groups formed and locational conflicts ensued as described previously. Road construction appeared on the political agenda as an environmental issue not a distributional one (Kirby 1982). The politics of mobility remains an insignificant component within the modern state despite its vital daily relevance to everyone.

THE GEOGRAPHY OF LOCAL GOVERNMENT: THE POLITICS OF BOUNDARIES

At the beginning of his classic *Semi-sovereign People* Schattschneider (1960) defines three related propositions underlying politics. First, he argues that the outcome of any conflict is not dependent on the immediate strengths of the combatants but rather that it depends on the scope of the conflict. The scope consists of all those brought into the conflict although not directly involved. Second, the most important political strategy in any conflict is to control the scope. A combatant who determines the composition of the ultimate decision-makers is obviously on a winner. Third, different scopes will differentially affect the different sides of a conflict: 'Every change in the scope of conflict has its bias; it is partisan in nature' (Schattschneider 1960: 4). In this discussion we will illustrate the operation of these three propositions in the context of local government. The scope will in practice be defined territorially in terms of local government areas or wards within such areas. The result is a particularly interesting politics of boundaries showing, for the final time, that all organization is indeed bias.

Local government units are not autonomous actors in the political sphere. They are the creation of national governments and make up an integral part of the spatial structure of the state. They are, therefore, in Helin's (1967: 483) words 'infra-sovereign' with sovereignty resting at the higher geographical scale. Local government is therefore distinct from federal state or provincial government which 'share' sovereignty with the national federal government. Whereas the boundaries of federal units are constitutionally sacrosanct, the boundaries of local government may be changed through legislative or executive action. In some countries this has meant frequent change as the priorities of national government change. This is particularly the case for highly centralized states: Poulsen (1971) reports on the numerous boundary changes within Eastern European states after the establishment of Communist Party regimes, for instance. But in all states local government units are subordinate and operate at the suffrance of the sovereign state.

This subordination is most clearly illustrated in revolutionary circumstances when new boundaries become part of the reconstruction of the state in the image of the new rulers. In 1789, for instance, the Abbe Sieyes drew up a completely new spatial structure for the French state which wiped away all the traditional provincial institutions. A series of regular shape and equal-area spatial units were created which cut through old social patterns of life. The delineation of these *departments* was an exercise in spatial-social engineering to break loyalties to the old provinces. To reduce local identification further, the names of the departments avoided any reference to historical, social or economic patterns of life. Instead the departments were named after 'neutral' physical features such as rivers and mountains. This strategy has become quite common. Poulsen (1971: 228) describes how the Yugoslav government established nine regions in 1931, 'neutrally named after river basins in order to weaken the nationalisms of the major ethnic groups'. Probably the best example of this is King Carol's reorganization of Roumania in 1938 into ten completely new districts. These were specifically designed to cut across the traditional ethnic and historical provinces so as not to provide rallying points for sectionalism (Helin, 1967: 492–3). Once again these were named after rivers, mountains and seas to avoid new regional identities emerging. This is another example of local government units contributing to the Napoleonic ethos of a 'unified and indivisible nation state'.

These examples highlight the problem of the increasingly popular use of the term 'local state'. From our discussion of the distinction between state and government in Chapter 4, it will be clear that there can be no local state 'within' a sovereign state except under federal arrangements. Local government is not 'a state' but is a *branch* of the state. In recent years it has become a very important aspect of state activity in organizing the legitimating function of social consumption. It is in this role of promoting the reproduction of labour that the term local state was originally coined (Cockburn: 1977). But as Duncan and Goodwin (1982,: 78) point out, 'in most discussions "local state" can in fact be easily replaced by "local government" with little effect on the argument'. They go on to suggest how the term local state might be usefully employed but we will not become involved in this discussion here. We continue to remain at the concrete level of government activity as it affects localities rather than dealing with the more theoretical themes associated with the state.

Changing the scope of a conflict in geographical terms means manipulating boundaries. We illustrate this politics of boundaries with three topics which have been thoroughly researched in recent years. The first involves removing boundaries, the second is based upon maintaining boundaries while the third concerns the redrawing of boundaries. In each case the purpose has been to change the political balance of local politics.

1. Removing boundaries: the reform of US city government

American cities inherited from Britain a local government tradition which involved election of local representatives to the city council on a ward basis. The combination of ward representation, class segregation and universal suffrage meant that by the end of the nineteenth century political control of American cities had been wrested out of the hands of the traditional local elite. This process is associated with the rise of corrupt machine politics under 'boss' control. Corruption and the general lowering of calibre of local councillors became a major political issue at the beginning of this century. According to orthodox versions of these events, ordinary citizens rose up against corrupt bosses and reformed city politics.

But, as Hays (1964) has pointed out this interpretation involves a major paradox. Whereas the reform movements claimed to be a popular force its reforms actually amounted to a centralization of government. In fact what we have is the use of a popular facade to change the scope of conflict in urban government.

Although the tammany machines were undoubtedly corrupt in their organization of city politics, they were much more than a collection of bad people loyal to a boss. They must be seen not as individuals but in a wider political-economy context. They performed several vital roles in the rapidly growing US city at the turn of the century. Although business interests had by this time generally lost direct control of city government, there remained an urgent need for mediation between dominant class and the dominated class who could control city hall. The boss-machine system evolved to fill this need. Corruption involved business gaining contracts in return for funds some of which were used to buy votes and 'organize' elections. On the other side of this relation the machine provided an informal social service for the newly arrived immigrants (Stretton 1969: 65–6). This included simple favours through to employment on the city pay-roll. In this way class conflict was largely diffused.

The system worked for a time but was obviously open to attack. As far as business interests were concerned it served as a temporary buffer against more extreme city government but was far from ideal. It was a compromise in sharing power but its very informality and illegality meant that it was unpredictable (Dearlove 1979: 202). Hence business interests began to back a reform movement. It is now well documented that far from being a mass movement, the progressive reformers were dominated by business interests and were backed by chambers of commerce. Hence the motives of the reformers were not so much to clean up city government as to redirect power within city government.

Using the argument that cities should be run like businesses the reformers proposed several new government structures. These invariably involved abolishing ward representation and replacing it by at-large elections. This change in scope undermined local power bases and favoured candidates with the necessary backing to mount a city-wide campaign. A good illustration of the effectiveness of this strategy can be seen in Dayton, Ohio in 1917 when the Socialists obtained 43 per cent of the vote city-wide but returned no councillors. Usually this reform was accompanied by restrictions on political parties so that elections became 'non-partisan'. Once again this favoured high-status candidates who would tend to be more well-known than lower status candidates who had relied on party identification to gain election. Finally, just in case these measures back-fired, city executive arrangements were commonly instituted to ensure the city was efficiently run. This council-manager form of government was only developed in 1911 but by 1920 it was used in 157 cities in USA and

Canada. By 1974 60 per cent of US cities over 25,000 had this form of government (Dearlove 1979: 211).

The whole scope of city politics was thus changed and the balance of forces moved decisively back to the business community and away from working-class localities. This can still be seen in recent treatment of black voters by this system. Sloan (1969) has shown that whereas in cities that still employ a partisan/ward electoral system the number of black representatives increases roughly in proportion to the number of black voters, in at-large/non-partisan electoral systems there is actually an inverse relationship. That is to say the more black voters in a city the fewer black representatives in city hall! However as the 'white flight' to the suburbs continues and central cities become more black, black representation has inevitably made its breakthroughs irrespective of the electoral arrangements (O'Loughlin 1980). No amount of reformist tickering can overturn this situation *within* the city. But in the meantime the key conflicts between localities has moved beyond the city boundaries.

2. Maintaining boundaries: the fragmented US metropolitan region

The most distinctive feature of current local government in the USA is the fragmented nature of the metropolitan regions. Cox (1973: 20), for instance, reports that the average number of government units per metropolitan area is eighty-seven. The larger metropolitan areas such as New York and Chicago have over a thousand local government units. As well as the sheer quantity of government units the relative size of the central city to the total metropolitan region is also politically significant. Both of these aspects of political fragentation are dealt with by Zeigler and Brunn (1980) who combine them in single measure which they term an 'index of geopolitical fragmentation'. This is defined as the ratio of number of units per 100,000 population to percentage of metropolitan population resident in the central city. This ratio is worked out for 264 standard metropolitan statistical areas (SMSA's which are loosely defined as daily urban systems). The largest index occurs in Johnstown, Pa., which has 116 local government units serving 266,000 people only 16.1 per cent of whom live in the central city. This produces an index of 274. The twenty-five SMSAs with the highest and lowest fragmentation indices are shown in Figure 25(a). This shows a very distinct geographical pattern following the frost-belt/Sun-belt cleavage.

The same pattern occurs when we look at the two ways in which the 'outmoded boundaries' can be eliminated (Zeigler and Brunn 1980: 84). Simple annexation of adjacent territory is the obvious strategy to reduce fragmentation and this has been pursued vigorously by some city governments. Figure 25(b) shows all those cities which added at least ten square miles of territory to their jurisdiction between 1970 and 1975. Once again it is the Sun-belt which is picked out and annexations are

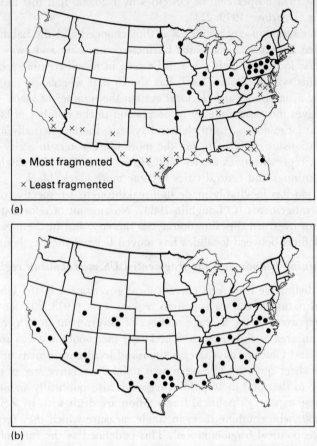

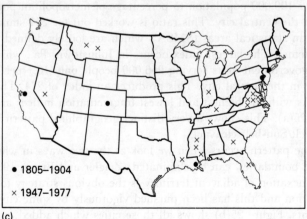

25. Fragmentation of metropolitan government in USA (a) Extreme indices of geopolitical fragmentation (b) Annexations, 1970–75 (c) City–county consolidations

conspicuous by their absence in the north. The most complete method of annexation to reduce fragmentation is the city–county consolidation strategy. Zeigler and Brunn (1980: 87) show that this second method has varied greatly over time. Until about the turn of the century city–county consolidations occurred for several big cities throughout the country. After a gap of forty years the strategy was rediscovered and employed with some success by several medium-sized cities. The pattern is shown in Figure 25(c) and once again we see that the recent changes are concentrated in the Sun-belt.

This consistent geographical pattern of fragmentation, and the strategies to overcome it, requires explanation. Zeigler and Brunn (1980: 85) favour institutional explanations such as rigid state statutes governing annexations and the need for mergers where a city is hemmed in by incorporated territory. However this does not explain why such institutional arrangements exist in the first place. By far the most sophisticated explanation has come from the public-choice theorists. They argue that fragmentation reflects a situation in which competition between local governments will produce efficient and sensitive administration and provision of services. As originally developed by Tiebout (1956) each local government will produce a different bundle of public goods which consumers/voters may choose between. Households will eventually settle in that jurisdiction which provides the bundle of services closest to its specific needs: in Tiebout's famous phrase – they 'vote with their feet'. Hence the fragmentation of American metropolitan areas is not a problem at all: quite the opposite in fact – it represents the evolution of a government structure to facilitate public choice in the democratic American tradition.

Of course not everybody accepts this explanation (Newton 1975; Cox and Nartowicz 1980). The theory was originally developed to complement the theory of the private firm by a theory of public agencies. As such it continues a long tradition of employing 'business logic' to local government which began at least in the progressive reform era as we have seen. The most obvious feature of the fragmented structure is that the boundaries correlate strongly with variations in material well-being. Cox (1973) has documented discrepancies between 'poor' central cities and 'rich' suburban governments although there are also major discrepancies between suburbs (Cox and Nartowicz 1980: 199). Rather than offering choice this structure has evolved to limit choice by constraining the residential mobility of the less affluent. This is achieved by exclusionary zoning procedures which can control which households or non-residential land uses can enter a jurisdiction (Cox 1973: 52). Furthermore the fragmentation prevents any 'pooling' of resources that may be redistributed from rich to poor areas. Quite the contrary, in fact, it has been shown for several cities that suburbanites 'free ride' on their central city neighbours by using services they do not pay for (Cox 1973). As Newton (1975: 246) so neatly puts it, fragmentation is a solution to a problem – the middle-class solution to preserve their neighbourhoods. The public-choice theory reduces to an apology for the inequality of the status quo and like the related pluralist theory of Dahl it manages to convert real constraints into theoretical choices.

Cox and Nartowicz (1980) have attempted to move beyond these critiques towards a more radical explanation for fragmentation. They emphasize divisions within capital and although there are examples of industrial capital and merchant capital using incorporation and land-use zoning to restrict taxes and competition, the major capital in this process is property capital which consists of that set of companies involved in the urban development process. According to Cox and Nartowicz (1980) property capital will use a variety of political strategies – annexation, suburban separation or special district designation – depending upon particular circumstances.

This explanation does not explain the very distinctive geographical pattern along the Sun-belt/frost-belt cleavage described by Zeigler and Brunn (1980). Why is annexation just a strategy of the south and west? A clue to answering this question can be seen in the city–county consolidation data (Figure 25(c)) which includes a time dimension. Annexation was a strategy in the north in the nineteenth century. This reminds us of Gordon's theory of quantitative and qualitative efficiency and the movement of industrial capital from the large cities of the north after 1898. According to Gordon (1976) annexation stopped when the business interests changed sides in the politics of annexation. With suburbanization of business, annexation stopped to produce a circle of suburban governments around the central city. In the latest phase of industrial development the rise of the sun-belt has been accomplished with city governments in the south and west remaining firmly pro-business. In these circumstances new corporate cities have emerged and corporations have remained in the central cities where they have not opposed annexations. The geography of local government fragmentation in USA is simply the inverse of the geography of business influence.

3. Redrawing boundaries: delocalization in Britain

In Britain local government is much more closely controlled by the central government. Major reforms have been imposed from above reflecting the particular balance of interests at the *national* scale. The first major reforms reflected the emergence of industrial capital in the political arena in the nineteenth century. First the Municipal Areas Act of 1835 and subsequently the setting up of County Boroughs in 1888 separated out urban areas from the traditional counties and made them independent. With the creation of the London County Council this created self-governing cities under the control of local business interests usually referred to as the 'city fathers'. This rural–urban cleavage was even extended into the counties where separate urban and rural districts were distinguished. These Victorian reforms represent the high point of a relatively independent local government system in Britain. With the extension of the suffrage the problem of political control of localities emerged in Britain as in USA. British solutions to this problem were at the same time less subtle, more direct and more ruthless. The end result is that the whole concept of local government is at risk in a process we may term delocalization. Let us briefly look at the history of this process in the twentieth century using the sequence of 'new politics' identified in the last chapter.

The first politics of crisis in the 1920s coincided with the rise of Labour as a major party. As Labour began to win political control of local government units a conflict emerged between the two levels of government. While central government was attempting to pursue austerity policies, some new Labour councils were developing incompatible expenditure programmes. Localities in different parts of the country became known as 'Little Moscows' because of their radical political leadership (Macintyre 1980). The most famous and far-reaching conflict occurred over poor relief and social services. This centred on the London borough of Poplar and local government rebellion is still referred to in Britain as *Poplarism* (Branson 1979). Part of the nineteenth-century reforms had transferred responsibility for poverty relief from parishes to larger districts. The relief was administered by 'guardians' who were elected. In Poplar the Labour majority on the Board of Guardians were dispensing relief which the central government considered too generous. Several strategies were developed to prevent this local democracy. After ruling out the possibility of restricting the franchise other rules were changed to force these communities to toe the line. First, parliamentary control over the guardians was tightened by the Default Act and Audit Act whereby guardians and councillors could be disqualified from holding office, personally surcharged for any excess expenditure and replaced by government-appointed commissioners. This led to suspensions of Labour authorities at West Ham in London and Chester-le-Street and Bedwellty on the Durham and South Wales coalfields respectively (Briggs and Deacon 1973). Second, the scope of the conflict was changed as the Board of Guardians were replaced by Public Assistance Committees elected from larger electorates. Instead of 635 Boards there were only 146 committees set up in 1929 (Briggs and Deacon 1973). Local government and its control was clearly an important element of this politics of crisis.

The politics of national interest are somewhat simpler. The ultimate solution to these local difficulties was embarked upon. In 1934 local involvement in the social security system was abolished and replaced by a new scheme run by civil servants for the central government. The result was a system which was 'centrally directed, uniformly fixed and removed from the vagaries and dissensions of party politics' (Runciman

1966: 78–9). Social security was removed from the local political agenda for the sake of the *national* interest.

In the era of the social democratic consensus local government expanded its functions as the responsibilities of the state in general increased. New planning and social-service functions compensated for loss of control over hospitals which were nationalized. This is a period of little or no conflict between the two levels of government although concern for planning issues led to dissatisfaction with the inherited administrative division between town and country which was to figure prominently in the subsequent reform debate.

The period of technocratic politics witnessed a complete redrawing of the local government map. Local government reorganization was an integral part of the whole technocratic ethos. There were separate reforms for Greater London and England, Scotland and Wales. In England after a major Royal Commission had reported, the 1972 Act reduced 1300 local government units to 401. The sequence of reform proposals are described by Honey (1981). For our discussion here we follow Dearlove (1979) who draws several interesting parallels with the earlier American local government reform movement. Councillor 'calibre' becomes a key issue as many urban councils are dominated by working-class representatives. It is assumed that larger councils will increase the likelihood of more business and professional representation in local government – a sort of return to the days of the Victorian city fathers. The first problem identified by the reformers, therefore, was a boundary problem. New boundaries were required to encompass larger areas covering a wider range of localities. In effect this meant abolishing the old urban–rural division in local government which had become increasingly antiquated with suburbanization. Nevertheless the social geography argument should not blind us to the intended *political* effects of increasing the scope of local government units.

To ensure that these political effects did occur the boundary problem was supplemented by concern for the management problem in local government. Traditional organization within councils was to be streamlined. An integrated approach was required and necessitated a corporate management structure. This strengthened the unelected officers at the expense of councillors. A new breed of officer emerged as 'chief executives' were appointed across the country. Although not going as far as the council-manager reforms in USA, the motives and purpose are the same. In Bennington's (1975) words 'local government becomes big business'. Streamlining organization simply meant making local government operate like a business. This is what Cockburn (1977) was referring to when she coined the term 'local state'.

In many ways this reorganization back-fired on the central government. Business organization is geared for expansion and this is what happened in local government. As such local government became part of the second politics of crisis with its new central government austerity programmes. Initially this was reflected merely in reduction of central government funding of local services. But as the crisis deepened the clash between local and central government became more obvious. Central government attempted to wrest control of local programmes from local government by direct funding of, for instance, inner-city policy which was marketed as a 'partnership'. The conflict between the two scales of government could not be hidden, however, in central government attempts to control local budgets. A system of penalties have been introduced which effectively fine local governments who 'overspend' as defined by central government criteria. Hence popularly elected councils can be directly prevented from implementing their programmes by central government (Boddy 1983). Is this the end of local government? Not quite . . .

In the current era of a new politics of national interest local government is finally being converted into mere local administration of central government policy. First in Scotland and subsequently in England and Wales the central government is taking direct control of council budgets in what is known as 'rate-capping'. This is a procedure whereby central government sets the maximum level at which local taxes can be set. Local governments effectively lose control of their budgets. Furthermore the metropolitan counties, which are usually Labour-controlled, are being abolished. These have represented centres of local opposition to central government policies and they are to be replaced by government-appointed boards. The parallels with the first politics of national interest are striking: quite simply central government cannot allow its national financial policy to be sabotaged by local politics. There are also parallels with US experience. Although not approaching the fragmentation of US metropolitan regions, British metropolitan regions are losing their political unity so that the more affluent districts will no longer be part of an administration dominated by 'low calibre' councillors.

British local government reform (or elimination) has been an ideal final topic for this book. Although only directly concerned with local issues it illustrates the geographical integration attempted by this study. We have provided an argument that encompasses issues ranging from geopolitical scenarios to who decides who sweeps the streets of British cities. We are now confident enough to quote a sceptic's view of our overall project. Pahl asserts that:

> (A) theory that the world capitalist crisis is responsible for everything from dirty streets to the closure of teacher-training colleges is . . . inadequate. (Pahl 1979: 42)

I have tried in this book to provide an adequate link between these topics as 'ideology separating experience from reality'. Our final example illustrates this clearly as local government is related to various 'new politics' which are in turn responses to the dynamics of the world-economy. A political geography perspective on the world-economy organized around geographical scales does seem to offer a fruitful approach to understanding our modern world.

BIBLIOGRAPHY

Abrams, P. (1978) 'Towns and economic growth: some theories and problems' in P. Abrams and E. A. Wrigley (eds) *Towns in Society* Cambridge U.P.

Agnew, J. A. (1981a) 'Structural and dialectical theories of political regionalism' in A. D. Burnett and P. J. Taylor (eds) *Political Studies from Spatial Perspectives*. Wiley: London and New York.

Agnew, J. A. (1981b) 'Political regionalism and Scottish nationalism in Gaelic Scotland', *Canadian Review of Studies in Nationalism*, **8**: 115–29.

Agnew, J. A. (1982) 'Sociologizing the geographical imagination: spatial concepts in the world-systems perspective', *Political Geography Quarterly* **1**: 159–66.

Agnew, J. A. (1983) 'An excess of 'national exceptionalism': towards a new political geography of American foreign policy', *Political Geography Quarterly* **2**: 151–66.

Ajami, F. (1978) 'The global logic of the neoconservatives', *World Politics* **30**: 450–68.

Alavi, H. (1979) 'The state in post-colonial societies' in H. Goulbourne (ed.) *Politics and State in the Third World*. Macmillan: London.

Almond, G. A. and **Verba, S.** (1963) *The Civic Culture*. Princeton U.P.: Princeton, NJ.

Almy, T. A. (1973) 'Residential location and electoral cohesion: the pattern of urban political conflict', *American Political Science Review* **67**: 914–23.

Alonso, W. (1964) *Location and Land Use*. Harvard U.P.: Cambridge, Mass.

Amin, S. (1980) *Class and Nation*. Monthly Review Press: New York.

Archer, J. C. and **Taylor P. J.** (1981) *Section and Party: A Political Geography of American Presidential Elections from Andrew Jackson to Ronald Reagan*. Wiley: Chichester and New York.

Ardrey, R. (1966) *The Territorial Imperative*. Atheneum: New York.

Atkins, S. T. (1977) 'Transportation planning: is there a road ahead?', *Traffic Engineering Control* **18**: 58–62.

Bachrach, P. and **Baratz, M.** (1962) 'Two faces of power', *American Political Science Review* **56**: 947–52.

Banks, A. S. and **Textor, R. B.** (1963) *A Cross-Polity Survey*. MIT Press: Cambridge, Mass.

Barker, C. (1978) 'The state as capital', *International Socialism* **2**: 16–42.

Barnett, R. J. and **Muller, R. E.** (1974) *Global Reach*. Simon and Schuster: New York.

Barraclough, G. (ed.) (1979) *The Times Atlas of World History*. Times Books: London.

Barratt Brown, M. (1974) *The Economics of Imperialism*. Penguin: London.

Beard, C. A. (1914) *An Economic Interpretation of the Constitution of the United States*. Macmillan: New York.

Bell, D. (1960) *The End of Ideology*. Free Press: Glencoe, Illinois.

Bennington, J. (1975) *Local Government becomes Big Business*. Community Development Project: London.

Bennett, S. and **Earle, C.** (1983) 'Socialism in America: a geographical interpretation of failure', *Political Geography Quarterly* **2**: 31–56.

Bergesen, A. and **Schoenberg, R.**
(1980) 'Long waves of colonial
expansion and contraction, 1415–1969'
in A. Bergesen (ed.) *Studies of the
Modern World System*. Academic: New
York.
Bergman, E. F. (1975) *Modern Political
Geography*. William Brown: Dubuque,
Iowa.
Berry, B. J. L. (1969) 'Review',
Geographical Review **59**: 450–1.
Blaut, J. M. (1975) 'Imperialism: the
Marxist theory and its evolution',
Antipode **7(1)**: 1–19.
Blaut, J. M. (1980) 'Nairn on
nationalism', *Antipode* **12**(3), 1–17.
Blechman, B. M. and **Kaplan, S. S.**
(1978) *Force without War: U.S. Armed
Forces as a Political Instrument*. Brookings
Institute: Washington, DC.
de Blij, H. J. (1967) *Systematic Political
Geography*. Wiley: New York.
Boddy, M. (1983) 'Central local
relations: theory and practice', *Political
Geography Quarterly* **2**: 119–38.
Bowman, I. (1921) *The New World*.
World Books: New York.
Bradley, J. E., Kirby, A. M. and
Taylor, P. J. (1978) 'Distance decay
and dental decay', *Regional Studies*
12: 529–40.
Brandt, W. (1980) *North-South: A
Programme for Survival*. Pan: London.
Branson, N. (1979) *Poplarism
1919–1925*. Lawrence and Wishart:
London.
Braudel, F. (1973) *Capitalism and
Material Life 1400–1800*. Weidenfield &
Nicolson: London.
Braunmuhl, C. von (1978) 'On the
analysis of the bourgeois nation state
within the world market context' in
J. Holloway and S. Picciotto (eds) *State
and Capital*. Arnold: London.
Brewer, A. (1980) *Marxist Theories of
Imperialism, A Critical Survey*. Routledge
& Kegan Paul: London.
Briggs, A. (1963) *Victorian Cities*.
Penguin: London.
Briggs, E. and **Deacon, A.** (1973)
'The creation of the Unemployment
Assistance Board', *Policy and Politics*
2: 43–62.
Brucan, S. (1981) 'The strategy of

development in Eastern Europe ,
Review **5**: 95–112.
Brunn, S. D. (1981) 'Geopolitics in a
shrinking world: a political geography
of the twenty-first century' in A. D.
Burnett and P. J. Taylor (eds) *Political
Studies from Spatial Perspectives*. Wiley:
Chichester UK and New York.
Buchanan, K. (1972) *The Geography of
Empire*. Spokesman: Nottingham.
Bukharin, N. (1972) *Imperialism and the
World Economy*. Merlin: London.
Bunge, W. (1982) *The Nuclear War
Atlas*. Society for Human Exploration:
Victoriaville, Quebec.
Burghardt, A. (1969) 'The core
concept in political geography: a
definition of terms', *Canadian Geographer*
63: 349–53.
Burghardt, A. (1980) 'Nation, state
and territorial unity: a trans-Outaouais
view' *Cahiers de géographie du Quebec*
24: 123–34.
Burnett, A. D. and **Taylor, P. J.** (eds)
(1981) *Political Studies from Spatial
Perspectives*. Wiley: Chichester UK.
Burnham, W. D. (1970) *Critical
Elections and the Mainsprings of American
Politics*. Norton: New York.
Busteed, M. A. (1975) *Geography and
Voting Behaviour*. Oxford U.P.: London.
Butler, D. E. and **Stokes, D. E.** (1969)
*Political Change in Britain: Forces Shaping
Electoral Choice*. Macmillan: London.

Cable, J. V. (1974) 'Glasgow's
motorways: a technocratic blight' *New
Society* (5 September) 605–7.
Castells, M. (1977) *The Urban Question:
A Marxist Approach*. MIT Press:
Cambridge, Mass.
Castells, M. (1978) *City, Class and
Power*. Macmillan: London.
Ceaser, J. W. (1979) *Presidential
Selection: Theory and Development*.
Princeton University Press: Princeton,
NJ.
Chase-Dunn, C. K. (1981) 'Interstate
system and capitalist world-economy:
one logic or two?' in W. L. Hollist and
J. N. Rosenau (eds) *World System
Structure*. Sage: Beverly Hills.
Chase-Dunn, C. K. (1982) 'Socialist
states in the capitalist world-economy'

in C. K. Chase-Dunn (ed.) *Socialist States in the World-System*. Sage: Beverly Hills.

Claval, P. (1984) 'The coherence of political geography: perspectives on its past evolution and future relevance' in P. J. Taylor and J. W. House (eds) *Political Geography: Recent Advances and Future Directions*. Croom Helm: London.

Cobban, A. (1969) *The Nation State and National Self-determination*. Collins: London.

Cockburn, C. (1977) *The Local State*. Pluto: London.

Cohen, S. (1973) *Geography and Politics in a World Divided* (2nd ed.). Oxford U.P.: New York.

Cohen, S. (1982) 'A new map of global political equilibrium: a developmental approach', *Political Geography Quarterly* **1**: 223–42.

Collins, I. (1957) *Liberalism in Nineteenth Century Europe*. Historical Association: London.

Coulter, P. (1975) *Social Mobilization and Liberal Democracy*. Lexington: Lexington, Mass.

Cox, K. R. (1969) 'The voting decision in a spatial context', *Progress in Geography* **1**: 81–117.

Cox, K. R. (1973) *Conflict, Power and Politics in the City: A Geographic View* McGraw Hill: New York.

Cox, K. R. (1979) *Location and Public Problems: A Political Geography of the Contemporary World*. Maaroufa: Chicago.

Cox, K. R. and **McCarthy, J. J.** (1982) 'Neighbourhood activism as a politics of turf: a critical analysis' in K. R. Cox and R. J. Johnston (eds) *Conflict, Politics and the Urban Scene*. Longman: Harlow, UK.

Cox, K. R. and **Nartowicz, F. Z.** (1980) 'Jurisdictional fragmentation in the American metropolis: alternative perspectives', *International Journal of Urban and Regional Research* **4**: 196–209.

de Crespigny, A. and **Cronin, T.** (eds) (1975) *Ideologies of Politics*. Oxford U.P.: London and New York.

Crewe, I. (1973) 'The politics of "affluent" and "traditional" workers in Britain: an aggregate data analysis', *British Journal of Political Science*

3: 29–52.

Crewe, I. and **Payne, C.** (1976) 'Another game with nature: an ecological regression model of the British two-party vote ratio in 1970', *British Journal of Political Science* **6**: 43–81.

Day, A. J. and **Degenhardt** (1980) *Political Parties of the World*. Longmans: London.

Deacon, A. and **Brigg, J.** (1974 'Local democracy and central policy', *Policy and Politics* **2**: 347–64.

Dear, M. (1978) 'Planning for mental health care: a reconsideration of public facility location theory', *International Regional Science Review* **3**: 93–111.

Dear, M. and **Clark, G.** (1978) 'The state and geographic process: a critical review', *Environment and Planning* A **10**: 173–83.

Dearlove J. (1979) *The Reorganization of British Local Government: Old Orthodoxes and a Political Perspective*. Cambridge U.P.

Deutch, K. W. (1953) *Nationalism and Social Communication*. Wiley: New York.

Deutch, K. W. (1961) 'Social mobilization and political development', *American Political Science Review* **55**: 494n5.

Dikshit, R. (1971a) 'Geography and federalism', *Annals, Association of American Geographers* **61**: 97–110.

Dikshit, R. (1971b) 'The failure of federalism in central Africa', *Professional Geographer* **23**: 27–31.

Dikshit, R. (1975) *The Political Geography of Federalism*. Macmillan: Delhi.

Dixon, R. G. (1968) *Democratic Representation: Reapportionment in Law and Politics*. Oxford U.P.: London and New York.

Dixon, R. G. (1971) 'The court, the people and "one man, one vote?"' in N. W. Polsby (ed.) *Reapportionment in the 1970's*. University of California Press: Berkeley.

Duncan, S. S. and **Goodwin, M.** (1982) 'The local state: functionalism, autonomy and class relations in Cockburn and Saunders', *Political*

Geography Quarterly **1**: 77–96.

Dunleavy, P. (1979) 'The urban basis of political alignment: social class, domestic property ownership, and state intervention in consumption processes' *British Journal of Political Science* **9**: 409–43.

Dunleavy, P. (1980) *Urban Political Analysis*. Macmillan: London.

Easton, D. (1965) *A System Analysis of Political Life*. Wiley: New York.

Emmanuel, A. (1972) *Unequal Exchange: A Study of the Imperialism of Trade*. Monthly Review Press: New York and London.

Engels, F. (1952) *The Condition of the Working Class in England in 1844*. Allen and Unwin: London.

Faris, R. E. L. (1967) *Chicago Sociology 1920–1932*. Chandler: San Francisco.

Fifer, J. V. (1976) 'Unity by inclusion: core area and Federal state at American independence', *Geographical Journal* **142**: 402–10.

Fifer, J. V. (1981) 'Washington, D. C. the political geography of a federal capital' *Journal of American Studies* **15**: 5–26.

Filkin, C. and **Weir, D.** (1972) 'Locality' in E Gittus (ed.) *Key Variables in Social Research*, Vol. 1. Heinemann: London.

Fitton, M. (1973) 'Neighbourhood and voting: a sociometric explanation', *British Journal of Political Science* **3**: 445–72.

Foeken, D. (1982) 'Explanation for the partition of sub-saharan Africa, 1880–1900', *Tijdschrift voor Economische en Sociale Geografie* **73**: 138–48.

Foster, J. (1974) *Class Struggle and the Industrial Revolution*. Weidenfeld and Nicolson: London.

Frank, A. G. (1967) 'Sociology of underdevelopment and the underdevelopment of sociology', *Catalyst* **3**: 20–73.

Frank, A. G. (1977) 'Long live transideological enterprise! The socialist economies in the capitalist division of labour', *Review* **1**: 91–140.

Frank, A. G. (1978) *Dependent Accumulation and Underdevelopment*. Monthly Review Press: New York; Macmillan: London.

Gallagher, J. and **Robinson, R.** (1953) 'The imperialism of free trade', *Economic History Review* (2nd series) **6**: 1–15.

Galtung, J. (1971) 'A structural theory of imperialism', *Journal of Peace Research* **8**: 81–117.

Gamble, A. (1974) *The Conservative Nation*. Routledge & Kegan Paul: London.

Gellner, E. (1964) *Thought and Change*. University of Chicago Press.

Gellner, E. (1983) *Nations and Nationalism*. Blackwell: Oxford.

Giddens, A. (1981) *A Contemporary Critique of Historical Materialism Vol. 1 Power Property and the State*. Macmillan: London.

Gold, D. A., Lo, C. Y. H. and **Wright, E. O.** (1975) 'Recent developments in Marxist theories of the capitalist state', *Monthly Review* **27**: 29–43 and **28**: 36–51.

Goldfrank, W. L. (1979) 'Introduction: bringing history back in' in W. L. Goldfrank (ed.) *The World-System of Capitalism: Past and Present*. Sage: Beverly Hills.

Goldman, R. M. (1980) 'The emerging transnational party system and the future of American parties' in L. Maisel (ed.) *Electoral Studies Yearbook* 5. Sage: Beverley Hills.

Gordon, D. M. (1976) 'Capitalist efficiency and socialist efficiency', *Monthly Review* **28**: 19–39.

Gordon, D. M. (1978) 'Class struggle and the stages of American urban development' in D. C. Perry and A. J. Watkins (eds) *The Rise of the Sunbelt Cities*. Sage: Beverly Hills.

Gottmann, J. (1951) 'Geography and International Relations', *World Politics* **3**: 153–73.

Gottmann, J. (1952) 'The political partitioning of our world: an attempt at analysis', *World Politics* **4**: 512–19.

Gottmann, J. (1973) *The Significance of Territory*. University Press of Virginia: Charlottesville.

Gray, C. S. (1977) *The Geopolitics of the Nuclear Era: Heartland, Rimlands and the Technological Revolution*. Crane, Russak: New York.

Gray, F. (1975) 'Non-explanation in urban geography', *Area* **7**: 228–34.

Gregory, R. (1968) *The Miners and British Politics, 1906–1914*. Oxford U.P.: London.

Gudgin, G. and **Taylor, P. J.** (1979) *Seats, Votes and the Spatial Organization of Elections*. Pion: London.

Hall, P. (1981) 'The geography of the fifth Kondratieff cycle', *New Society* 26th March: 535–7.

Hall, P. (1982) 'The new political geography: seven years on', *Political Geography Quarterly* **1**: 65–76.

Hartshorne, R. (1950) 'The functional approach in political geography', *Annals, Association of American Geographers* **40**: 95–130.

Hartshorne, R. (1954) 'Political geography' in P. E. James and C. F. Jones (eds) *American Geography: Inventory and Prospect*. Syracuse University Press: Syracuse, NY.

Harvey, D. (1973) *Social Justice and the City*. Arnold: London.

Haseler, S. (1976) *The Death of British Democracy*. Elik: London.

Hayek, F. A. (1975) 'The principles of a liberal social order' in A. de Crespigny and J. Cronin (eds) *Ideologies of Politics*. Oxford U.P.: London and New York.

Hays, S. P. (1964) 'The politics of reform in municipal government in the progressive era', *Pacific Northwest Quarterly* **55**: 157–69.

Hechter, M. (1975) *Internal Colonialism. The Celtic Fringe in British National Development, 1536–1966*. University of California Press: Berkeley.

Hechter M. and **Brustein, W.** (1980) 'Regional modes of production and patterns of state formation in Western Europe', *American Journal of Sociology* **85**: 1061–94.

Helin, R. A. (1967) 'The volatile administrative map of Rumania', *Annals, Association of American Geographers* **57**: 481–502.

Henige, D. P. (1970) *Colonial Governors from the Fifteenth Century to the Present*. University of Wisconsin Press: Madison.

Henrikson, A. K. (1983) '"A small, cozy town, global in scope": Washington, D.C.', *Ekistics* **50**: 123–45.

Herz, J. H. (1957) 'Rise and demise of the territorial state', *World Politics* **9**: 473–93.

Hillman, M , Henderson, I. and **Whalley, A** (1973) *Personal Mobility and Transport Policy*. Political and Economic Planning: London.

Hillman, M., Henderson, I. and **Whalley, A.** (1976) *Transport Realities and Planning Policy*. Political and Economic Planning: London.

Hinsley, F. A. (1966) *Sovereignty*. Watts: London.

Hobson, J. A. (1902) *Imperialism: A Study*. Allen & Unwin: London.

Hobson, J. A. (1968) 'Sociological interpretation of a general election' in P. Abrams (ed.) *The Origins of British Sociology 1834–1914*. University of Chicago Press.

Hodgart, R. L. (1978) 'Optimising access to public services', *Progress in Human Geography* **2**: 17–48.

Hollist, W. L. and **Rosenau, J. N.** (1981) 'World system debates' in W. L. Hollist and J. N. Rosenau (eds) *World System Structure*. Sage: Beverley Hills.

Holloway, J. and **Picciotto, S.** (eds) (1978) *State and Capital: A Marxist Debate*. Arnold: London.

Honey, R. (1981) 'Alternative approaches to local government change' in A. D. Burnett and P. J. Taylor (eds) *Political Studies from Spatial Perspectives*. Wiley: Chichester, UK and New York.

Hunt, A. (1980) 'Introduction: taking democracy seriously' in A. Hunt (ed.) *Marxism and Democracy*. Lawrence and Wishart: London.

Isaacs, A. (1948) *International Trade: Tariff and Commercial Policies*. Irwin: Chicago.

Inkeles, A. (1975) 'The emerging social structure of the world', *World Politics* **27**: 467–95.

Jackson, W. A. D. (1964) *Politics and Geographic Relationships.* Prentice Hall: Englewood Cliffs, N.J.

Jahnige, T. P. (1971) 'Critical elections and social change', *Polity* **3**: 465–500.

Janelle, D. (1977) 'Structural dimensions in the geography of location conflicts', *Canadian Geographer* **21**: 311–28.

Janelle, D. G. and **Millward, H. A.** (1976) 'Locational conflict patterns and urban ecological structure', *Tijdschrift voor Economische en Sociale Geografie*, **67**: 102–13.

Jefferson, M. (1939) 'The law of the primate city', *Geographical Review* **34**: 226–32.

Jessop, B. (1974) *Traditionalism, Conservatism and British Political Culture.* Allen and Unwin: London.

Jessop, B. (1982) *The Capitalist State.* Robertson: Oxford, UK.

Johnston, R. J. (1973) *Spatial Structures.* Methuen: London.

Johnston, R. J. (1977) 'The electoral geography of an election campaign', *Scottish Geographical Magazine* **93**: 98–108.

Johnston, R. J. (1979) *Political, Electoral and Spatial Systems.* Oxford U.P.: London and New York.

Johnston, R. J. (1980a) 'Political geography without politics', *Progress in Human Geography* **4**: 439–46.

Johnston, R. J. (1980b) 'Electoral geography and political geography', *Australian Geographical Studies* **18**: 37–50.

Johnston, R. J. (1980c) *The Geography of Federal Spending in the United States of America.* Wiley: Chichester, UK.

Johnston, R. J. (1982) *Geography and the State.* Macmillan: London.

Johnston, R. J. (1983) 'The neighbourhood effect won't go away: observations on the electoral geography of England in the light of Dunleavy's critique', *Geoforum* **14**: 161–8.

Jones, K. and **Kirby, A.** (1982) 'Provision and wellbeing: an agenda for public resources research', *Environment and Planning* A **14**: 297–310.

Jones, S. B. (1954) 'A unified field theory of political geography', *Annals,*

Association of American Geographers **44**: 111–23.

Jones, S. B. (1959) 'Boundary concepts in the setting of place and time', *Annals, Association of American Geographers* **49**: 241–55.

Kaldor, M. (1979) *The Disintegrating West.* Penguin: London.

Kaplan, S. S. (1981) *Diplomacy of Power.* Brookings Institute: Washington, DC.

Kasperson, R. E. and **Minghi, J. V.** (eds) (1969) *The Structure of Political Geography.* Aldine: Chicago.

Kerr, C. and **Siegel, A.** (1954) 'The inter-industry propensity to strike' in A. Kornhauser (ed.) *Industrial Conflict.* Wiley: New York.

Kirby, A. (1976) 'Housing market studies: a critical review', *Transactions, Institute of British Geographers* NSI: 2–9.

Kirby, A. (1982) *The Politics of Location: An Introduction.* Methuen: London and New York.

Kirby, A. (1983) 'Neglected factors in public services research', *Annals, Association of American Geographers* **73**: 289–95.

Kleppner, P. (1979) *The Third Electoral System: 1853–1892.* University of North Carolina Press: Chapel Hill.

Knight, D. B. (1982a) 'Canada in crisis: the power of regionalisms' in D. G. Bennett (ed.) *Tension Areas of the World.* Parte: Champaign, Ill.

Knight, D. B. (1982b) 'Identity and territory: geographical perspectives on nationalism and regionalism', *Annals, Association of American Geographers* **72**: 514–31.

Knox, P. (1982) *Urban Social Geography: An Introduction.* Longman: London and New York.

Koves, A. (1981) 'Socialist economy and the world-economy', *Review* **5**: 113–34.

Kristof, L. D. (1959) 'The nature of frontiers and boundaries', *Annals, Association of American Geographers* **49**: 269–82.

Kubalkova, V. and **Cruickshank, A. A.** (1981) *International Inequality.* Croom Helm: London.

Laski, H. J. (1935) *The State in Theory and Practice*. Allen & Unwin: London.

Laski, H. J. (1936) *The Rise of European Liberalism*. Allen & Unwin: London.

Lees, L. H. (1982) 'Strikes and the urban hierarchy in English industrial towns, 1842–1901' in J. E. Cronin and J. Schnear (eds) *Social Conflict and the Political Order in Modern Britain*. Croom Helm: London.

Levinson, C. (1980) *Vodka Cola*. Biblios: Horsham, UK.

Lewis, P. F. (1965) 'Impact of negro migration on the electoral geography of Flint, Michigan, 1932–62: a cartographic analysis', *Annals, Association of American Geographers* **55**: 1–25.

Ley, D. and **Mercer, J.** (1980) 'Locational conflict and the politics of consumption', *Economic Geography* **56**: 89–109.

Libby, O. G. (1894) 'The geographical distribution of the vote of the thirteen states on the federal constitution, 1787–1788' *Bulletin of the University of Wisconsin* **1**: 1–116.

Lichtheim G. (1971) *Imperialism*. Penguin: London.

Liebman, M. (1964) '1914: the great schism', *Socialist Register* 1964. 283–92.

Liebowitz, R. D. (1983) 'Finlandization: an analysis of the Soviet Union's "domination" of Finland', *Political Geography Quarterly* **2**: 275–88.

Lijphart, A. (1971) 'Class voting and religious voting in European democracies', *Acta Politics* **6**: 158–71.

Lijphart, A. (1982) 'The relative salience of the socio-economic and religious issue dimensions: coalition formation in ten western democracies, 1919–1979', *European Journal of Political Research* **10**: 201– a11.

Lockwood, D. (1966) 'Sources of variation in working class images of society', *Sociological Review* **14**: 249–67.

Lowenthal, D. (1958) 'The West Indies chooses a capital', *Geographical Review* **48**: 336–64.

McColl, R. W. (1969) 'The insurgent state: territorial bases of revolution', *Annals, Association of American Geographers* **59**: 613–31.

McCormick, R. P. (1967) 'Political development and the second party system' in W. N. Chambers and W. D. Burnham (eds) *The American Party Systems*. Oxford U.P.: London and New York.

McCormick, R. L. (1974) 'Ethnocultural interpretations of American voting behaviour', *Political Science Quarterly* **89**: 351–77.

Macintyre, S. (1980) *Little Moscows*. Croom Helm: London.

Mackenzie, R. T. and **Silver, A.** (1968) *Angels in Marble: Working Class Conservatives in Urban England*. Heinemann: London.

Mackinder, H. J. (1904) 'The geographical pivot of history', *Geographical Journal* **23**: 421–42.

Mackinder, H. J. (1919) *Democratic Ideals and Reality: A Study in the Politics of Reconstruction*. Constable: London; Holt: New York.

Mackinder, H. J. (1943) 'The round world and the winning of the peace', *Foreign Affairs* **21**: 595–605.

McLafferty, S. (1982) 'Urban structure and geographical access to public services', *Annals, Association of American Geographers* **72**: 347–54.

McLafferty, S. (1984) 'Constraints on distributional equity in the location of public services', *Political Geography Quarterly* **3**: 33– a48.

McPhail, I. R. (1971) 'Recent trends in electoral geography', *Proceedings of the Sixth New Zealand Geography Conference* **1**: 7–12.

Manning, D. J. (1976) *Liberalism*. Dent: London.

Mansergh, N. (1949) *The Coming of the First World War: A Study in the European Balance, 1878–1914*. Longmans: London.

Mayhew, D. R. (1971) 'Congressional representation: theory and practice in drawing the districts' in N. W. Polsby (ed.) *Reapportionment in the 1970's*. University of California Press: Berkeley.

Mellor, R. (1975) 'Urban sociology in an urbanized society', *British Journal of Sociology* **26**: 276–93.

Miliband, R. (1961) *Parliamentary Socialism.* Allen & Unwin: London.
Miliband, R. (1969) *The State in Capitalist Society.* Quartet: London.
Miliband, R. (1977) *Marxism and Politics.* Oxford U.P.: London.
Minghi, J. V. (1963) 'Boundary studies in political geography', *Annals, Association of American Geographers* **53**: 407–28.
Modelski, C. (1978) 'The long cycle of global politics and the nation state' *Comparative Studies of Society and History* **20**: 214–35.
Muir, R. (1981) *Modern Political Geography* (2nd ed.). Macmillan: London.
Mumford, L. (1938) *The Culture of Cities.* Secker & Warburg: London.
Murdie, R. A. (1969) *The Factorial Ecology of Metropolitan Toronto, 1951–1961.* Department of Geography Research Paper; University of Chicago.

Nairn, T. (1977) *The Break-up of Britain.* New Left Books: London.
Navari, C. (1981) 'The origins of the nation-state' in L. Tivey (ed.) *The Nation-State.* Robertson: Oxford, UK.
Nelund, C. (1978) 'The national world picture' *Journal of Peace Research* **315**: 273–8.
Newby, H. (1977) *The Deferential Worker.* Allen Lane: London.
Newton, K. (1975) 'American urban politics: social class, political structure and public goods', *Urban Affairs Quarterly* **11**: 241–64.

O'Connor, J. (1973) *The Fiscal Crisis of the State.* St Martin's Press: New York.
O'Loughlin, J. (1980) 'The election of black mayors 1977', *Annals, Association of American Geographers* **70**: 353–70.
O'Loughlin, J. (1984) 'Geographic models of international conflicts' in P. J. Taylor and J. W. House (eds) *Political Geography: Recent Advances and Future Directions.* Croom Helm: London.
O'Sullivan, P. (1982) 'Antidomino', *Political Geography Quarterly* **1**: 57–64.
Openshaw, S. and **Steadman, P.** (1982) 'On the geography of the worse case nuclear attack on the population

of Britain', *Political Geography Quarterly* **1**: 263–78.
Orridge, A. (1981a) 'Varieties of nationalism' in L. Tivey (ed.) *The Nation-State.* Robertson: Oxford, UK.
Orridge, A. (1981b) 'Uneven development and nationalism I and II', *Political Studies* **24**: 1–5 and 181–90.
Orridge, A. and **Williams, C. H.** (1982) 'Autonomous nationalism', *Political Geography Quarterly* **1**: 19–40.
Osei-Kwame, P. and **Taylor, P. J.** (1984) 'A politics of failure: the political geography of Ghanaian elections, 1954–1979', *Annals, Association of American Geographers* **74**.

Paddison, R. (1983) *The Fragmented State. The Political Geography of Power.* Blackwell: Oxford, UK.
Pahl, R. E. (1970) *Whose City?.* Longmans: London.
Pahl, R. E. (1979) 'Socio-political factors in resources allocation' in D. T. Herbert and D. M. Smith (eds) *Social Problems and the City.* Oxford U.P.: London.
Park, R. E. (1916) 'The city: suggestions for the investigation of human behaviour in the urban environment', *American Journal of Sociology* **20**: 577–612.
Parker, W. H. (1982) *Mackinder. Geography as Aid to Statecraft.* Clarendon: Oxford, UK.
Parkin, F. (1967) 'Working class Conservatives: a theory of political deviance', *British Journal of Sociology* **18**: 278–90.
Parkin, F. (1971) *Class Inequality and Political Order.* Holt, Rinehart & Winston: New York.
Peele, S. and **Morse, S. J.** (1974) 'Ethnic voting and political change in South Africa', *American Political Science Review* **68.1: 1520–41.**
Piepe, A., Prior, R. and **Box, A.** (1969) 'The location of the proletarian and deferential worker', *Sociology* **3**: 239–44.
Pirie, C. H., Rogerson, C. M. and **Beavon, K. S. O.** (1980) 'Covert power in South Africa: geography of the Afrikaner Broederbond', *Area*

12: 97–104.

Polanyi, K. (1977) 'The economistic fallacy', *Review* **1**: 9–20.

Poulantzas, N. (1969) 'The problem of the capitalist state', *New Left Review* **58**: 119–33.

Poulsen, T. M. (1971) 'Administration and regional structure in east-central and south-east Europe' in G. W. Hoffman (ed.) *Eastern Europe*. Methuen: London.

Pounds, N. J. G. (1951) 'The origin of the idea of natural frontiers in France', *Annals, Association of American Geographers* **41**: 146–57.

Pounds, N. J. G. (1954) 'France and "les limites naturelles" from the seventeenth to the twentieth centuries', *Annals, Association of American Geographers* **44**: 51–62.

Pounds, N. J. G. (1963) *Political Geography*. McGraw Hill: New York.

Pounds, N. J. G. and **Ball, S. S.** (1964) 'Core areas and the development of the European states system', *Annals, Association of American Geographers* **54**: 24–40.

Prescott, J. R. V. (1965) *The Geography of Frontiers and Boundaries*. Hutchinson: London.

Prescott, J. R. V. (1969) 'Electoral studies in political geography' in R. E. Kasperson and J. V. Minghi (eds) *The Structure of Political Geography*. Aldine: Chicago.

Read, D. (1964) *The English Provinces c 1760–1960. A Study in Influence*. Arnold: London.

Redfield, R. (1941) *The Folk Culture of Yucatan*. University of Chicago Press.

Reissman, L. (1964) *The Urban Process. Cities in Industrial Societies*. Free Press: New York.

Renshon, S. A. (1977) 'Assumptive frameworks in political socialization' in S. A. Renshon (ed.) *Handbook of Politics Socialization*. Free Press: New York.

Research Working Group (1979) 'Cyclical rhythms and secular trends of the capitalist world-economy: some premises, hypotheses and questions', *Review* **2**: 483–500.

Reynolds, D. R. and **Archer, J. C.**

(1969) 'An inquiry into the spatial basis of electoral geography', *Discussion Paper* 11. Department of Geography, University of Iowa.

Robinson, R. (1973) 'Non-European foundations of European imperialism: sketch for a theory of collaboration' in R. Owen and B. Sutcliffe (eds) *Studies in the Theory of Imperialism*. Longman: London.

Robinson, R., Gallagher, J. and **Denny, A.** (1961) *Africa and the Victorians* Macmillan: London.

Rokkan, S. (1970) *Citizens, Elections, Parties*. McKay: New York.

Rokkan, S. (1975) 'Dimensions of state formation and nation building: a possible paradigm for research on variations within Europe' in C. Tilley (ed) *The Formation of Nation States in Western Europe*. Princeton U.P Princeton, N.J.

Rokkan, S. (1980) 'Territories, centres and peripheries: towards a geoethnic-geoeconomic-geopolitical model of differentiation within Western Europe' in J Gottman (ed.) *Centre and Periphery*. Sage: Beverley Hills.

Rumley, D. (1979) 'The study of structural effects in human geography', *Tijdschrift voor Economische en Sociale Geografie* **70**: 350–60.

Runciman, W. G. (1966) *Relative Deprivation and Social Justice*. Routledge & Kegan Paul: London.

Russett, B. M. (1967) *International Regions and the International System: A Study in Political Ecology*. Rand McNally: Chicago.

Russett, B. R. et al. (1963) *World Handbook of Political and Social Indicators*. Yale U.P.: New Haven.

Rustow, D. A. (1967) *A World of Nations: Problems of Political Modernization*. Brookings Institute: Washington, DC.

Sack, R. D. (1981) 'Territorial bases of power' in A. D. Burnett and P. J. Taylor (eds) *Political Studies from Spatial Perspectives*. Wiley: Chichester UK and New York.

Sack, R. D. (1983) 'Human territoriality: a theory', *Annals,*

Association of American Geographers
73: 55–74.
Salvadori, M. (1977) The Liberal
Heresy. Origins and Historical Development.
Macmillan: London.
Sarkissian, W. (1976) 'The idea of
social mix in town planning: an
historical review', Urban Studies
13: 231–46.
Sauer, C. O. (1918) 'Geography and
the gerrymander', American Political
Science Review 12: 403–26.
Scase, R. (1977) Social Democracy in
Capitalist Societies. Croom Helm:
London.
Scase, R. (1980) The State in Western
Europe. Croom Helm: London.
Schattschneider, E. E. (1960) The
Semi-Sovereign People. Dryden: Hinsdale,
Illinois.
Schultz, H. J. (1972) English Liberalism
and the State: Individualism and
Collectivism?. Heath: Lexington, Mass.
Schumpeter, J. A. (1951) Imperialism
and Social Classes. Kelley: New York.
Seliger, M. (1976) Ideology and Politics.
Allen & Unwin: London.
Semmel, B. (1960) Imperialism and
Social Reform. English Social-Imperialist
Thought 1895–1914. Allen & Unwin:
London.
Shevky, E. and Bell, W. (1955) Social
Area Analysis. Stanford University
Press: Stanford, Co.
Short, J. R. (1982) An Introduction to
Political Geography. Routledge & Kegan
Paul: London.
Siegfried, A. (1913) Tableau Politique
de la France de l'Ouest. Colin: Paris.
Skinner, Q. (1978) The Foundation of
Modern Political Thought Vol. 2.
Cambridge U.P.
Sloan, L. (1969) '"Good government"
and the politics of race', Social Problems
17: 161–75.
Small, M. and Singer, J. D. (1982)
Resort to Arms. International and Civil
Wars 1816–1980. Sage: Beverley Hills.
Smith, A. D. (1979) Nationalism in the
Twentieth Century. Robertson: Oxford,
UK.
Smith, A. D. (1981) The Ethnic Revival
in the Modern World. Cambridge U.P.
Smith, A. D. (1982) 'Ethnic identity

and world order', Millennium: Journal of
International Studies 12: 149–61.
Smith, D. (1978) 'Domination and
containment: an approach to
modernization' Comparative Studies in
History and Society 20: 177–213.
Smith, N. (1984) 'Isaiah Bowman:
political geography and geopolitics',
Political Geography Quarterly 3: 69–76.
Smith, T (1981) The Pattern of
Imperialism. Cambridge U.P.
Soja, E. W. (1971) The Political
Organization of Space. Association of
American Geographers: Washington,
DC.
Spate, O. H. K. (1942) 'Factors in the
development of capital cities',
Geographical Review 32: 622–31.
Stretton, H. (1969) The Political
Sciences. Routledge & Kegan Paul:
London.
Szymanski, A. (1982) 'The socialist
world system' in C. K. Chase-Dunn
(ed.) Socialist States in the World-System.
Sage: Beverley Hills.

Tabb, W. K. and Sawers, L. (eds)
(1978) Marxism and the Metropolis.
Oxford U.P.: New York.
Taylor, C. and Hudson, M. (1971)
World Handbook of Political and Social
Indicators. Yale University Press: New
Haven, Conn.
Taylor, P. J. (1973) 'Some
implications of the spatial organization
of elections', Transactions, Institute of
British Geographers 60: 121–36.
Taylor, P. J. (1978) 'Progress report:
political geography', Progress in Human
Geography 2: 153–62.
Taylor, P. J. (1981a) 'Political
geography and the world-economy' in
A. D. Burnett and P. J. Taylor (eds)
Political Studies from Spatial Perspectives.
Wiley: Chichester UK and New York.
Taylor, P. J. (1981b) 'Geographical
scales within the world-economy
approach', Review 5: 3–11.
Taylor, P. J. (1982a) 'The changing
political map' in R. J. Johnston and
J. C. Doornkomp (eds) The Changing
Geography of the United Kingdom.
Methuen: London.
Taylor, P. J. (1982b) 'A materialist

framework for political geography', *Transactions, Institute of British Geographers* NST: 15–34.

Taylor, P. J. (1984) 'Accumulation, legitimation and the electoral geographies within liberal democracies' in P. J. Taylor and J. W. House (eds) *Political Geography: Recent Advances and Future Directions.* Croom Helm: London.

Taylor, P. J. and **Gudgin, G.** (1976a) 'The statistical basis of decision making in electoral districting', *Environment and Planning* A **38**: 43–58.

Taylor, P. J. and **Gudgin, G.** (1976b) 'The myth of non-partisan cartography: a study of electoral biases in the English Boundary Commission's Redistribution for 1955–1970', *Urban Studies* **13**: 13–25.

Taylor, P. J. and **Johnston, R. J.** (1979) *Geography of Elections.* Penguin: London.

Taylor, P. J. and **Johnston, R. J.** (1984) 'Political geography of Britain' in A. D. Kirby and J. R. Short (eds) *Contemporary Geography of Britain.* Routledge and Kegan Paul: London.

Thompson, E. P. (1968) *The Making of the English Working Class.* Penguin: London.

Thompson, E. P. (1980) 'Notes on exterminism, the last stage of civilization', *New Left Review* **121**: 3–31.

Tiebout, C. M. (1956) 'A pure theory of local expenditures', *Journal of Political Economy* **64**: 416–24.

Tietz, M. (1968) 'Towards a theory of urban public facility location', *Papers of the Regional Science Association* **21**: 35–51.

Tilly, C. (1975) 'Reflections on the history of European state-making' in C. Tilly (ed.) *The Formation of Nation States in Western Europe.* Princeton U.P.: Princeton, NJ.

Tilly, C. (1978) *From Mobilization to Revolution* Addison-Wesley: Reading: Mass.

Tivey, L. (1981) 'States, nations and economies' in L. Tivey (ed.) *The Nation-State.* Robertson: Oxford, UK.

Tufte, E. R. (1973) 'The relationship between seats and votes in two party systems', *American Political Science Review* **67**: 540–54.

Urry, J. (1981) 'Localities, regions and social class', *International Journal of Urban and Regional Research* **5**: 455–73.

Valkenburg, van S. (1939) *Elements of Political Geography.* Holt: New York.

Wachs, M. and **Kumagai, T. G.** (1973) 'Physical accessibility as a social indicator', *Socio-economic Planning Sciences* **7**: 437–56.

Waddington, I. (1977) 'The relationship between social class and the use of health services in Britain', *Journal of Advanced Nursing* **2**: 609–19.

Wagner, P. (1969) 'Rank and territory' in R. E. Kasperson and J. V. Minghi (eds) *The Structure of Political Geography.* Aldine: Chicago.

Wallerstein, I. (1974a) *The Modern World System. Capitalist Agriculture and the Origins of the European World-Economy in the Sixteenth Century.* Academic Press: New York.

Wallerstein, I. (1974b) 'The rise and future demise of the capitalist world system: concepts for comparative analysis', *Comparative Studies in Society and History* **16**: 387–418.

Wallerstein, I. (1976a) 'A world-system perspective on the social sciences', *British Journal of Sociology* **27**: 345–54.

Wallerstein, I. (1976b) 'The three stages of African involvement in the world-economy' in P. C. W. Gutkind and I. Wallerstein (eds) *The Political Economy of Contemporary Africa.* Sage: Beverly Hills.

Wallerstein, I. (1977) 'The tasks of historical social science: an editorial', *Review* **1**: 3–8.

Wallerstein, I. (1979) *The Capitalist World-Economy.* Cambridge University Press.

Wallerstein, I. (1980a) *The Modern World-System II. Mercantilism and the Consolidation of the European World-Economy 1600–1750.* Academic Press: New York.

Wallerstein, I. (1980b) 'Maps, maps, maps', *Radical History Review* **24**: 155–9.

Wallerstein, I. (1980c) 'The future of the world-economy' in T. K. Hopkins and I. Wallerstein (eds) *Processes of the World-System*. Sage: Beverly Hills.

Wallerstein, I. (1980d) 'Imperialism and development' in A. Bergesen (ed.) *Studies of the Modern World-System*. Academic: New York.

Wallerstein, I. (1982) 'Socialist states: mercantilist strategies and revolutionary objectives' in E. Friedman (ed.) *Ascent and Decline in the World-System*. Sage: Beverly Hills.

Wallerstein, I. (1983) *Historical Capitalism*. Verso: London.

Walters, R. E. (1974) *The Nuclear Trap: An Escape Route*. Penguin: London.

Wambaugh, S. (1920) *A Monograph on Plebescites*. Oxford U.P.: New York.

Wambaugh, S. (1936) *Plebescites since the World War*. Carnegie: New York.

Watson, J. W. (1970) 'Image geography: the myth of America in the American scene', *Advancement of Science* 27: 71–9.

Whittlesey, D. (1939) *The Earth and the State: A Study in Political Geography*. Holt: New York.

Wilkinson, H. R. (1951) *Maps and Politics: A Review of the Ethnographic Cartography of Macedonia*. University Press: Liverpool.

Williams, C. H. (1980) 'Ethnic separation in western Europe', *Tijdschrift voor Economische en Sociale Geografie* **71**: 142–58.

Williams, C. H. (1981) 'Identity through autonomy: ethnic separatism in Quebec', in A. D. Burnett and P. J. Taylor (eds) *Political Studies from Spatial Perspectives*. Wiley: Chichester and New York.

Williams, C. H. (1984) 'Ideology and the interpretation of minority cultures', *Political Geography Quarterly* **3**, 105–26.

Williams, O. (1971) *Metropolitan Policy Analysis*. Free Press: New York.

Wolpert, J., Mumphrey, A. and **Seley, J.** (1972) *Metropolitan Neighbourhoods: Participation and Conflict over Change*. Association of American Geographers: Washington, DC.

Young, C. (1982) *Ideology and Development in Africa*. Yale U.P.: New Haven.

Zeigler, D. J. and **Brunn, S. D.** (1980) 'Geopolitical fragmentation and the pattern of growth and need: Defining the cleavage between Sunbelt and Frostbelt metropolises' in S. D. Brunn and J. O. Wheeler (eds) *The American Metropolitan System: Present and Future*. Arnold: London.

Zolberg, A. R. (1981) 'Origins of the modern world system: a missing link', *World Politics* **33**: 253–81.

INDEX